For nearly thirty years, the artists that passed through the gates of Disney Animation, and even non-artists like myself, were influenced by the craft, skill, wisdom, writings and sketches of Walt Stanchfield.

—Roy Disney

Walt was a kind of Mark Twain for us at Disney. He always taught with humor and skill. You learned to see the world through his eyes. I remember him one day encouraging us to leap into our drawings with boldness and confidence, "Don't be afraid to make a mistake. We all have 10,000 bad drawings in us so the sooner you get them out the better!" Sitting in Walt's class was as much a psychology course as it was a drawing class. One couldn't help walk away with your mind and soul a little more open than when you entered.

—Glen Keane, Walt Disney Animation Studios

Walt Stanchfield's classes and writings were little distillations of the man: quirky, strongly stated in a genial voice, and brimming with a lifetime of sharp observations about story telling and graphic communication. Whether he drew with a ball point pen or painted with a brush dipped in his coffee cup, he got to the essence of things and was eager to share what he learned with his eager disciples, myself among them. He was grizzled and he was great and proof that there was more than one Walt at the Disney Studio that could inspire a legion of artists.

—John Musker, Walt Disney Animation Studios

Walt Stanchfield was one of Disney Animation's national treasures. His classes and notes have inspired countless animation artists, and his approach to drawing of caricature over reality, feeling over rote accuracy, and communication over photographic reproduction gets to the heart of what great animation is all about. Huzzah to Don Hahn for putting it all together for us!

—Eric Goldberg, Walt Disney Animation Studios

During the Animation Renaissance of the 1990s, one of the Walt Disney Studio's best kept secrets was Walt Stanchfield. Once a week after work, this aged but agile figure jumped from drawing board to drawing board, patiently teaching us the principles behind the high baroque style of Walt Disney Animation drawing. Being in a room with Walt made you feel what it must have been like to have been taught by Don Graham. Having one of your life drawings be good enough to be reproduced in one of his little homemade weekly bulletins was akin to getting a Distinguished Service medal! Senior animators vied with trainees for that distinction.

—Tom Sito, Animator/Filmmaker/Author of Drawing The Line: The Untold Story of the Animation Unions from Bosko to Bart Simpson

This exciting collection of master classes by the great teacher Walt Stanchfield is destined to become a classic on the order of Kimon Nicolaides' exploration of the drawing process. Stanchfield (1919–2000) inspired several generations of Disney animators and those of us outside the studio fortunate enough to happen upon dog-eared copies of his conversational notes, which we passed around like Leonardo's Codex Leicester. Stanchfield beautifully communicates the essence and joy of expressing ideas through the graphic line and accumulating a visual vocabulary. Drawn to Life is a treasure trove of cogent, valuable information for students, teachers and anyone who loves to draw.

—John Canemaker, NYU professor and Academy Award®-winning animation filmmaker

Walt Stanchfield, in his own unique way, taught so many of us about drawing, caricature, motion, acting, and animation. Most important to me was how Walt made you apply what you had observed in his life drawing class to your animation. Disney Animation is based on real life, and in that regard Walt Stanchfield's philosophy echoed Walt Disney's: "We cannot caricature and animate anything convincingly until we study the real thing first."

—Andreas Deja, Walt Disney Animation Studios

Walt Stanchfield's renewed emphasis on draftsmanship at the Disney Studios transformed the seemingly moribund art of animation. His students were part of a renaissance with The Little Mermaid and Who Framed Roger Rabbit, a renaissance that continues with films ranging from The Iron Giant to Lilo and Stitch to Wall-E.

—Charles Solomon, Animation Historian

DRAWN TO LIFE

GENE
4/19/97

DRAWN TO LIFE

20 GOLDEN YEARS OF DISNEY MASTER CLASSES

Walt Stanchfield
Edited by Don Hahn

AMSTERDAM • BOSTON • HEIDELBERG • LONDON
NEW YORK • OXFORD • PARIS • SAN DIEGO
SAN FRANCISCO • SINGAPORE • SYDNEY • TOKYO
Focal Press is an imprint of Elsevier

Focal Press is an imprint of Elsevier
30 Corporate Drive, Suite 400, Burlington, MA 01803, USA
Linacre House, Jordan Hill, Oxford OX2 8DP, UK

Library of Congress Cataloging-in-Publication Data
Application submitted

British Library Cataloguing-in-Publication Data
A catalogue record for this book is available from the British Library.

ISBN: 978-0-240-81107-9

For information on all Focal Press publications
visit our website at www.elsevierdirect.com

09 10 11 12 5 4 3 2

Printed in Canada

Working together to grow
libraries in developing countries

www.elsevier.com | www.bookaid.org | www.sabre.org

ELSEVIER   BOOK AID
            International   Sabre Foundation

Dedicated with love to Dee

It is management's wish that the "Disney Tradition" be revitalized and maintained. The tradition, as we see it, reflects the desires and aspirations of Walt, who, when alive strove to bring animation to a highly developed art. In attempting to recapture the quality attained in former years, we need but refer to the letter Walt wrote to Don Graham in 1935. It expresses the needs of the animation artist and the means he felt were necessary to develop and fulfill those needs.

Walt not only encouraged his employees to better themselves by bringing teachers and lecturers to the studio but he demanded constant improvement. We don't have Walt with us today but we do have the great heritage of animation he left, plus the facilities and the talent with which to uphold that heritage and, hopefully improve on it.

Nevertheless, there will be an attempt to reinstate the learning atmosphere that once permeated this studio. There will be various classes, conducted by numerous instructors. There will be suggested reading and film study; discussion on action analysis and its application to our media.

There will be no attempt to return to any particular era of the past, but to incorporate a composite of all the great accomplishments of the past into a future product that we can all be proud of.

Stan Walsh 2/10/81

Contents

Foreword

Once in a lifetime, a truly exceptional teacher crosses your path and changes your life forever. To me and to many, many of my colleagues in the arts, Walt Stanchfield was that teacher.

Part painter, part poet, part musician, part tennis bum, part eccentric savant, part wise professor, Walt inspired a generation of young artists not only with his vast understanding of the animator's craft, but also his ability to teach that craft and share his enthusiasm for a life in the arts.

Born in 1919 in Los Angeles, Walt began his career in animation in 1937, right out of high school, at the Charles Mintz Studio. He served in the U.S. Navy, then joined the Walter Lantz Studio prior to his lengthy tenure at The Walt Disney Studios. There he worked on every full-length animated feature between *The Adventures of Ichabod and Mr. Toad* (1949) and *The Great Mouse Detective* (1986).

Walt's writing started in the 1970s, when veteran animators at the Disney Studio were at the end of their illustrious careers and new talent was pouring into the studio. Frank Thomas and Ollie Johnston turned to writing their iconic book *The Illusion of Life* and Stanchfield focused on establishing a training program for new animators with veteran animator and director Eric Larson. Walt held regular weekly drawing classes and lectures for the crew. Among the young talent: Brad Bird, John Lasseter, Don Bluth, Joe Ranft, John Musker, Ron Clements, Glen Keane, Andreas Deja, Mark Henn, and so many others.

By the mid 1980s Walt started weekly gesture drawing classes for the entire studio. At the end of each class, he grabbed a few drawings that inspired or challenged him, then pasted them up with his typewritten commentary as a handout for everyone in the class. These weekly lecture notes along with his early writing for the animation training program are the basis for this first-time publication of his complete and prolific work.

In late 1987, I asked Walt to come to London to train the crew on *Who Framed Roger Rabbit*. The artists led by legendary director Richard Williams would crowd around him on the vacant third floor of the Edwardian factory building that was our studio. They would hang on his every word and absorb every line of his drawings. When it came time to pose, we had a leggy supermodel dressed up like Jessica, but Walt was the one who moved like her and helped us see what made her beautiful and sexy.

Walt's writing became the bible of animation for a very young enthusiastic crew of artists that would eventually create films like *The Little Mermaid*, *The Lion King*, *Aladdin*, and *Beauty and the Beast*. Because of Walt's informal approach to these notes, many of the drawings included here are a generation or two away from the artist's original. This photocopied style is very much in keeping with Walt's casual, conversational style of teaching.

The text herein has largely been left alone, as written by Walt. His conversational style is so completely accessible to the artist, it seemed wrong to formalize or edit his voice out of the material in any way. Parts of the text are very heavy with animation terms and technique, but remain as written because they apply to the art of drawing in any medium. Topics appear in no particular order and the sections are meant to be browsed as either instant inspiration, or week-long immersion into any array of subjects. The random nature of topics is also a signature of Walt's personality and approach. He saw life as a unified experience. Drawings inspired paintings, which inspired poetry, which inspired architecture, which inspired travel, which inspired tennis — all connected parts of an artist's life experience.

Drawn to Life is one of the strongest primers on animation ever written. The material spares no detail on the craft of animation, but also digs deep into the artistic roots of the medium. We get a chance to see Walt grow personally as an artist over the span of 20 years represented in these two books. It's a journey that takes him from admired production artist, to technical teacher, to beloved philosopher.

Walt's affect on his students extended way beyond the drawing board. It's not just that he drew better than everyone else, or taught better than everyone else — I admired Walt so much because he seemed to live better than everyone else. When he was not drawing, he was playing guitar, writing poetry, tending his vegetable garden, or making baskets in the style of the Chumash Indians. He was never without a pen and would often color his drawings by dipping a brush into his cup of coffee at breakfast. The drawings were always loose, improvisational, impressionistic and alive, just like their creator.

He passed away in the year 2000 leaving behind a thousand pages of lecture notes and a generation of magnificent animators. With thanks to Dee Stanchfield, Focal Press and The Walt Disney Studios, and special thanks to my co-editors, Connie Thompson and Maggie Gisel, it is with great pleasure that the genius of Walt Stanchfield is now available to you in the pages of *Drawn to Life*.

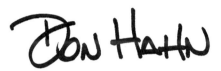

Acknowledgements

EDITED BY:
Don Hahn

CO-EDITORS:
Maggie Gisel
Connie Thompson

EDITORIAL CONSULTANT:
Dee Stanchfield

EDITORIAL STAFF:
Kathy Emerson
Christopher Gaida
Josh Gladstone
Kent Gordon
Charles Hayes
Fumi Kitahara
Tracey Miller-Zarneke
Stephanie Van Boxtel

BUSINESS AFFAIRS:
Kevin Breen

FOCAL PRESS/ELSEVIER:
Jane Dashevsky
Paul Gottehrer
Amanda Guest
Georgia Kennedy
Chris Simpson
Katy Spencer
Anais Wheeler

DESIGNED BY:
Joanne Blank
Dennis Schaefer

WALT DISNEY PUBLISHING CLEARANCES:
Margaret Adamic

ADDITIONAL CLEARANCES:
Ashley Petry

DISNEY ANIMATION RESEARCH LIBRARY:
Fox Carney
Doug Engalla
Ann Hansen
Kristen McCormick
Lella Smith
Jackie Vasquez
Mary Walsh
Patrick White

ARTIST RESEARCH AND LOCATION:
Chantal Bumgarner
Ginger Chen
Tenny Chonin
Howard Green
Tiffany Herrington
Bill Matthews
Robert Tiemans
Pamela Thompson

TRANSCRIPTIONS:
Patti Conklin
Kathleen Grey
Rhiannon Hume

INITIAL DESIGN CONCEPTS:
Kris Taft Miller

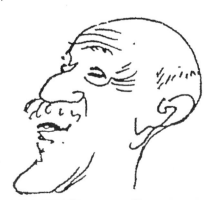

1

Innovation

1 Review and New Approach

Some of you have been studying in our gesture analysis class for a long time now. The subject has been drawing and the emphasis has been drawing specifically with animation in mind. We have covered such areas as "Animation and Sketching," wherein I implored you to carry a sketchbook with you and sketch, sketch, and sketch.

I did a paper on "Mental and Physical Preparation" wherein I extolled the benefits of keeping in good shape. No illustration here for good shape does not refer to developing an Adonis-like body or a genius-like mind, not that we could if we tried, but at least a healthy mental and physical state that will help withstand the rigors they will be put to in pursuing an animation career.

I introduced the subject of angles in "Using Angles" and have pushed that subject as a very important element in capturing the gesture in drawing from the model and in creating movement in animation.

We covered "Doodling and Drawing" several times. The idea behind it was that doodling leads you to something, whereas if you have a specific gesture you are after — drawing will get you there.

Then "Simplicity for the Sake of Clarity." How many times have we lost our original idea in a maze of complications? One remedy for that is to back off and try to recapture that all-important first impression. To illustrate that lesson I used Frank Thomas's seemingly simple animation and (probably) Dale Oliver's seemingly simple cleanup drawings. I say seemingly simple because though it appears to be simple, still a great deal of thought went into each function to make it appear simple. Not for the sake of simplicity, but for the sake of readability. There was an idea to put over and any complication would only have been detraction.

"The Opposing Force." Angle against angle, squash against stretch, close proximity against openness — potent tools in both drawing from the model and in animation.

"Action Analysis: Hands and Feet." This was a short paper, but a revealing one. It was prompted by the tendency of students to leave the hands and feet (and props) off their drawings. Using some illustrations, I attempted to prove that you can tell more what a character is doing by their hands and feet than you can from their body.

There was a lesson, "For the Action Analysis Class." The class used to be called "Action Analysis" because years ago we used animation paper and drew 3 action poses on portable pegs. We did a preparation, anticipation, and action drawing for each gesture. The accompanying illustrations were some suggestions for a simplified approach to drawing from the model — they were taken from Glenn Vilppu's article on Life Drawing.

We followed that lesson with a couple of sessions where we used cylinders in place of body parts while drawing from the model. This was, and is, especially helpful when faced with a foreshortening problem.

I introduced you to Bruce McIntyre's rules of perspective. On the surface these may seem overly simple, even infantile, but in drawing they become genuine symbols that are easily applicable as drawings helps.

There was "Note Taking and Sketching." You've probably seen the American Express commercial where Karl Malden says, "Don't leave home without it." That goes for notebooks and sketchbooks too. There was more on "Sketching," "Essence Drawing," "Feeling the Pose," "Living Model to the Living Gesture," "Creative Energy," and many more. When I realized the next picture, "The Little Mermaid," will have hundreds, perhaps thousands, of head and shoulder shots, I offered some things on heads, suggesting we start with a simplified approach to head drawing. And we began devoting a portion of the sketch class to heads.

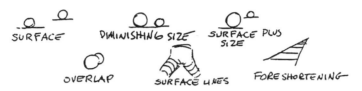

Finally, one that I think is of supreme importance, "Drawing and Caricature." We study from a live model, but we draw and animate caricatures. The ability to be able to know the human head and figure and to transfer that knowledge into cartoons is of utmost importance.

Along with all this we have been using pen and ink to help us focus on those points and to encourage (force) the mind to see first what we want to draw before attempting to put it down. Everyone has been most cooperative in going along with all these suggestions. Perhaps it is time to explore some other aspects of drawing and some other approaches. So let's for a time put away the pens and bring out the soft pencils. For a couple of sessions let's throw caution to the winds and have a graphite orgy. Forget (for now) the subtleties we have been striving for and go for bold. Try still to capture the gesture, but in the most flamboyant manner. Be extravagant, be bold, be loose, be adventurous, even careless. Try to make the most powerful statement you have ever made, with no thoughts of right or wrong, good or bad. "Let," as the old saying goes, "it all hang out."

2 Artist/Actor

An actor's training and his later daily exercises and observations might run something like this: he imagines he is in church — what is the mood of the church and how do the types of characters he plays react in this situation? Likewise in a cemetery, a nightclub, at the dentist, at a wedding, watching a comedy — the list goes on and on.

But the problem is deeper than just that. How different would he act if it were happening in ancient Rome or Egypt, or in the Colonial days, or in England in the days of King Arthur? Or what if he were a comedian with not a serious bone in his body, and took all this as a big joke? What kind of background would he need, or what type of research would he have to do, what kind of reading should he do?

How would he portray the simple things in everyday life — sitting on a couch, reading a magazine, drinking a cup of coffee, watching a ball game on TV, or looking out a window, reacting to something happening on the street or at his neighbor's house?

How would he act if it's dusty, hot, freezing, or windy?

Can he express different ways of showing happiness for roles of different ages, social standing, and different physical makeup? Would an optimist express happiness differently than a pessimist?

Does etiquette, custom, or convention effect the manner in which he expresses laughter, for instance how loud, how long, or how spirited? How would he laugh if he had a pain in his side, or if he had just lost a friend, or if he didn't get the joke but was laughing out of politeness?

Again the list goes on and on. I posed these questions as if it were an actor in question, but I was thinking of you as artist/actor. Acting is the parallel between you and the stage or movie actor — the difference being, you act with a pencil, he acts with his body. But the background, training, and preparation are the same — the knowledge and understanding of human (and animal) nature.

In the evening drawing classes we have been trying to grasp the process of how and why the model arrives at the various poses and gestures. The audience goes to see cartoons to be entertained. They are interested in *what* happens (in the story). But we who fabricate them also have to know *why* and *how*. So we concern ourselves with why and how people (characters) act the way they do under the multitude of situations we subject them to in our stories.

Last week Craig Howell modeled for us. First of all he is post middle age, meaning he has a slight pot (belly), his cheeks are beginning to hang down, he has a double chin, and he is beginning to get that stoop-shoulder that most elderly people end up with. His hands are large, fingers fat — those of a worker. He is very serious minded. You would not know it to look at him but he is a walking encyclopedia. He is a professional model and he knows how to play-act. He has done for us a carpenter, a waiter, a gardener, a farmer, a navy shore patrolman, a hunter (for McLeach), and last week a doctor and a construction worker. And whether you draw him realistically or caricature him, all these things have a bearing on your approach to drawing him.

Let's explore some of the applications of these physical traits to drawing. Here is an intern's drawing of Craig carrying a long rod. In my sketch next to it I have suggested a more stooped over back by projecting the head and neck forward. To balance the weight of the metal rod, I angled the head away from the rod. Figuring the metal rod had some weight to it, I extended his hand forward to better balance the part that hangs over his shoulder behind him. I also lifted his shoulder a little to make a kind of shelf so the rod would not slip off:

Here's another intern's drawing of Craig prying something with the metal rod. The student seemed concerned with drawing all the parts. He has the head isolated and the arms and hands out in the clear. In my suggestion sketch I tried to show more tension and power by folding those elements up into a grouping of forces. It is like the difference between trying to arm wrestle with your arm outstretched, or with your arm, shoulder, neck, and chest all marshaled together in support of each other.

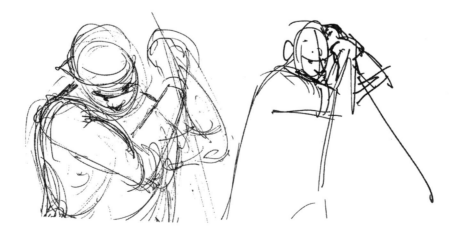

Here is a rather nice drawing of Craig about to clean the wax out of a patient's ear. In my sketch I carried the concept a bit further by utilizing Craig's bent-over upper back, plus his intense interest in what he was doing, to force the attention toward the object of the pose.

Here is an instance where even if the character was not stoop-shouldered or paunchy, he would bend forward to look into his black medical bag. However, a person with a paunch would have to make an extra effort to bend over so he could see over his stomach:

As you can see these are all things an actor/artist must *think*, *feel*, and *do*.

Here are two more poses where in my sketch I not only tried to capture the essence of the gesture but attempted to use as few lines as possible, applying two of Craig's physical attributes — the paunch and the bent-over upper back. When you know the *what*, *how*, and *why* of the gesture and the physical characteristics and traits of your character, you can go right to it in a matter of seconds. These are not meant to be finished drawings — only the necessary foundation for a drawing.

3 Don't Be Ordinary

Ever try to take the lid off a jar that was stuck tight? You end up bent over with the jar between your knees, all doubled up, your face all contorted in the exaggerated effort. Only an Arnold Schwarzenegger could twist the lid off by just holding it at a normal position in front of him.

When my wife, Dee, asks me to unscrew a tight lid, I first try to do it the Schwarzenegger way — to show how strong I am. If that fails, I most certainly ignore the ordinary way, that is to hold it under the hot water tap until the cap expands, but go right into the face-saving, cover-up routine — the overexaggerated cartoon version, exclaiming, "Boy, this cap is really welded on!"

So the next time you have to draw or animate a guy unscrewing a stuck jar lid, how will you approach the problem? The Schwarzenegger way? The only time you do that is when you are Arnold or when you are trying to show off, and are more interested in your ego than you are in the visual interest. I am sure my wife enjoys it more when I am wrestling with this tiny little beast. Even my dog enjoys it. Actually, come to think of it, I enjoy it more, too.

I always enjoy drawing a more exaggerated version of action. If I drew a character just standing there twisting off the lid as if it were already loosened — how would anyone know it was stuck, unless it was a caricature of Arnold? Even then, for the sake of entertainment it might be funnier if he fails, goes into the overexaggerated routine, only to have the gal he is with take the lid off easily with two fingers. It depends on the character, too. Tinker Bell would simply sprinkle a little pixie dust on the lid. Roger Rabbit might go to the workshop and come back with pipe wrenches, a vice, and a blowtorch. Donald in his inevitable fury might try explosives.

Still, if the two-finger approach was staged properly it could be delightfully funny. Perhaps the story calls for some understatement. It may not even be humor you are after, in which case you would have to find an entertaining way to put over whatever it is. Whichever, it would probably take some thought, much like I am doing here. It may seem terribly involved, but usually good entertainment can only be acquired through hard work. And to make it even more challenging, no matter how much hard work goes into it — it has to appear spontaneous.

There is a rather recent style of cartooning in the newspapers and magazines that uses a technique where things are explained in a caption. For instance, a guy gently holding a jar, the caption reading, "Elmer twists off one of those stubborn fruit jar lids, effortlessly, a la Arnold Schwarzenegger." That type of humor can be funny, but without the written explanation the drawing is practically meaningless. Like if you had a drawing of a waffle, it would mean nothing special, but with the caption like "A non-skid pancake," it suddenly becomes humorous.

Pantomime has to do its thing without that written or verbal explanation. And that is what good animation and good drawing from the model does.

In the evening drawing class, many of the poses are of the Arnold S. type, that is, rather confined. So I encourage the artists not to copy what is before them, but add some zest to the gesture — to become the comic actor, so to speak, and step out of the ordinary.

Here is a student's drawing that I interrupted soon after he started. Any further work on it would have been like trying to high jump with a scuba outfit on. The pose was saying something like "What the hell is this?" or "How do I straighten this out?" or "I've forgotten how to use this thing"' or one of a hundred other fabricated stories. Any of which would supply motivation for the artist to make a clear and perhaps exiting drawing. In my sketch I simply wanted to assure the viewer that the character was concerned about whatever he is holding. So I bent him over in a sort of bewildered way, straightened out the front of his body (thinking that it would be nice to use a straight against the curve of his back) so the look goes rocketing down to the object of the gesture:

Here is another one where the model was combing his hair in a hand mirror. I do not have any hair to comb, but if I did, I would do it with a little flurry. I would pull my upper body, arm, and shoulder back, getting all that out of the way so I had a good look at the hair (the purpose of the pose), then thrust my head forward toward the mirror as if I were ducking something — perhaps by doing that I imagine I can see the top of my head and farther around the sides. I lowered his right arm to show that he was pulling down on a comb full of hair. I tried to clear the path of his look to the mirror that is being held up by the left arm (so up goes the left elbow). His right knee has to be higher than his left because the lower part of his right leg is more vertical.

One of the things we have to overcome in drawing gestures is our non-gesture type of anatomy training. For instance, we are taught that the shoulders are attached to the upper chest area and protrude (on males especially) upward and outward. But when a person bends over and stretches his arms downward — the shoulders are capable of helping that downward motion with great flexibility.

Here is a similar problem. The back is bent and the shoulders are pulled forward because of the nature of the gesture. Try this pose. You will feel your elbows jut way out and your shoulders follow suit. The elbows seem to fold up while the knees spread apart. Why? Because the top of the chair back is very narrow so the elbows have to squeeze together to fit. Contrariwise, the bottom of the chair is wider, forcing the knees apart:

4 Sketcher

The cartoonist, when he sketches is going through a process of study. He concentrates upon the model, plumbs its movement, bulk, and outline. Then he sets it down, remembering that he wants only the spirit — the "guts" of the thing he's after. He puts into his drawing (even though it may be as big as your thumbnail) all his experience. He simplifies. He plays with his line. He experiments. He isn't concerned with anatomy, chiaroscuro, or the symmetry of "flowing line." There's nothing highbrow about his approach to the sketchpad. He is drawing because he likes to draw!

Lawrence Lariar

Sketching is to the artist what shadow boxing is to a boxer; keyboard practice is to a concert pianist; practice is to a tennis player, or a participant in any sport (or endeavor). I have often quoted artists and cartoonists who swear by and recommend sketching as a necessary part of an artist's daily ventures (adventures). And occasionally I reproduce drawings from sketchbooks for the purpose of promoting interest in sketching and for just plain old inspirational purposes. This week I feel privileged to bring some of animator Ron Husband's work to you.

Ron appears to be a quiet guy who just goes about his business in an even-mannered way. But he is an inveterate sketcher — his pen is constantly searching and probing for incidents of every day life, attempting to push them beyond the ordinary — into the realm of entertainment. The 100 filled sketch books in his room (there are a 100 more at home) might hoodwink you into thinking that is all he does when not animating, but he has several "irons in the fire," and is more than capable of doing justice to all of them. He is an illustrator for children's magazines, and is involved in some very imaginative books of his own; Ron does not confine his drawing to just the small sketchbook format, either.

I recall an exhibit a year or so ago where he displayed many drawings about 17 × 22 inches. They ranged from humorous to dramatic, and were most elegantly done.

Ron believes quick sketching is an aid to animation. He maintains sketching will enhance drawing ability, quicken your eye, help you to analyze action in a shorter period of time. He says the benefits of quick-sketching are the ability to capture the essence of a pose, to acquire believability in your drawing, and to sharpen your awareness of "grid" or ground planes and backgrounds. A greater familiarity with depth, perspective, and third dimension also frees you from thinking in terms of the standard 3/4 front or rear view.

I had only time to go through a few of his sketchbooks, but in those few was a wealth of material. Here is a sampling.

5 Plus or Minus

Years ago I got into developing color film. I do not know how it is done now but I used to have to keep the developing chemicals plus or minus one-half degree. In sketching, if you keep within plus or minus one-half degree of the pose, you will end up with an uninteresting tracing. To do the pose any justice at all, you have got to go at least 10 or 15 degrees on the plus side. Drawing is unique in that sense. We are so used to being herded into that one-half degree plus or minus syndrome: set your carburetor mixture just so or you will waste gas, use the right amount of baking powder or your cake will either fall or blow up, adjust your radio to the station or you will get static, etc. Realism for the cartoonist is not copying things from nature to the nth degree, it is caricaturing those things — turning them into entertainment (and having fun at the same time).

I found a new positive thinking statement I am trying to put into practice: IT IS OKAY TO HAVE FUN. And who of all people should have more fun than cartoonists, except maybe the audience those cartoonists draw for. It thrills me to see artists come into the class after a grueling day of hard work, and still dig into their fun bag to come up with some delightful "pot shots" at their fellow artists. Here are a few by Hans Bacher.

Here is one by Dan Boulos:

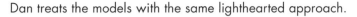

Dan treats the models with the same lighthearted approach.

If I were a cleanup artist, those are the kind of animation drawings I would like to clean up. They are teeming with expression, the gestures are unmistakable, and the drawings are unencumbered by superfluous lines. They are far from being finished drawings, but the raw material is all there. "Tracings" of the model show only that the artist is capable of copying what is before him. There are so many possibilities beyond that.

There is always a lot of intense looking while drawing from a model, but intensity in itself does not ensure an entertaining drawing. We often see what we are taught to see, or what we are comfortable in seeing. I have been in the business of drawing since 1937 and I still do not trust my ability to see. I am a master of looking — but I have a filter system like everyone else. This system blanks out things my unconscious does not want to recognize. But it will accent those things I want to see. I have a notoriously bad memory, so I cannot trust that, and being a right-brained person, I realize I take the elements that are before me and reorganize them into something different — something I can call my own.

In the latest *Natural History* magazine, there is an article by Stephen Jay Gould, wherein he tells about some experiments made on college students. One of them was showing a film of an accident, followed later by a misleading question: "How fast was the sports car going when it passed the barn while traveling along the country road?" (There was no barn in the film.) A week later 17 percent of the group stated that they had seen the nonexistent barn.

"Thus," the author says, "We are easily fooled on all fronts of both eye and mind; seeing, storing, and recalling. The eye tricks us badly enough; the mind is infinitely more perverse. What remedy can we have but constant humility, and eternal vigilance and scrutiny? Trust your memory as you would your poker buddy."

We also have habits that stick to us like glue. It seems like the first way we do something or see something is the way we remember it.

It might take two minutes to learn something the wrong way and then five years to unlearn it. When I started playing tennis years ago, the way to hit a topspin was to roll the racket over the top of the ball. When the method changed to hitting the ball with the racket going from low to high, it took me years to change the groove my body had gotten into. The body has a memory that is harder to change than the mind, and it takes part in drawing, too. If it learns to draw something a certain way, your creative spirit may be hard pressed to try something new. That is why changing hands gives your drawing a new look. Your "left" hand does not even know how to hold the pen or pencil, and has no memory of how to draw anything.

What's more, your left-brain mode will back up the body 100 percent. "Yeah," it will say, "hip bone connected to the thigh bone, thigh bone connected to the knee… just the facts man — none of that gesture, mood, and caricature stuff — just the facts." The poor, sometimes suppressed, right brain is saying, "Darn, I see something cute or funny here but I just can't seem to get this pencil to loosen up. It feels like there's a groove in the paper that the point is stuck in." Like that sign on a country road that says, "Be careful which rut you pick, you're gonna be in it for the next twenty miles."

Boy! You just have to keep your wits about you, 'cause the more wheels that go over that rut — the deeper it gets.

On the following page are some examples of plus and minus drawing. The student's drawings are all on the minus side. Angles were un-angled, tension was un-tensed, and the whole gesture straightened up. In a word, they were nonplussed. My suggestion sketches were an attempt to go maybe 10 percent on the plus side:

6 Mood Symbols

Recently I came across these symbols buried in the archaeological-like layers in my studio. They were done many years ago, I think by Richard Haines, artist, painter, and teacher, who conducted some classes at Disney Studios. Originally they were done in wash, but I transposed them into grease pencil so they could be Xeroxed. There was no explanation other than the suggestions accompanying each drawing. Although they speak for themselves, I would like to comment on them from my point of view. They suggest moods, states, conditions, or behavior. They seem to be inherent in the nature of things, or at least in our interpretation of them. If this is so, then these symbols can work as sort of emotional short-hand, and when used in a drawing or action, can subconsciously arouse in the observer the emotion with which they are associated.

Drawings are but symbols. They are an arrangement of lines and shapes that merely *represent* real things to the extent that these symbols can be incorporated in a scene (layout, background, or animation drawings) and to the extent that the emotion communicated will hopefully be kindled in the audience. Using these symbols will not only enhance the scene but will actually work as a short cut to illustrating your ideas.

These symbols may be a little harder to apply to drawings than are the common everyday gestures we are so well-acquainted with, but they do have a psychological effect on a viewer or audience, so they are worth investigating. They are applicable to all phases of animation. If indeed any of these symbols are used in the evolution of the story (story development, story sketch, or layout), the animators should be made aware of them so there might be a more perfect marriage of ideas.

The psychology of color can greatly enhance the effects of these symbols. I am sure Judith Crook, who recently conducted a color seminar at the studio, could add much to the enlightenment on the subject. There has been much research done in that field, not only for artistic purposes but also in the realm of physical and mental healing.

We in animation are mainly involved in motion, which is the thing that attracts the eye, delineates the movement, and carries the story. However, these symbols, along with color, are part and parcel in setting the proper mood, although the audience is rarely consciously aware of them.

My current involvement is in the realm of gesture (acting) and I strongly feel that in body gesture, people (and cartoons) make use of certain of these symbols. We had Harry Frazier, a Shakespearian actor, model for us. On each of the three nights I had him deliver a speech from a Shakespeare play. I watched him carefully as he twisted his body into shapes that described the text. I suspect he has either made a study of something similar to these symbols or he is just a "natural" actor who feels those means of expression intuitively.

These symbols as presented may seem static and possibly only helpful in a still life or some other type of painting, but that is only one aspect of their value. They represent a dynamic force, not a fixed, changeless, immobile design. It appears that Richard Haines must have spent some time in gathering and classifying these symbols, but that does not mean he has exhausted their possibilities. Perhaps a similar study could be done for gesture as applied to animation.

In the meantime, look these over carefully. Mull them over in your mind and see if you can use them to embellish your gesture drawings (or your story development, story sketch, or layout drawings).

SYMBOLS OF VIBRATION

DOTS, DASHES, BROKEN LINES
VIBRATION OF COLOR, AND DESIGN.

FOUNTAIN

SPONTANEOUS, CAREFREE,
IRRESPONSIBLE, GAY.

CASCADE

PLEASUREABLE, PLAYFFUL,
SWIFT, POWERFUL, RHYTHMIC

UNSUPPORTED DIAGONAL

MOVEMENT ACROSS OR IN AND OUT
OF SPACE.

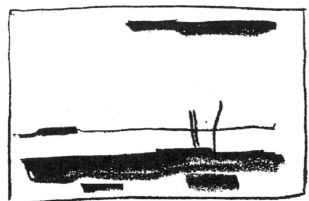

HORIZONTALS
REPOSE, CALM, PEACE, RESTFULNESS
FINALITY, SPACE, QUIET, DEPTH.

VERTICALS
DIGNITY, AUSTERITY, HEIGHT,
IMPERIOUS, TENSION.

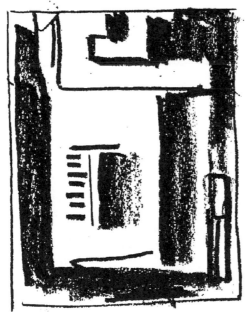

VERTICAL & HORIZONTAL
STOLIDITY, ENDURING, SOLIDITY,
PROTECTIVE, STUBBORNNESS!

GOTHIC ARCH
MYSTERY, CONTEMPLATION,
ASPIRATION, SPIRITUAL, AWE.

SPHERES

COMFORT, OPULENCE, SENSUOUS, LUXURIANCE, ABUNDANCE, RICH

CONFLICTING DIAGONALS

CONFLICT, DISSONANCE, DRAMATIC, PHYSICAL, OR EMOTIONAL DISTURBANCE.

SPIRAL

GERMINATION OF LIFE, GREAT FORCE, MYSTICAL, AWE-INSPIRING

ZIGZAG

ANIMATION, EXCITEMENT, RESTLESS.

WAVE - CURVE
GRACEFUL ENERGY, RHYTHMIC, YOUTH.
ELASTICITY, ORGANIC, STORM WAVE,
TURBULENCE, UNREST.

FLAME
VEHEMENCE, ASPIRATION,
ORGANIC GROWTH, INTENSITY,
FRANTIC, MENACING, TRAGIC.

POINTED SHAPES

ALERTNESS, PENETRATION,
VIVACITY, ACTIVITY.

GRIEF LINE
FATIGUE, SORROW, TRAGEDY

7 Breaking the Constraint Barrier

We spend a great percentage of our lives talking to people who are either in a standing pose or in a sitting position. The predominance of these poses is very apt to become burned into a sort of permanent image on our retinas and in our brains. The more active gestures such as sports and other activities are so fleeting that unless we pay special attention they flit by without making a good impression. A sketcher can spot these fleeting moves having trained himself in looking for and getting them down in graphic form.

Some of us though, when faced with a gesture that doesn't fit our familiar impression of how a human looks and acts (while in that conversational pose), straighten the pose up to conform. We being humans, are lovers of the status quo, comfort, familiarity, routine; life being less a problem when we follow the established way, the confirmed, the typical, even the systematic. It's sometimes difficult to break away from that entrapment — to "let ourselves go," so we can venture off into more creative realms.

Maybe that's why caricatures are usually a little wilder in gesture and countenance. We manage to step over a kind of barrier into an area of freedom — a kind of visual "sound barrier." Here are some caricatures made in the evening classes. It's as if the artist just decided to overstep the boundaries of restraint. The artist being, in this case, James Fujii:

This may seem like a repeat of a recent "handout" but there are things that have to be said and these drawings help me to say them. I often reproduce Dan Boulos' drawings for this very reason — he seems to have crossed the barrier. Even his drawings from the model are caricature-like. I never have to suggest to him, "push it farther" or "loosen up." Actually, occasionally I suggest that he "tie himself down" in a few areas for the sake of solidity and definition — but never to the point where he might take a backward step back into "copyland."

Here are some of his recent drawings from the class.

Here is one of Dan's "pot shots" at a fellow classmate. It may at first appear to be just a lot of random lines, but on closer examination you will see that every line plays an important part in the drawing. It is *loose* and free, and at the same time a good *solid* drawing.

Who says we have to draw the model? If there were any rules in the class they most certainly would have something to do with creativity, to loosen up, and (yes, you're going to have to hear this again) *don't try to trace the model*!

But just making an exaggerated drawing doesn't ensure a feeling of gesture or action. For instance, here is a pose where the doctor (Craig Howell) was getting his stethoscope off the shelf. Actually it was a complicated pose, carefully designed by Craig to show the grab of the instrument, with the upper back beginning to pull away, creating a tension, as if a rubber band was going through his body. In the next frame his right shoulder (with upper body) will pull back a little more, and his left arm (elbow) will straighten out (the hand will stay there). With the whole action started, his right shoulder will relax, the body straightens up, and the hand with the stethoscope will be pulled toward him. It's a kind of whip-like action. His right hand then comes in to assist and he'll be in a good position to go into his next move:

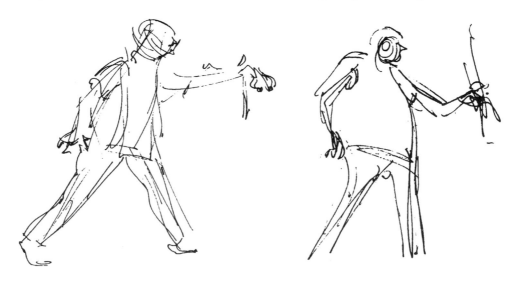

Sometimes when I make a suggestion sketch, I go to extremes. It is my way of showing the possibilities that are in the pose, plus an attempt to get the artist to loosen up. For instance, in this sketch what was meant to be a provocative, come-hither pose, the student simply went for the parts — and sure enough they are all there, but the seductive attitude is missing:

Here is a drawing of a "bag lady" taking a swig from a bottle. The student portrays her as very unenthusiastic about it. Perhaps that is the way a tired and discouraged old lady would go about it, but on the other hand it just seems like she could get the last drop out better by leaning back and tipping the bottle up more. Besides, it is a clearer gesture and a more entertaining picture.

Maybe the key to getting more out of the model's pose is to think of it as a drawing for some Disney cartoon, and to concoct your own story to fit the gesture. That way you have added incentive and direction. The models can only go so far, they are not cartoons and can only do so much with their stiff old bodies. (I engage mostly elderly models. They have more character and though the athleticism may not be there — the essence is.) The breaking of the barrier is up to you.

8 The Agony and the Ecstasy

Here we go again! New production, new director, new characters, and perhaps a new lease on life. A variation on the ancient maze, a new and distinctive color concept, and more incentive to get to work early (to find a parking spot). But whether or not you work on the Beauty or on the Beast — it should prove to be exciting.

Of course there are a few afflictions that need to be healed and others that will have to be accepted as normal occupational aftereffects. Here are some of the things we will have to deal with.

Inbetweener's elbow is a malady that is not necessarily confined to elbows, and it attacks the strong as well as the weak. No one in the business is immune to this indisposition. It will assault inbetweeners, assistants, animators, directors, and computer operators alike.

Management seems to be the only department that is immune. Although a few of them have had minor annoyances of the throat from excessive dictation and from delivering acceptance speeches at awards dinners.

Another strange and as yet unnamed malady is what might (after more research is done) be called look-alike-itess. Simply put, this is when an artist working on a particular character for great lengths of time, begins to take on its characteristics. You need only observe your fellow artists to identify the character they worked on. So far the only known cure is to be cast on a character that will tend to draw things back to normalcy (if indeed that seems more desirable). One especially susceptible artist was bundled up in his scene and carried off to camera. He was sent back when they couldn't locate him on the exposure sheet.

Another devastating condition is spot-itess. This is purely and simply the result of long hours of grueling overtime, plus overdoses of coffee and soft drinks. Spots before the eyes can be devastating for artists who use line in their drawing. In one extreme case, an assistant animator cleaned up a fifteen foot scene in pointillism. Further complications developed when his inbetweener contracted staccato elbow while trying to follow the extremes.

Another so far unnamed affliction is a kind of loss of control in general. The artist's hands (and mind) spasm uncontrollably. One scene animated in such a condition is being turned over to the *Beauty and Beast* staff for possible use in one of the Beast's scenes of rage.

There are many other random problems that crop up in everyday life that baffle even the experts, for instance, trying to pass off a Corby card as a credit card. One pitiful victim called the auto club because her card wouldn't open her car door.

The fact that most artists can't deal with reality even under normal circumstances is hampering the study of an increase in that dreaded disease work-a-holicism. A few layoffs and a few vacations may prove to be beneficial for those artists who choose to dive right into the next production, but there is fear that those addicted will push for even tighter schedules.

A complete list of casualties is beyond the scope of this handout, but here is a partial tabulation: Marshall Toomey, Eric Pigors, Carl Bell, Karen Lundeen, Rick Hoppe, Theresa Martin, Lee Dunkman, James Fujii, Lori Noda, Brian McKim, and Dolly Baker.

In the evening classes I have addressed the problem and am conducting the sessions with therapy in mind. I think much progress has been made along these lines; for instance, here is a joint on the part of two "drifters." (See the following paragraph for definition.) In this case the troubled artists are Mark Kennedy and Dan Boulos.

Not a few artists who have worked too far beyond their "norm", have drifted to a point of no return. Their pitiful condition is called "space-itess". The feeling they are experiencing is much like that of an astronaut who has drifted away from his spaceship and is wandering aimlessly in space.

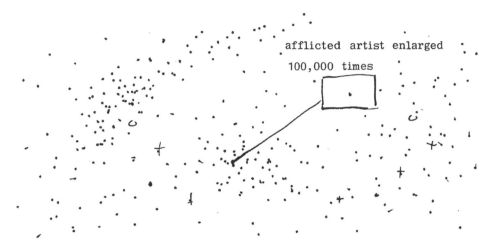

Maybe old "Salt's" situation is slightly different, but he has a poignant way of putting it.

Well, I have tried to make light of the agony — but there is ecstasy, too. The last few pictures have been absolutely delightful. And in the drawing class there have been moments of ecstasy when a student, grappling with the problems of drawing, makes a major breakthrough and begins to see a little clearer what drawing/acting is all about.

This caricature was done by one of the students with his left hand.

Here are a few drawings that their creators, Bill Perkins, Jesse Cosio, James Davis, and Dan Boulos, can be proud of.

9 Making All Parts Work Together to Shape a Gesture

First of all, I did another booboo! The latest one is not just the latest one — it's a mistake I've made twice. They say the third time is a charm, so I hope you're charmed by this one. Twice I've reproduced this wonderful drawing, giving credit to someone other than the person who drew it — Mark Kausler. My apologies, Mark.

I explained a drawing I had made as if it was an extreme in a scene — the shoulders pulling back, the arms straightening, leaving the hand there for a frame or two (for a little overlapping action). In a scene of animation you have to time these things to avoid everything moving at the same speed and all coming to a stop at the same time. It's a little more difficult to work those elements into a still drawing, but it's good practice to think about them as you are drawing. It will add the dimension of flexibility and action to your drawing. If you fail to think of the action while drawing from the model, much of the gesture can easily be lost.

For instance, here are two attempts at a pose that are in themselves attractive, but there is no feeling of life or movement in them. In my accompanying suggestion sketch, I show how the left elbow is pulled back, causing the arm hole in the dress to stretch out of shape and the cloth to fold and wrinkle as a result:

But more than just pulling the elbow back — which happens in this kind of a move — the head comes forward, stretching the neck in front, while squashing it in back, and the back bends forward, allowing the dress to hang down from the shoulders in front (the curve of the back against the straight of the hanging dress is a nice touch). The point is you are drawing an action (gesture — same thing) not a head, a neck, a shoulder, a back, etc., as such. The parts may be many, but the action is one.

Here is another, but similar problem, where the whole body is twisted, and the shoulders pulled completely at right angles to the feet. The model is pulling her dress around with the twist that causes it to cleave to her back and the hem to protrude out in front. There are a lot of things going on, but (as in any pose) *everything works as one*:

In this next corrective sketch, I left the clothing out and addressed only the figure. It doesn't matter as they work in cahoots. The model is somewhat at ease resting her lower arm in her lap and leaning on her other arm. In such a move (think of it as a move, not as a pose) her right shoulder follows the elbow as it rests in her lap. This does two things: (1) it suggests a period of rest and (2) it pulls her right shoulder down so her look has a clear path to travel in. Her left shoulder pushed up causes a stretch on her left side, setting up a squash on her right side. Squash and stretch are an animator's "Man Friday."

Here is another pose where in my suggestion sketch you may detect a concentration of attention on what the model is looking at or listening to. She not only turns her head, but her shoulders, too (it swings the whole attention around in that direction). Bending her forward intensifies her interest in what she sees or hears. Again, it is making everything in the drawing work toward telling the story.

Nothing on the character can remain static — everything is alive and moving. And Merleau Ponty's statement, "my body....does not have a spatiality of position but one of situation," in our situation means story. And finally that his whole body, his "entire posture" takes an active part in the act of leaning upon the desk with both hands — all the parts of his body working together as one.

Gesture (acting) can be a lot of fun!

10 Forces (Energy, Animation, Power, Vim, Vigor, and Vitality)

Webster defines dynamic as "relating to energy or physical force in motion." Stanchfield defines drawing as depicting a motion graphically, using the proper forces that affect the particular move or gesture being drawn.

For instance, if you're going to draw a character reaching forward with his hands, the forces that make that move possible are going to affect more than just the outstretched hands. Actually it is not the muscles in the hands that extend the hands forward — it is the cooperation of many muscles throughout the body that are mustered by the forces behind that move. Those forces are actuated by the intellectual desire to do something. They inform the sensory nerve endings in the muscles to produce the feeling of stretching the arm forward. You don't have to see this to do it — even with your eyes closed you know whether or not you are stretching. You don't have to see it visually to do it, but you do have to see it mentally and feel it kinesthetically to draw it. Just seeing the hand outstretched means nothing unless you have felt the forces in the shoulder, the back, the bend at the waist, the reach of the neck, head, and even the look of the eyes.

In drawing an action or a gesture it will help to think of the body parts as having come from a "normal" front-on position, and then to feel the exertion of the forces required to get to that gesture. Though the body has stopped moving, the forces are still at work. If the muscles relax their tensions, the pose would change — the figure would tend to return to "normal," or maybe even fall down to the floor in a tensionless heap. If you don't feel those forces at work in your drawing, you will tend to return the pose to "normal." You will "straighten everything up." Putting it bluntly, your drawing will be gutless.

Let's look at some drawings from the evening class to illustrate the possibilities in using those forces. Here's one where the "workman" is buckling on his tool belt. His right hand holds everything up while his left hand reaches around to attach the buckle. He leans away from the problem area so the folds in his shirt won't block out his view. And notice how he forms a shelf out of his hip to support those heavy tools. In my sketch I also had him lean over toward us a little so he can have a better view of the buckle. Can you feel the force behind this move and how every part of the body is supporting the activity?

Here is a difficult view — a straight-on, bending toward us. In my sketch I cheated a little by bending him slightly to his right. It's still essentially a straight-on, but the slight bend plus the curved line on his upper back says "bending over." It also got his elbows down to his knees where they belong — if he's going to lean on them. That allowed me to drop the "crystal" down into the opening below his seat and out in front of his knees. Can you feel the third dimensional space in that area? I call that area the "stage" of the drawing — the arena where the story is being told, where all the forces congregate, supported by all the parts of the body working as a unit.

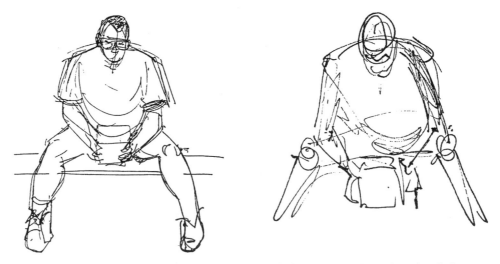

Here's the same pose from another angle. I stopped the artist early in his sketch because I felt he was headed for trouble. In my sketch I pointed out the desirability of getting the foundation built before trying to put up the windows. I first established his bend forward, and where his buttock was situated so I could get his knees situated, where his elbows were going to have to be, and of course the important thing — the crystal. There is a "school" of drawing that advocates drawing the center of interest first, then adjusting everything else to suit. That approach would require a great amount of visual skill. I think the sculptor's method is the safest — first comes the armature, then build it up from the inside out. Anyway, here's the drawing, and incidentally, can you see that third dimensional area in this drawing that I mentioned in the above sketch?

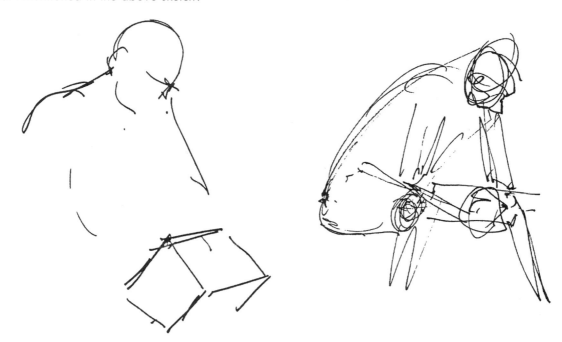

Here's an interesting one. The model (our own Kevin Smith) is holding the crystal at an arm's length (and then some). In my sketch I tried to show that the more you can show the continuity of the forces, the clearer the statement will be. I'm not suggesting that everything you draw should go to such extremes; I merely wanted the forces to be apparent. Even in a more subtle action the forces should be felt. And because of the tremendous thrust, I cupped his right hand around the front side of the crystal (half in jest) so it couldn't get away from him:

Here's the same pose from the opposite side. As you can see, in my sketch the leg was kept back farther to emphasize the arm stretch. Notice also that I staged the hands in the reverse of the above illustration:

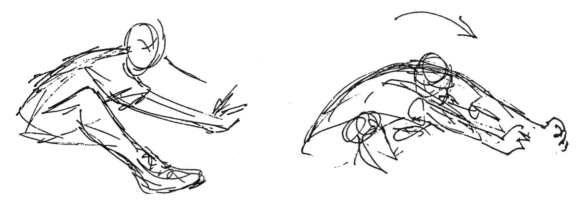

In this next sketch the model is fumbling through his bag for something. What are the forces at work? Well, I see his left hand holding the case open (and up so it doesn't collapse) and pushing down with his right hand, poking into the corners. There is a certain fascination about the student's drawing. As he is searching in the bag, he gazes off, looking at nothing — after all, what he's searching for has to be found by feel, so why look into the bag? My sketch simply suggests another possible use of the forces.

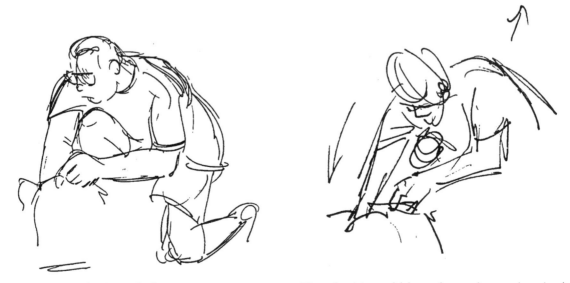

As Don Graham said after critiquing a painting, "So what! It could have been done a hundred different ways and all of them been correct." Of course that was in a painting class. In animation there are certain rules that determine the best staging and the best acting. You may get away with "murder" in modern painting but at Disney Studios, the story has to come through loud and clear.

In this last drawing, the student has made a very powerful statement — you can feel the tremendous stretch of the left arm and the pulling up of the right shoulder, the nice knee bend and spread of the feet (which in my haste I missed in my sketch). The reason I picked on this drawing was because the student had copied some very nebulous shapes on the back of the model. I suggested that a simple bent back would be clearer. Also the arms are both pointing in the same direction, creating an undesirable parallel. In addition, they are both the same length, and have the same amount of bend in them, making them a bit static. I took advantage of the stretched arm and featured it as the stretch, making the other arm a squash. (The upper back is a stretch, while the stomach is a squash.)

Many fine drawings were made that evening (as usual), and I wish I could reproduce all of them, but here is at least one artist's accomplishment — the work of Michael Surrey. You can feel the whole body working as a unit and the forces are not wasted on superfluous moves or distracting details:

11 Pure Performance

It's very gratifying to see someone in the evening class break loose from the "run-of-the-mill" copying of the model. It happens often, and each time I'm tempted to reproduce them for you. (Instead, I assault you with those tedious critiques.) When those delightful times occur, it seems that the artist has suddenly become freed of all self-consciousness and entered the realm of pure performance in the form of acting/drawing.

In a recent class, Bobby Ruth Mann modeled for us. She posed as a Hawaiian hula dancer — even played some Hawaiian music, via recording, for mood setting. The costume she wore was rather confusing. If you copied what was before you it would have been indefinable. On that evening two artists transcended the difficulties and came up with some delightful drawings. One of them, James Fujii, seemed to catch the spirit in which the poses were presented. These are, at the same time, realism and caricature. And they are the epitome of Bobby Ruth. James somehow defied or ignored the confusion of the costume and went straight for the essence.

The other artist, Dan Boulos, seemed playfully audacious in his approach to drawing the model. He sees things most of us are too conservative to ever dare to even look for, let alone be able to see. If you could watch him draw! It's as if he were hacking his way through a small 11″ × 17″ jungle; a chop here, a chop there — and suddenly you realize he has cut a path to that illusive clearing — performance. Suddenly there is a gesture that is more Bobby Ruth than Bobby Ruth.

I'm not trying to "sell" James or Dan. I singled their drawings out only because I felt they were outstanding. On a scale of 1 to 10 the other artist's works may have been a 9 1/2, or a 9 9/10, but these to me were 10s. I acknowledge that many of you, as James and Dan, have worked hard; have drawn a lot; have attended my classes twice a week, and have somehow gotten into the spirit of gesture drawing. I don't mean to infer that these two have "arrived." I don't know that anyone ever actually "arrives ." Drawing/acting is a lifetime adventure. There is no "formula" for becoming a proficient artist. It is just a lifetime of search and discovery. Teachers can only hint at some direction — the artist has to latch on to some personal method of finding and applying the facts for himself. My highest wish is that all of you will continue to develop your own means of expressing yourselves as performers.

Trying to reach a "goal" is not so much *narrowing down* to a fine point as it is *opening up* to a wider range of realization. You *concentrate* your efforts only by *broadening* your knowledge and understanding and skill. I hope these drawings will serve as an inspiration for you to do just that.

12 Different Concepts

It needn't be thought of as conflicting information if one teacher says draw all the details and go for a finished drawing, while another encourages you to be loose and flexible. Similarly, some may suggest using a square to block in the head, while others will say use a circle. Still others will advise, think of the head as a series of planes. Many will declare that everything is design, design, design. All they're trying to do is give you a compatible concept in your approach to drawing. What may give one a clear concept may confuse another. If you have a concept that works for you — don't change. If you're struggling, it's not demeaning to experiment with another.

As for finished drawing as opposed to sketching — there is a place and a need for both, and every artist at Disney Studios should be adept at both. Since more time has been spent on final drawings than on roughs, I have been trying to get everyone in the evening (and day) classes to loosen up. These sessions afford an opportunity to fashion your own personal gestures, rather than cleaning up another's work. Approaching gesture drawing with a cleanup concept is an extremely difficult thing to pull off. That is why I use all the underhanded tactics available to get everyone to untether and run free — this is a time to stretch! This is an opportunity to exaggerate, to push beyond the old limits.

After an intensive period of working on production drawings with their demands of exactitude, clean lines and narrow tolerances, one is apt to get a little "tight" — one's concept narrows down. Tightness or tension has a lot to do with becoming self-conscious and inflexible while drawing (especially acting/drawing.) To be creative, one must be in the "mood," that is, in a flexible, open, bold, daring, and searching attitude. The desire to entertain should accompany every line you put down. In one of the afternoon sessions I attempted to get everyone to loosen up. I insisted that no one try to "draw" anything — especially not a tight, clean, detailed drawing. Rather than try to turn people on with their pretty drawings, I suggested they turn people off with some loose, grubby, besmeared, messy sketches — sketches that tell not what the model looks like, but rather what the model is doing. To assist them in doing this I had the model do three related segments of an action, which were to be drawn on top of each other. I was hoping for a more entangled mess, but most artists came through with some looser than usual, but still rather articulate drawings. Here are some real nice composites of 3 out of the perhaps 20 artists present. The first group is from the pen of Wendie Fischer.

Wendie's two head drawings are in keeping with my request (during the head sketching period) to stay away from "portraits," and to lean toward loose caricatures. They have a light, comical air about them.

These drawings by Ed Gutierrez may not appear grubby, besmeared, and messy to you, but for him they must seem so — he usually draws in an extremely neat and finished style.

This is a good way for animators to study from the live model. It adds a sense of movement to the drawings. Look from drawing to drawing and you can see the action happening. An animator should never make a drawing as if it were a plaster of paris statue — even one drawing alone should have a sense of movement like these groups of three have.

Jane Krupka was another artist whose work I confiscated that day. Though she did draw three figures, one on top of another, she was careful to use only the essentials in order to keep them neat. I called for messy drawings to free the artists of the responsibility of clean drawings so they could more easily capture the movements, but most of the class, including Jane, strove for clarity.

I have heard it said that while under hypnosis the subject cannot be made to do something that is against their morals. It seems that in drawing a similar thing happens. If you have been drawing long enough with a particular style or technique — even hypnotism would not turn you aside. This is not a criticism — it's one of the many facts of life. What I am attempting to do is pry my students away from copying what is before them. Andrew Loomis in his book *Figure Drawing* says "Try to get the meaning behind the drawing much more than the drawing itself." You have to realize it's entirely possible to train someone to copy what is before them without knowing one thing about anatomy, or how anatomy works; gesture, or how gesture ties in with acting; or without the slightest notion that acting is fundamental to animation.

Most of the characters in our cartoons are far from anatomical specimens — à la Hogarth or Bridgeman. They are lizards and mice, etc., and in the next production, a candelabra, a teapot, a footstool, a music box, etc. How are you going to make a teacup say, "Pardon me, Master... But your supper's getting cold," if you are paying more attention to the construction of a teapot than you are the "meaning behind the drawing?"

Well, as Ollie Johnston used to say, "It ain't easy."

Afterthought: A drawing has a right to metamorphosis, the first stage of which is a rough (often messy) sketch. Sometimes, in attempting to capture an illusive gesture, the sketch may even be nebulous, ambiguous, and even downright obscure.

13 A Time for This and a Time for That

If I may misquote the *Bible*, "There is a time for this and a time for that." And that's just what we've been doing. There is a time for hard-core study, with your nose in an anatomy book or attending lectures and studying animation. And there is a time for quick sketching and gesture drawing — a period of stretching the imagination and loosening up.

In one of the Thursday afternoon drawing classes everyone seemed to loosen up. There was an air of freedom of expression. Lighthearted attitudes allowed for much freer sketching — at times there was a definite release of tension, becoming apparent audibly. There were even "hotspots" of hilarity as one or another artist got a little light-headed and ventured into the realm of cartooning. I encouraged it, for I believe it's okay to be funny at times — after all we *are* cartoonists.

Even the poses were innovative that day, which by the way, were done by the students. I think it is good practice to have to search within to come up with a pose that is worthy of drawing — especially for artists involved in animation. In keeping with the heightened preoccupation of the moment, someone brought in a bike to pose with. Here is Ron Westlund's rather nice sketch on one of the bike poses. To the right of that is a more lighthearted version by Eric Pigors.

On top of the next page is another nice sketch (artist unidentified, sorry) and next to it a sketch by Kris Heller — done with her left hand.

And of course Eric Pigors on the other side of the room "slides into home" with this imaginative version of the same pose. To its right is a drawing by Pres Romanillos, where he turned the handles of the bike into something more meaningful to him.

I'd like to show you more of Kris's sketches made with her left hand. She succeeded in breaking all the habits formed with the right hand and found a new freedom of expression. The left hand was incapable of drawing any detail so Kris got a real nice, loose drawing of the gesture. I think these are very expressive.

But don't go away! Kris, in her inspired state, decided to hold the pen in one place and move the paper. I don't think even Betty Edwards thought of that.

In the meantime, on the other side of the room, Eric, who by the way, did some nice realistic drawings also, was busy soaring off into cartoon land — turning the model into animals, mechanical men, and other aberrant creatures.

Even the rather reserved (at least on the surface) Laurey Foulkes got in the spirit of the moment and rendered a male model in this slightly unorthodox way.

Of course the session was not all party and games. I hovered over them as usual (about 25 artists that day) and they knew who was the next victim when they heard my pen snap open behind them, and my old knees crack as I knelt beside them. Sometimes I would get "two birds with one stone," saying to the artist in the next seat, "That goes for you, too." Anyway, here are some student's drawings with my suggestions beside them. This is a typical "waterloo" of poses — the figure bent over, leaning on an elbow. I like to think of the head (the mind) as instigating the move. It (the mind) says "I will stretch forward to pick up something. Since I am seated and my buttock is fairly glued to the chair, I will have to stretch from that point with the top half of my body."

The spine is a key ingredient in this move, for it extends from the buttock to the head. Better yet, from the buttock to the look, for looking at the object that is to be picked up is vital to this pose.

More important than looking for things on the model to draw, is getting the feeling of what the model is doing. All the parts may be drawn, but if they aren't integrated to tell the story — they become just so many parts. Here's another view — same problem — same solution.

Here again the student got all the physical elements down but lost the tensions and forces in the figure. Notice how I kept his right leg turned toward us to set up a tension as the body is forced against it. Stretching out his left leg helped the overall thrust of the action.

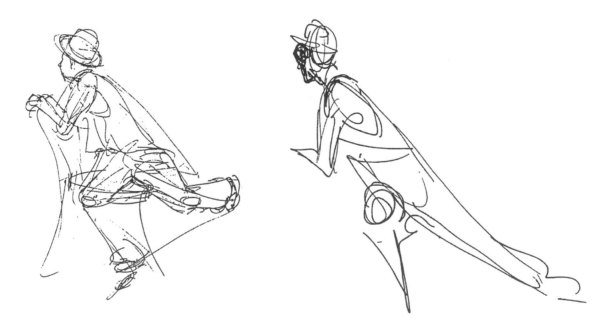

When I was learning animation, I heard the word "staging" a lot. In this pose, the student copied what he saw. In my sketch I staged the drawing so it would "read" clearly. In doing this I used the principle of perspective — overlap. That is, his left shoulder is in front of (overlapping) the shirt; the shirt is overlapping the neck; the neck is in front of the pectoralis major, and that is in front of the right shoulder. As you can see it sets up a nice feeling of third dimension.

14 Look to This Day

My friends, it is good to be back in the swing of things again. My wife, Dee, who was hit head-on on Highway 101 on October 17, has recuperated most of her injuries and can at last spare me for a few days a week. For two months I haven't had time to draw or write (or play tennis), so my finger joints are squeaking and my brain is staggering like an inebriated jellyfish. I did miss you all — and I missed writing a handout each week. I often think maybe there aren't any more handouts. After all, how many different ways can this stuff be presented? I have done 139 of these lessons. That's around 139,000 words. End to end, that would reach to over a mile. Maybe I'm due for burn-outs-ville.

One of the things that keeps me going is like once in a while someone says to me, "Hey, Walt, I sure got a lot out of last week's handout." Well, I'm a sucker for that kind of compliment. Not that I've done something great, but because I've helped someone. That's the name of the game... my game, anyway.

Some of you are probably sick and tired of the New Year's resolution thing, but I recently read an interesting "New Year's Resolutions" article by Douglas Smith, Ph.D., who practices in nearby Los Olivos. It was written specifically for people who are trying to lose weight and/or are on other physical health and exercise programs. I'm going to quote the part that I think can be applied to artists.

I think artists fall into two major categories (generally speaking): those who study hard, learn fast, and retain what they've learned; and those who have to plug away all their lives, learning, learning, learning. Read what Dr. Smith has to say, and as you read, apply what he is saying to your life as an artist:

Every year at about this time I write my annual article on New Year's Resolutions. I imagine that my article has stimulated a few people to gather up their emotional resources and try, once again, to make some major changes in their lives. Unfortunately, most of the people who make New Year's resolutions have failed by the end of January. Why do people fail to make lasting changes?

To understand these failures we need to understand the nature of problems and how we typically try to remedy those problems in our lives. To make problem solving easier to grasp, you can view it in one or two ways. One type of problem solving is like building a house; the other style is similar to planting a garden.

Building a house is a major project that takes good planning and careful execution. Fortunately, once it is done, it is done.

The second major type of problem is like that of growing a garden. Like building a house, this too needs careful planning and execution. But unlike building a house, you are never finished with the task of growing a garden. Every day you need to control weeds, fertilize and water, trim overgrown plants, replace dead growth, and plant new seeds to replace old crops. Everyone who has ever grown a garden knows that it is a never-ending task.

If you approach a growing garden as you do building a house, you will have an initial success; however, the garden will soon become weed-infested, overgrown, and dead. The same is true if you approach a "growing garden" type of problem. If you take a house building approach to a garden-like problem, you will soon fail.

Skipping to the end, he continues:

We choose these large goals in the hope that we can somehow be healthy and stay that way without any further work. We unconsciously believe that we can approach exercise (*drawing*) as if we were building a house. The truly healthy (*talented*) individual knows that health (*drawing*) is a daily task.

This year, as you think of making New Year's resolutions, get into the mind-set of growing a healthy emotional garden. Choose a goal that you can incorporate in your life each and every day. Recognize that almost every goal will need to be reaffirmed a day at a time. We are never done in our lifelong task of personal growth and health.

Nicely put, and pertinent to us artists. We all know how soon we go to pot when we neglect sketching and studying every day. Here are some drawings from our classes at the studio that can be likened to flowers from a well-tended garden. I say that because it was only after much study and practice (controlling weeds, fertilizing, watering, replacing dead growth, and planting new seeds) that this high caliber of drawing began to emerge (blossom).

Those were just a few of the many excellent drawings made from a model, and implanting life of Maurice as they were sketched.

Mark Kausler did this very same drawing the same night.

Here are four versions of one pose done with the confidence that comes with constant practice and a target of gestural expression. I'm sorry, but the names of the artists who did these have eluded me. All I remember is the regulars in the class had reached a very high standard.

I must confess, I don't indulge in New Year's resolutions, but I do indulge in gardening. I feel like God when, out of a patch of dirt I can raise tasty, nutritious vegetables and fruits. Drawing is similar to gardening in that out of nothing (blank paper, not blank minds) emerges these delectable drawings. I happen to be of the second category of artist — the kind that has to plug away in study all their lives. But I can handle that — I'm a gardener at heart.

Make this a year of growth. Have a good one!

The title of this handout is *Look To This Day*, which is the first line of an old Sanskrit poem that I thought you might enjoy. It proclaims the real value and meaning of each day.

Look to this day
for it is life
the very life of life
In its brief course lie all
the realities and truths
of existence.
The joy of growth
the splendor of action
the glory of power
For yesterday is
but a memory
And tomorrow is
only a vision
But today well lived
makes every yesterday
a memory of happiness
And tomorrow a vision
of hope
Look well, therefore,
to this day!

15 Entertainment

Just before I took off in October, I was conducting four drawing classes a week. The momentum of improvement was awesome. I had gotten everyone to relax and quit trying to make drawings like finished Norman Rockwell or Michelangelo paintings. We have different problems than the so-called illustrator or fine artist. In the time it took those guys to do one painting, an animator will have had to do maybe a hundred drawings. That's not to say that the great artists of the past, whom we all admire and study, could not or did not zap out a bunch of gesture drawings as studies of or preliminaries to their more complex (and painstaking) paintings.

My occasional reference to the "masters" may seem far afield, but actually it is not. We all revere the great masters of the past. They are an inspiration and a source of artistic information. They were not unlike ourselves in that they spent every day of their lives as we do — searching for knowledge and wisdom to express ourselves. The only difference is that their goal was easel painting or murals, and ours is animation. Look at some of the sketches of those artists (reproduced here). At that point in their work, they are on a level with us as we sketch in class or at work, attempting to capture a gesture or a series of gestures that will tell the story we are either depicting in a painting, or acting out in drawings for a film.

Some of these sketches (preliminaries for paintings, called cartoons) are extremely rough and detail-less, but certainly not lacking in expression. They had to tell a whole story in one painting, so a concerted effort had to be made to get the proper gestures. Most of these sketches are in a serious vein, but are nonetheless entertaining.

That is the kind of probing and exploring needed in preliminary drawings for the more final creation or performance. It was necessary for some of those masters to spend months, even years, on a single painting to complete it. An animator's searching and probing resemble those of the master's in many ways, but the animator has to move on immediately. He must do dozens of them in the time it took Rembrandt to prime his canvas.

Here are some sketches done by some Disney artists that are every bit as praiseworthy as those reproduced above. That area of getting down the gesture is of prime importance in both cases. Perhaps more so for the animator, for he doesn't have weeks or months to adjust and re-adjust his drawings. He must train himself to capture the gesture in moments and then move on. That's why in the Tuesday and Wednesday evening classes, we are concentrating on gesture, which in a series of drawings becomes acting. Incidentally, the model was our own master of gesture sketching, Tom Sito.

ARTIST: Mark Kausler

ARTIST: James Fujii

ARTIST: Lureline Weatherly

ARTIST: James Fujii

ARTIST: Joe Haidar

16 Follow-Up Department

Last week I touched on New Year's resolutions. Several people responded favorably to the handout; however, none of them professed any resolution making. Actually, what I was suggesting was a lifetime resolution, one that becomes so much a part of life that it can no longer be thought of as a resolution.

The *LA Times* had an interesting bit in the column, "View Finder." The author listed some recent resolves. Here are a few samples: "...to get a life," "...to remain tall, happy and increasingly stupendous," one guy resolved to continue his sex education, a gal resolved not to get caught, and another gal hopes her troubles last as long as her New Year's resolutions. They all kinda' make sense, don't they?

But, in the form of resolutions or not, *do* commit yourself to the studying of drawing, animation, humor, drama, acting, and that matrix which holds all of those together — gestures.

17 Entertainment II

In an ongoing attempt to get the students to loosen up and quit trying to draw exact replicas of the model, I remind the class the audiences that come to see the films we make like to be entertained. They are not interested in how well we can draw. And as any cartoonist worth his pencil dust would do, Dan Boulos latched on to that one and turned it into "entertainment."

"You work for Disney ... You don't have to draw well."

My thanks to Dan for inadvertently helping me put over a point. The point is that there is a need, of course, to improve our ability to draw anatomy (especially hands and faces), drapery, textures, etc., but what is done with that skill is what the gesture class is all about. Dan has an approach to drawing that is worth analyzing. He manages to overcome the tendency to get involved in surface details, and goes straight to the essence of the gesture.

Compare one of his sketches that clearly reveals the story behind the pose, with the sketch of another artist who was attempting to copy what he saw, and missed the clarity necessary. I think the difference is, one artist had his mind on the gesture, which was a clown balancing on a tight rope (or wire), and the other artist had his mind on the model. If he had been intent on putting over the gesture, he might have adjusted the arms (which got all glued together into an objectionable tangent) to create that feeling of balancing on a rope. I suggested three alternative arm positions — one a variation on his drawing and two more imaginative extremes.

I think a lot of it has to do with the artist's attitude or concept of what he is drawing. I often try to explain it is "play-acting," which simply means you put your whole heart and soul into it — you play like it's real. I think that "playful" attitude while drawing is both important and good. We are involved in the field of entertainment and our drawings should reflect that fact. We have a responsibility to bring entertainment to the audience.

So many times in the evening classes we get so serious in our attempts to make a nice looking drawing that we get all tied up, stiff, and inflexible. So much so that sometimes the drawings are not fun to look at. Even a serious or dramatic drawing should be entertaining.

Last week the title of my handout (Chapter 15) was "Entertainment." I started out in that direction but my mind wandered into something about comparing Disney artists with the "masters." I had been perusing

Eric Larson's extensive writings on "Entertainment" and had desired to pass some of his thoughts on to you. Eric worked for Disney Studios for over 50 years. His contributions to the field of entertainment are immeasurable. Much of his later years were spent teaching young animators at the studio. The heart of his teaching seemed to focus on entertainment. He taught timing, drawing, squash and stretch, and other phases of animation, but all with entertainment in mind. Becoming an animator usually requires an infinite amount of study, preparation, practice, self-determination, and dedication. Yet, in spite of the torturous, grueling, exhausting nature of such an exciting art — the product has to be entertaining.

I am reminded of the opera *I Pagliacci* (The Players) where the clown, in spite of his fouled up love life, is supposed to go out and make the audience laugh. Are we so different? We have problems with our our love life, our car payments, our eviction notices, our wayward children, etc., but when we pick up our pencils, a transformation has to take place, the "actor/artist" (the play-actor) takes over, the show must go on. Laugh clown, laugh. Today you are Canio, King Lear, Mickey Mouse, Ariel, and you have to step out of the life of the townsperson or the art student and become the professional actor — the entertainer.

My mind is wandering again. Let me quote Eric for a while:

In discussing entertainment and ways to achieve it, we are going to repeat thoughts and facts we have considered and reconsidered time and again because, as Stanislavsky wrote: "Reproduction of life by actors (animators) is a challenge and a responsibility."

It would be impossible to list so-called "creative steps" in a tight progressive order of importance. *The fact is, every effort and thought going into our scenes will be important* — our attitude, our planning, imagination, acting, drawing, action, and personality analysis; our approach to pantomime, caricature, and dialogue interpretation and phrasing; our views of comedy, drama, fantasy, and the whimsical; our sense of staging, our use of the silhouette, of perspective, of music, of the rhythmic flow of movement in a pose, and the need for weight and balance in that pose; our sense of timing and the value of a "change of pace" in the action we do, remembering that what we have to say must be said with the whole body, and that in simplicity there is strength. All are important.

Well, WOW! Now that's a whole course in animation in two paragraphs. He never lets you forget the close relationship those things have to entertainment. As he begins his analysis of each subject, he starts out like this: "Let's begin our approach to entertainment by checking our..."

I would like to quote one more short paragraph and then get on to some drawings from my classes where we "do battle" with these concepts. Stanislavsky wrote:

In striving for entertainment, our imagination must have neither limits nor bounds. It has always been a basic need in creative efforts. Imagination must be cultivated and developed; it must be alert, rich, and active. An actor (animator) must learn to think on any theme. He must observe people (and animals) and their behavior — try to understand their mentality.

My wife, Dee, who reads my stuff for errors of all kinds (my writings would be unintelligible without her input) was reading this back to me and when she got to Eric's writing she switched to a Swedish dialect. Now that's what I call "play-acting." All of a sudden it all became more meaningful, more expressive — like an artist interpreting a gesture in a drawing. It was strictly a subconscious thing. She didn't know Eric Larson, nor did Larson speak in a Swedish dialect — the name must have sparked the spontaneous embellishment. The process is the same when an artist draws on the subconscious (right brain) to make an entertaining drawing. Anyway, it took me about five minutes to laugh that one off.

Here is a drawing by a young man who is fairly new to drawing but not new to dedication. He is determined to find a place for himself in animation. In this sketch he drew what he knew to be true — a human with two arms, two legs, one head, etc., but locking into that kind of reporting netted him a less than entertaining drawing. I pointed out to him how, in keeping his mind free and flexible he could in a sense, mentally orbit the model and see what the pose looked like from other angles in order to better understand it from the angle he was drawing it. Doing that helps to not only draw things from left to right, but in and out of the picture plane third dimensionally.

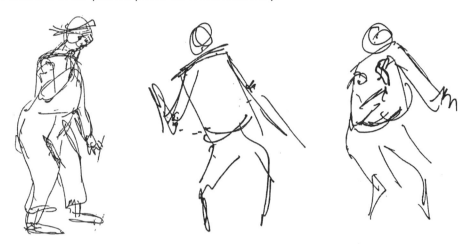

In my first sketch you can see how I imagined the pose from another view. It allowed me to see how low the model's right shoulder was and how the whole upper body was angled toward me. It also helped me see how the legs had to be supporting the body.

Here is a pose that presents the problem of foreshortening. Searching for lines on the model is sometimes futile. Clothing doesn't always know the rules of drapery. For solving the foreshortening dilemma, I recommend the principle of perspective called "overlap." It is simply drawing one thing in front of another (works every time). Maybe you can get the gist from my crude explanatory sketches. In my sketch of the pose, I simply used that rule, drawing the knees first, the hip behind that, the chest behind that, the head behind that, and, finally, the arm overlapped by both chest and head. My sketch is in a very elemental stage, but as you can see, the principle gets you of to a pretty solid start.

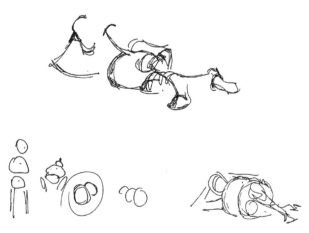

Let me do one more drawing critique for you. First let me say that when acting, you assume the role of someone other than yourself, so you go through the motions almost as if you are mimicking that character. No transformation will happen if you don't mentally and physically take on another role — act out the person. I like to call it "play-acting," because if you think of it as play, you don't get so uptight.

Now if you were going to have to take off a sweater, you would have to go through all the antics that describe the action. The antics you go through are what you understand of a real life, natural (or caricatured) moves required to get that sweater off. If you can't get the sweater off in your imagination, you're not going to get it off in a drawing. In my sketch below, I showed how the girl's left arm is pulling up on the sweater, while her right arm is pulling out and down in an attempt to get her arm out of the sweater sleeve. In doing this, her left hip is thrust out for additional power. Also it makes a lively drawing, angling up to the right, then to the left, then to the right again. You can see and feel the struggle, the tension, and the movement. As I have said many times before, every line on your drawing should help the action and make it more entertaining.

18 Playing to the Balcony

Some time ago I did a handout online. It was a rather frivolous paper, but it met with such acclaim that I started to plan others on dots, spaces, shapes, angles, etc., but it got so mind-boggling that I had to see my psychiatrist. His analysis was that I was given my first set of crayons at too young an age. He may be right. I remember munching on those things thinking they might color my life. Well, they did. I started dreaming in color very early in life — mostly in blue (blue was the tastiest crayon). Even now you'll notice that I wear nothing but blue. Every time I get a blood test the little glass adapter fills up with a blue liquid. The nurse says "Okay, that's it, your majesty."

When I got into animation I had to give up color for line. Looking at a line as opposed to a splotch of color is like looking at everything from the side. That is, an area of color

from the side looks like this.

Eventually, after much academic work, art school, soul-searching, and the final submission to the great possibilities of line, I discovered that interesting shapes could be made by connecting those lines.

I found that dots could be made by chopping those lines up into tiny bits. Heads, for instance, were merely shapes with a purpose.

with one of those tiny bits of chopped line for an eye. Angles are plain lines looking for a place to lie down

(or get up, depending on your interpretation or need).

Lines soon took on a life of their own. They were living things which, if I was not quite firm in my conviction while drawing, would take over and assert themselves, usually simply as lines minus any resemblance to what I was trying to portray. I knew I had to come to terms with this dilemma, so I put lines into categories which in effect gave them new identities, and thus limited their power to be "just lines." Thusly made subservient to my wishes, they became instruments to express bends, stretches, squashes, shapes, areas, angles, tension, action, large and small, far and near, this way and that, etc. Drawing "ain't easy," as Ollie said, but at least I have some reliable tools to work with.

I almost dread the time when I retire and want to go back to color. It may require a complete reversal of the process. Maybe a week or so of poached crayon for breakfast, crayon on whole wheat for lunch, and for dinner, crayon pizza with Neapolitan ice cream for dessert will do the trick.

Well, so much for silliness. It's very often trauma time when we are faced with a living, third dimension, line-less model and must condense all that complexity into a line drawing. We can't draw the color, the shadows, the density, or the fleshiness. Often the personality is evasive. The gesture is at best only suggestive. So what we have to do is put ourselves in the model's character and circumstance (the gesture) and draw from within our own experiences, much like a stage or movie actor does. It has to be fabricated first in the mind, then transposed to the "stage." That way, though we may not be able to express the things we are called upon to illustrate in our own lives (physically), we can still, through "play-acting," express them in drawing.

In the book, *On Method Acting* the author Edward Easty says, regarding the problem of acting out certain emotional or physical action:

...the average actor experiences extreme difficulty in bringing onto the stage that which an ordinary human being feels and thinks every day of his life. Because most of us have all our lives been taught to suppress many of our natural feelings, instincts, and emotions from childhood, we are now faced with the issue of expressing them as actors to an audience while still unable to express them in our own lives. This is indeed a problem that forces the teacher (of acting) to emphasize to the student the need for honest expression in his personal relationship with life before he can expect to come to terms with a particular role.

That "personal relationship with life" is certainly open to discussion. But in my estimation, one doesn't have to experience all the complexities of life (human, animal, and bird) to draw or animate them. I think reading, studying acting, drawing, sketching, and observation will suffice. If you and I had to act on stage what we are called upon to act out on paper we might become embarrassed, blush, perspire, or maybe even become terrified. But on paper we can lose our imagination and if it doesn't come off we tear the drawing up and start over.

Drawing from the model is very much like drawing from the imagination. A mental picture is formed and we proceed to capture it on paper. The advantage of a live model is that there is a suggestion of a pose before us as a constant reference when needed. The disadvantage is that there is something tangible that tempts us to merely copy. That would be something like playing golf with cement channels to drive your balls along right into the hole.

I have some drawings here from our evening classes that may help to sort out the problems I posed above. For instance, here is a student's sketch where an awful lot of time was spent around the head area. I think that as the whole body contributes to a gesture, so should the drawing reflect that wholeness at any given time in its construction.

If after 15 seconds the model should leave, you should have enough of the gesture down so that tomorrow you could finish it. If you have only the head, then by tomorrow you almost certainly will have forgotten what the body was doing.

Here's another student's sketch where all the elements are present, the pipe is held up to the mouth, the beer can held in the other hand, they are there...but just there. In my sketch I tried to show that at this particular time, the "hobo" was interested in the pipe, so she was leaning into it in a much more covetous manner. "Mmm," she is saying, "this is goooood." The beer, on the other hand, is "set aside" for the time being, so is stretched out away from the center of interest — the primary action. That "story concept" that I concocted allowed me to get a feeling of movement into the sketch and to pull the audience's attention to the action that I thought was taking place.

Here is another student's sketch, interrupted in its early stages, that didn't seem to be acting like an actor would if he were before a thousand people at some large theater, or for a cartoon feature that will be shown to millions of people all over the world. It might help to realize that if you were acting on a stage, you would have to act (play) to the farthest person from you. You've probably heard the saying "play to the balcony." It means if you make a lot of subtle moves of say an inch or two, no one past the third row is going to detect it. To put it in plain language (bad plain language), "It ain't gonna read." There's not only nothing wrong with caricaturing a gesture, but it will invariably make a more entertaining drawing, and those in the farthest row in the "balcony" can read it.

2

Drawing

19 A Sack of Flour

In the book, *Psycho-Cybernetics* by Maxwell Maltz, there is a pithy paragraph with the heading, "The Secret of 'Natural' Behavior and Skill." It goes:

> The Success Mechanism within you can work in the same way to produce "creative doing" as it does to produce "creative ideas." Skill in any performance, whether it be in sports, in playing the piano, in conversation, or in selling merchandise, consists not in painfully and consciously thinking out each action as it is performed, but in relaxing, and letting the job do itself through you. Creative performance is spontaneous and "natural" as opposed to self-conscious and studied. The most skilled pianist in the world could never play a simple composition if he tried to consciously think out just which finger should strike which key — while he was playing. He has given conscious thought to this matter previously — while learning, and has practiced until his actions become automatic and habit-like... conscious effort inhibits and "jams" the automatic creative mechanism..."

I think the interesting thing is that the artist can and must, sooner than the pianist, cease that conscious effort and go for the spontaneous performance. If I remember correctly, it was Robert Henri who said, "If an artist had limited knowledge but used that limited knowledge creatively, he could paint a masterpiece." We're trying to do these things in the evening Gesture Classes. Not to use the class to study anatomy, the details of attire, or shadow, but to take what we know — no matter how little and go for the creative performance — the gesture. Anatomy is something every artist should know, but not to the neglect of gesture. All the characters we will be called upon to draw do not have the kind of anatomy we learn in the typical anatomy class, but they all carry out their roles by means of gestures.

In our gesture classes the goal is to take that quantum leap from the self-conscious drawing of anatomy or a blatant copying of the model, to an unself-conscious and unstudied, spontaneous sketching of the gesture (acting on paper). Here are two examples where the artists (both not directly involved in animation) were able to assume, in a matter of a few minutes, a change of attitude while drawing. The drawings on the left are the rather stiff approach they had been using. Then after my suggestion on how to loosen up I drew a goal-seeking sketch, but in a careless, carefree, and casual manner with my eye on the goal — the gesture. Then their successful attempt to do the same is shown.

The square and the circle was my way of pointing out that they are not drawing something built with rectangles made of wood, or metal, but of organic, third dimensional, living, growing things — beings made of flesh, blood, bones, nerves, with a will to live, move, and be active.

At bottom are the student's two sketches after the "loosening up" lecture. I never cease to be amazed at the impact attitude has on drawing. Needless to say we were both pleased at these results.

The objective is to be able to mentally picture a gesture (first impression — because the first impression is usually the strongest), then sketch that picture loosely and freely, whether you use human anatomy, frog anatomy, or a sack of flour. And incidentally here is an example of creating gesture with a sack of flour (from *Illusion of Life: Disney Animation* by Johnston and Thomas).

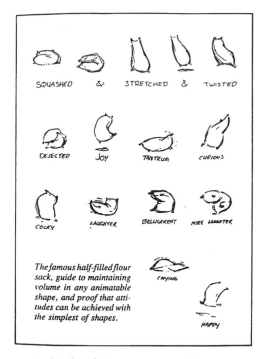

SQUASHED   &   STRETCHED   &   TWISTED

DEJECTED   Joy   TANTRUM   CURIOUS

COCKY   LAUGHTER   BELLIGERENT   MORE LAUGHTER

The famous half-filled flour sack, guide to maintaining volume in any animatable shape, and proof that attitudes can be achieved with the simplest of shapes.

CRYING

HAPPY

As Maxwell Maltz says, certain kinds of "...conscious effort inhibits and 'jams' the automatic creative mechanism...." So don't be afraid of making mistakes — or a bad drawing. You, in a sense, learn from making bad drawings. William Gladstone, the British Statesman, said, "No man ever became great or good except through many and great mistakes. I have learned more from my mistakes than from my successes."

Missiles are in our current news and thoughts. Some missiles are guided by their mistakes. They are projected toward a target (as we are in drawing), but they are continually corrected by their guidance system — learning, as it were, from their mistakes. Our correction mechanism is not quite so mechanical or automatic — we need textbooks, teachers, and continual sketching to keep our "missile" on track.

Here is a nice sketch where you can almost feel the guidance system keeping the pen within the borders while on its way to the gesture. I think the artist is Mary–Jean Repchuk (an Alzheimer's attempt at recall).

In the following drawings you can sense the first impression was so strong that the guidance system had little correcting to do. The artist is James Fujii.

20 Pantomime (Drawing) Preparation

Each week I try to reproduce some student's sketches with my suggestion drawings beside them, with a commentary on what goes through my mind to come up with a "storytelling" gesture. When those thoughts are written down, it seems like it must cover quite a span of time. While I am sketching and talking it takes but 10 or 15 seconds, but when just sketching, it usually takes but a split second to ferret out the manner in which the constituent parts tell the story. In doing this I am not suggesting that you have to think like me to make a good gesture drawing. Individuality is one of our chief contributions to creativity, so you will develop your own line of investigation. That will make all of our drawings different, but will assure that they have all been thought through to entertaining conclusions.

My experience on the stage, in animation, and in study has steered me to my way of thinking through a drawing. If you're at the beginning of your career, now is the time to start searching for your concepts of acting/drawing. You may even choose not to get involved in the thinking part and just sort of let it all happen. But let me remind you of the chap who was a loyal Disney person, a likeable guy with a good sense of humor, who rather than delve into his chosen career full sail, was drifting along, "waiting for the light to come on." The "light" isn't likely to just "come on." You have to find the light switch and turn it on yourself. In these handouts I'm attempting to suggest as many ways to the light switch as I can.

Well, I got sidetracked — let's go back to the first paragraph. Usually, the essence of the gesture hits you in a "flash." That first impression can usually be trusted, for it's like seeing familiar things anew, like something that's never happened before. Those are moments of pure Zen which spark up one's day. And perhaps they'll never occur again — so it becomes a very precious thing. But along with that first impression you have to draw upon your sense of logic, your desire to entertain, your ability to figure out how and why you were so struck with the pose. A gesture isn't some magic happening — it doesn't come in a vacuum-sealed container with a label that states: "This is a 100% organically grown gesture." Your character (or model) decides to strike a pose — every muscle and bone in the body are suddenly rallied as one, all taking an active part in constructing and fulfilling that gesture. When you draw that gesture, you have to simulate that bodily expression in line. What the model did with his or her hundreds of bones and muscles, you have to do with a greatly reduced number of lines.

When you write a letter, you are careful to choose words that express what you are trying to say. So it is in drawing. You pick shapes, angles, perspective, squash, and stretch (which are analogous to words and syntax in a sentence) that will express the gesture clearly. If you are oblivious of those things, your audience is going to be oblivious to what you are trying to say in your drawing.

Some of you may already have this lesson/article, "Pantomime Preparation," from *The Stage and the School* by Katherine Ommanney and Harry Schanker, so bear with me, for those who don't have it, should. It illustrates how a mime must prepare himself for a performance. I think it's doubly urgent for the artist, because unlike an actor, who gets to use his body which all his life has served him in his communicating, the artist has to translate those bodily moves into line, and that involves some major cerebral gymnastics. As you read this article, substitute yourself in place of the mime student.

Pantomime Preparation

In your imitation of a real person, you should first determine his chief characteristics. Is he friendly? Timid? Boisterous? Suspicious? Glamorous? Physically vigorous? Discontented? Next, note mentally the details of his habitual facial expression, especially his eyes and mouth. Observe how he holds his head, the kinds of hand movements he makes, and the way in which he walks. Decide what makes him different from any other human being. Then place him in a situation. Take plenty of time to think through his exact reactions to your imaginary situation. Visualize them as if you were watching him on a television screen. Finally, imitate what you have imagined he would do.

In your imaginary characterizations, you should follow much the same procedure. You will, however, have to begin by inventing the details which will characterize the person you plan to play. What is his age? What are his physical traits? How does he dress? What makes him a distinctive individual? Only when you can see him as clearly as someone you actually know will you be able to make him live.

Whether your character is imitated or imaginary, you must work out in detail the situation in which you plan to place him. Have your character enter a definite environment in a clear-cut state of mind and body. Invent something that will change his mood. The conclusion of your pantomime should leave no uncertainty in the mind of your audience about the mental state of the character as he leaves the stage.

While working out your individual pantomime, keep the following directions constantly in mind.

1. Set your mental stage in detail — location of furniture and props.
2. Imagine yourself to be dressed in the clothes of your character, making your audience see the weight, shape, and material of each garment and its effect upon you in your particular mood and situation.
3. Visualize the appearance and emotional state of your character in minute detail.
4. Remember that in all dramatic work the thought comes first — think, see, and feel before you move. Let your eyes respond first, then your face and head, and finally the rest of your body. This is a "motivated sequence."
5. Keep your action simple and clear-cut.
6. Keep every movement and expression visible at all times to your entire audience.
7. Never make a movement or gesture without a reason. Ask yourself, "Does it make clear who I am, how I feel, or why I feel as I do?" Take time to make every movement clear and definite.
8. Try out and analyze every movement and gesture until you are satisfied that it is the most truthful, effective, and direct means of expressing your idea or feeling.
9. Make only one gesture or movement at a time, but coordinate your entire body with it and focus the attention of the audience upon it.
10. Rehearse until you know that you have created a clear-cut characterization and that the action has begun definitely, remained clear throughout, and come to a conclusion.
11. Plan your introduction very carefully. It may be humorous or serious, but it must arouse interest in your character and the situation in which he is placed. It also must make clear all the details of the setting and preliminary situation.
12. Plan the ending very carefully. You should either leave the stage in character or come back to your own personality and end with a bow or a smile.

After creating a single study which satisfies you with its clarity, build up a sentence of events which brings about a change of mood and situation. Finally, build up to a definite emotional climax and conclusion. Such a pantomime will require hours of preparation before it will be ready for class presentation.

(Remember M. Marceau (Marcel) said,"It takes years of study...no one can just walk out on the stage and do it.")
    Under bibliography, she lists Agna Enters book, *On Mine*, Wesleyan, Middletown, Connecticut, 1965. Under Applications, she asks the student to check the performances of others by this checklist:

a. Has the pantomime been carefully prepared?
b. Are the characters interesting, lifelike, and vivid? Do you become emotionally involved with them?
c. Do the gestures and movements seem sincere, convincing, clear, and properly motivated?
d. Does all of the action help to delineate the characters and their situation for you?
e. Is the action clear-cut, realistic, prolonged sufficiently, and exaggerated enough to be seen by the whole audience?
f. Can you visualize the setting, the props, and the clothing of the characters?
g. Does the pantomime have a definite beginning and ending?

Under Characterization she states:

Relating each to an imagined situation, show fear, agony, appeal, embarrassment, hate, sympathy, indecision, power, weariness, and joy. First employ your face, next your hands, and then your feet. Finally express these emotions with your entire body.

In *The Natural Way to Draw* Kimon Nicolaides says:

The study of gesture is not simply a matter of looking at the movement that the model makes. You must also seek to understand the impulse that exists inside the model and causes the pose which you see. The drawing starts with the impulse, not the position. What the eye sees — that is, the various parts of the body in various actions and directions — is but the result of this inner impulse, and to understand one must use something more than the eyes. It is necessary to participate in what the model is doing, to identify yourself with it. Without a sympathetic emotional reaction in the artist there can be no real, no penetrating understanding.

Here are some excellent sketches by Joe Haidar (who thinks he should have done better — while some of the rest of us wish we could do partly that good). Look at them with that "Pantomime Preparation" in mind and you will sense all those things having taken place in the process of making these drawings. They go deeper than just copying the model. They, in subtle ways, depict that model and the manner in which that particular model depicted his inner impulses.

Here are two views of the same pose. Examine them using the checklist above. In my suggestion sketches I figured if he is leaning over looking at something, his right arm should look like there is weight on it as he uses the chair rung for a support, and his left arm should act as a stabilizer — keeping him from falling over. Both arms are stretched taut in carrying out their opposite functions; that is, one pushing and the other pulling. The rest of his body can be fairly loose and relaxed, for its stability has been taken care of. The push/pull action makes for good contrast, too. I should explain that the analysis of my sketches are not after-the-fact diagnosis — they are part and parcel of the "first impression" and the sketches were whisked along under their influence, substance, suggestion, relevance, and energy. (How can you go wrong with all that behind you?)

21   That Darned Neck

The neck has been a difficult area for many of the students in the evening Gesture Class. When asked for help, I usually just sketch for them my simple, "shorthand" version of the neck in question; hoping that will suggest at least one more step out of the quagmire. I remind them that the back of the neck is a continuation of the backbone, and is usually shorter than the front of the neck. The front of the neck starts under the chin and extends down into the chest area, culminating at the point where the clavicle bones attach to the sternum. I also caution that parallel lines make the neck stiff and "pipe like." Here are some examples from the class — I often add a simple "diagram" sketch (in circle) to suggest the general construction. As usual the student's drawings are on the left.

In cartooning we rarely (if ever) draw those prominent sternomastoid and trapezius muscles that play such a big part in the neck workings. Even a smattering of what takes place there, though, structure-wise, will be useful, so I have picked a few "text book necks" that should help your understanding of that area a little better. Here are some from Victor Perard's, *Anatomy and Drawing*.

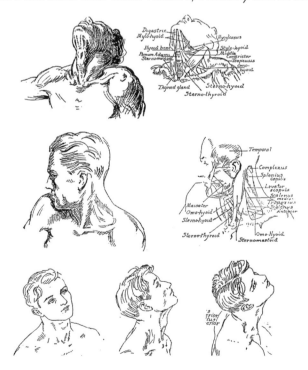

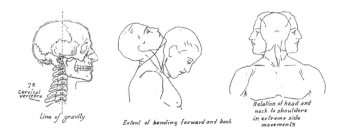

Here are a few from *Constructive Anatomy* by George Bridgman. By studying a variety of teach-ers one should get a more comprehensive view of a subject. And as Thoreau said: "The symbols of an ancient man's thought become a modern man's speech."

Glen Keane did these studies of neck and head shapes.

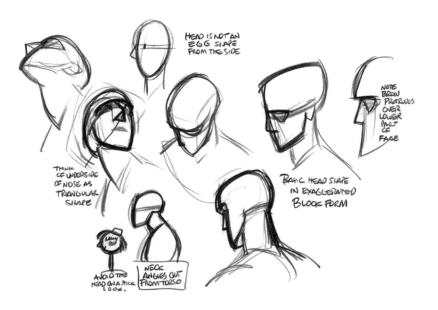

As in any study, one must not get too caught up in the style of the teacher (no matter how appealing). Although it is said that you may be attracted to a certain style, because that is the direction in which you would probably naturally go. However the sensible approach is to glean from the teacher only the things that are meaningful and useful.

Necks vary greatly, from the spindly, unlikely necks of young children (they look like they could never hold up those outsized heads), youths, mature adults; the sexy, fat, muscular, weak, rigid, short, long, stiff, etc. Oh, and the older people whose necks project forward from their "dowager's humps." And those whose necks begin to sag just behind the chin. As was suggested in Chapter 20, Pantomime (Drawing) Preparation, you must decide upon your character's age, his physical traits and what makes him a distinctive individual. The neck is a very distinctive and visible part of anyone's anatomy and character. Traditionally, Mickey's neck has not been very visible. As a matter of fact, some versions have him with no neck at all. Lounsbery's booklet, *How to Draw Mickey Mouse*, shows the body "connected to a point within the head." Freddy Moore, however, intuitively drew a neck on some of his Mickeys.

Goofy's neck is an integral part of his character. But noticeably absent from most cartoon characters are any indications of sternomastoid or trapezius muscles.

A simple shape plus squash and stretch are all the anatomy you need for cartoon characters. Any similarity to the human anatomy will be found in the extent and limits of movement, and of course, the fact that the neck is an extension of the backbone (which applies to all characters, cartoon or real). Whatever the cartoon neck shape, there is a similarity to human gesture in its action.

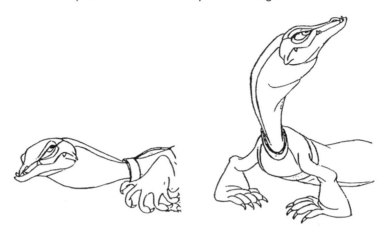

Needless to say, most of the Disney feature characters, at present, are humans, which makes a good understanding of the neck a must. I didn't reproduce any here, because everyone probably has several of them pinned up around them — even as we speak.

In class, when I see someone struggling with a neck, I suggest a very simplified version. I am a believer in simplicity (though I like to think of myself as a very complicated intellectual type). Let me refer to Chapter 20 again, specifically:

9. Make only one gesture or movement at a time, but coordinate your entire body with it and focus the attention of the audience upon it.

With the proper manipulation of line, shape, angles, perspective, and an appropriate neck shape to fit the character, you *can* keep it simple, and you *can* express the story point effectively.

To finish off this handout I sketched some very uncomplicated, manageable, squash, and stretchable necks that at least you can use in your "starter kit," either in drawing from the model or in animation.

22 Crayolas?

A couple of weeks ago I mentioned Crayolas in the handout and it spurred many a moment. One girl said she had eaten oil paint rather than crayons. Bill Perkins brought a book for me to read, called *All I Really Need to Know I Learned in Kindergarten* by Robert Fulghum. In it there is a chapter on Crayolas that I thought you might enjoy.

> Good friends finally put their resources together and made themselves a child. Me, I'm the god-father in the deal. I take my job seriously. So far I've introduced the kid to the good things in life — chocolate, beer, cigars, Beethoven, and dirty jokes. I don't think he cares much for Beethoven. But he's only a year old, and he'll get tired of chocolate, beer, cigars, and dirty jokes. I haven't told him about sex yet, but he's got some ideas of his own already. I won't go into details here, but if you have ever had a little kid or have ever been a little kid, then you know what I mean. Also, I introduced him to crayons. Bought the Crayola beginner set — the short, fat, thick ones with training wheels. Every few weeks I would put one in his hand and show him how to make a mark with it. Mostly he just held it and stared at me. He had a cigar in his other hand and couldn't tell the difference between it and the Crayola. Then we went through the orifice-stuffing phase, where the Crayola went in his mouth and ears and nose. Finally, last week, I held his hand and made a big red mark with the Crayola on a sheet of newsprint. And WHAM! He got the picture. A light bulb went off in a new room in his head. And he did it again on his own. Now, reports his mother, with a mixture of pleasure and pain, there is no stopping him.

> Crayolas plus imagination (the ability to create images) — these make for happiness if you are a child. Amazing things, Crayolas. Some petroleum-based wax, some dye, a little binder — not much to them. Until you add the imagination. The Binney Company in Pennsylvania makes about two billion of these oleaginous sticks of pleasure every year and exports them to every country in the United Nations. Crayolas are one of the few things the human race has in common. That green-and-yellow box hasn't changed since 1937. In fact, the only change has been to rename the "flesh" color "peach." That's a sign of progress.

> The way I know about "flesh" and "peach" is that, when I bought my godson his trainer set, I indulged myself. Bought my very own set of sixty-four. In the big four-section box with the sharpener built right in. Never had my own set before. Seems like I was always too young or too old to have one. While I was at it, I bought several sets. Got one for the kid's mother and father and explained it was theirs, not his.

> What I notice is that every adult or child I give a new set of Crayolas to goes a little funny. The kids smile, get a glazed look on their faces, pour the crayons out, and just look at them for a while.

> Then they go to work on the nearest flat surface and will draw anything you ask, just name it. The adults always get the most wonderful kind of sheepish smile on their faces — a mixture of delight and nostalgia and silliness. And they immediately start telling you about all their experiences with Crayolas. Their first box, using every color, breaking them, trying to get them in the box in order again, trying to use them in a bundle, putting them on hot things to see them melt, shaving them onto waxed paper and ironing them into stained glass windows, eating them, and on and on. If you want an interesting party sometime, combine cocktails and a fresh box of Crayolas for everybody.

> When you think about it, for sheer bulk there's more art done with Crayolas than with anything else. There must be billions of sheets of paper in every country in the world, in billions of boxes

and closets and attics and cupboards, covered with billions of pictures in crayon. The imagination of the human race poured out like a river. Ronald Reagan and Mikhail Gorbachev used crayons, I bet. So did Fidel and the emperor of Japan and Rajiv Gandhi and Mrs. Thatcher and Mr. Mubarak and maybe even the Ayatollah. And just about everybody else you care to name.

Maybe we should develop a Crayola bomb as our next weapon. A happiness weapon. A Beauty Bomb. And every time a crisis developed we would launch one. It would explode high in the air — explode softly — and send thousands, millions, of little parachutes into the air. Floating down to earth — boxes of Crayolas. And we wouldn't go cheap either — not little boxes of eight. Boxes of sixty-four, with the sharpener built right in. With silver and gold and copper, magenta and peach and lime, amber and umber and all the rest. And people would smile and get a little funny look on their faces and cover the world with imagination.

Guess that sounds absurd, doesn't it? A bit dumb. Crazy and silly and weird. But I was reading in the paper today how much money the Russians and our Congress just set aside for weapons. And I'm confused about what's weird and silly and crazy and absurd. And I'm not confused about the lack of, or the need for imagination in low or high places. Pass the crayons, please.

"Crayons," in one form or another, belong to the very great artists, too. In *The Agony* and *the Ectasy*, author Irving Stone has the thirteen-year old Michelangelo thinking:

With rapid strokes of the crayon he began redrafting his features, widening the oval of the eyes, rounding the forehead, broadening the narrow cheeks, making the lips fuller, the chin larger. "There," he thought, "now I look better. Too bad a face can't be redrawn before it's delivered."

Now there's a thought. Who, of the artists you know, would you trust to redraw *your* face? Or what would you do if you had to redraw a friend's face? Pretty sobering, isn't it?

I'm not doing all this just for entertainment's sake. I think what goes into the making of an artist is a stretching of the imagination — on a vast scale. Everything you read, see, hear, and experience goes into your arsenal of drawing weapons. I think you have to be "impressed" before you can "express." Drawing isn't only knowing bones, muscles, perspective, etc. A certain amount of wisdom has to be present to use those things effectively.

In the book, *Psycho-Cybernetics*, the author, plastic surgeon Maxwell Maltz, tells how the personality itself seems to have a "face." "This non-physical 'face of personality' seemed to be the real key to personality change. If it remained scared, distorted, 'ugly', or inferior, the person himself acted out this role in his behavior regardless of the changes in physical appearance."

That applies to drawing as well. Just "copying" the live model in class, or "sticking to the model" in animation does not ensure a faithful depiction of a character's action or personality. The "face of personality" can be found as much in the gesture as in the physical makeup.

Dr. Maltz goes on to say, "…the 'self-image,' the individual's mental and spiritual concept or 'picture' of himself, was the real key to personality and behavior." Again, applying that to drawing — isn't it our character's "self-image" that we are drawing? We have to create the illusion that it is our character who is thinking — who has decided to perform the action.

I hope you understand these meanderings are directed mainly to the students in my drawing classes. The "old pros" know all this stuff. This is just all "stuff" I wish I'd heard when I was a newcomer to the business (back in 1937). And let me interject that credit for the pictures we have made and are continuing to make goes far beyond those who are "sweating" over the character's personalities on the drawing board. In Ollie and Frank's book, *Disney Animation: The Illusion of Life*, they so fittingly point out that:

Everyone who has worked on a picture will feel that he made the personal contribution that caused the cartoon character to come alive on the screen. The story man naturally will feel the character is his, because, after all, it was the story work that determined what kind of an individual this figure would be; and the story sketch man smiles. Because he drew the new character, made the expressions, showed how he would look; and the director knows that it was he who pulled all these talents together and kept insisting that the figure act a certain way; and all the time the actor who did the voice is saying, "Well, I know he's my character because he's me; I did him!" And the animator nods knowingly, because no one can deny that he set the final model and brought him to life, and the assistant (animator) knows that without his work the character would never have reached the screen. The person who selected the colors, those who painted the cels, even those who carefully checked to see if this character had all his buttons; the cameraman who shot the scenes; the sound mixer who gave the special sound to the voice — to all of them, he is their character! This is as it should be. Unless everyone feels this closeness to the end product, the dedication will not be there and the necessary care will not be taken to ensure that the end result will be the finest anyone can do.

I might add, too, that in a very real sense, management, the secretaries, security, and all other peripheral departments influence the final product. And, oh, the cafeteria! What in God's name would we do without that salad bar, those entrees, those deli sandwiches in croissant rolls...and that frozen chocolate yogurt?!

I don't know if any of you are into poetry or not, but Edgar Lee Masters wrote a monumental work called, *Spoon River Anthology*. It's a series of 244 poetic monologues by former Spoon River inhabitants. They speak these monologues from their graves as epitaphs. These three lines from one of them could apply to all of you — after you've "gone." (I'm not trying to be gruesome — just poetic.) Simply supplant "Spoon River" with "Disney Studios."

It is all very well, but for myself I know
I stirred certain vibrations in Spoon River
Which is my true epitaph, more lasting than stone.

Okay! After all that intellectual stuff, let's see if we can apply some of it to drawing. Here's a student's drawing that has some nice loose line work in it. However, I saw that the model sat down by a chair for some relaxation, reverie, or perhaps to listen to some music. That required that she assume a relaxed pose (as the student's drawing suggests), but that she would also gather her upper body into a more cuddly posture and then gently lay her head against the resting place her hands had made for that purpose.

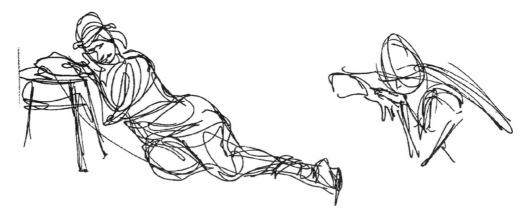

When drawing an action (gesture) there has to be some force or forces at work to bring it about. First of all there is the mental force, that is, what makes the character decide what it's going to do. Once you have that figured out (your first impression) you look for the physical forces that carry out that decision. In the next gesture, the model was adjusting her hat. She was pulling down with her right hand and arm, while pushing up with her left (opposing forces!) It was a stiff hat but I still bent it slightly to emphasize the action. Because the left arm is upraised, that formed a "stretch" on the whole left side of her body, and conversely a "squash" on the right side. Compare the two drawings and you can see how important "squash and stretch" is in drawing — not just in animation, but in drawing.

Notice that I used the wrists as the "primary action" and let the hands and fingers become the "secondary action." As a little touch, to show the delicacy of the pursuit, I raised the little finger of her left hand. It not only adds a feminine touch, but it helps augment the whole upward movement on that side. And notice the ever so slight tilt on her head (not as much as the hat — but like a "drag" — the wrists leading, the hands following, the hat following them, and then the head, the last and least to react). It suggests that she is looking in a mirror, and is pleased with what she sees.

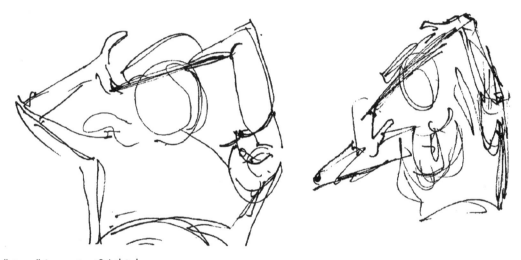

Is "story" important? I think so.

23 Hands (Those Darned?)

In Chapter 21 I dealt briefly with a problem area, the neck. The neck, being a very visible and expressive part of the body, should be drawn with the finesse it deserves. There is another seemingly insignificant area that too often, in the evening Gesture Classes, is just sloughed off as not worthy of further consideration. Let me remind you that the hands are second only to the tongue in communication. The tongue and facial expression are almost always backed up by the hands for extra emphasis. We have all seen actors use hands alone to express ideas and emotions.

It's tempting to say that hands have a personality all their own, but actually the hand is just the outer extremity of the composite personality of the character. Consider the hands (and wrists) of a laborer, a ballerina, a pianist; or the busy hands of a mime. Take hands away from any one of them and you take away a vital means of expression. Regardless of the character's personality or vocation, the hands are a very important part of their ability to make them understood, or to carry out *any* of their daily activities.

Ages ago I did a handout titled Action Analysis: Hands and Feet, wherein I suggested that the hands and feet could sometimes tell more of the action than the body and head. Here are a couple of the illustrations from that handout.

The hand can be very complicated if you try to "photograph" it in line. For the purposes of gesture drawing it is best to learn a simple method of recording your impressions. For the types who are usually overwhelmed by the complexities of the hands, I recommend a simple formula. It consists of a square or rectangle shape that represents the bulk of the hand. This is a groovy way to draw the hand in difficult views.

Once you have your perspective — simply add five pork sausages (or other suitable finger shapes).

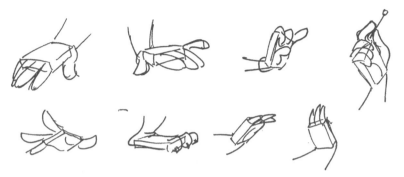

That simple hand construction allows you to get down the gesture without getting sidetracked by those difficult-to-draw knuckles, wrinkles, and other construction problems. Most important it makes for a sharply defined gestural signal.

The wrist is an important ally in the battle for expression (influenced by the war news). It not only establishes where the arm ends and the hand begins (important), but it helps *set up* the hand gesture.

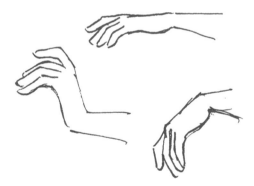

For instance, if you have a hand in this somewhat expressionless configuration, it might be enhanced by lifting it up from the wrist. Suddenly there is an alertness to it, or perhaps an air of dignity. Bend the wrist the other way, and you have a hand that might suggest relaxation or disappointment.

As you can see the change of attitude was brought about by the wrist. So when you're talking hand gesture — include the wrist.

I lean toward a crisp bend at the wrist, but that is a personal preference. Look at this beautiful result James Fujii has gotten with a long gentle curve at the wrist. Ordinarily, I don't like such long, curved lines, but this one seems to fit right in with the relaxed reading attitude of the character. Notice how simple the hands are, yet how expressive.

Again, I am reproducing some drawings of hands from various anatomy books (some out of print) to show that there are a variety of approaches to anatomy study. These are just for information, for eventually it all has to be adapted to the "Disney Studios" style of drawing. The first group is from Victor Perard's *Anatomy and Drawing*.

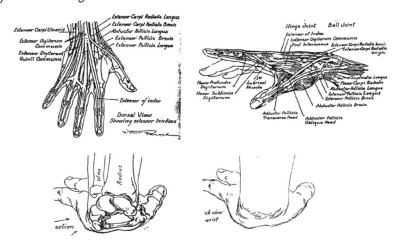

The drawing below shows studies of hands with use of imaginary lines for proportion.

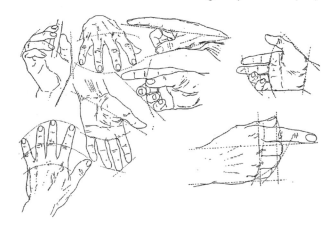

Here are some of Bridgman's hands from *Constructive Anatomy*.

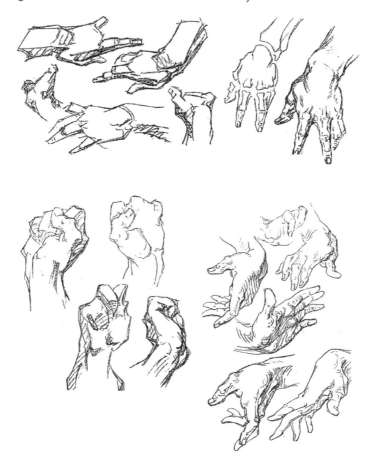

Schider's hands are realistic in a kind of supernatural sense.

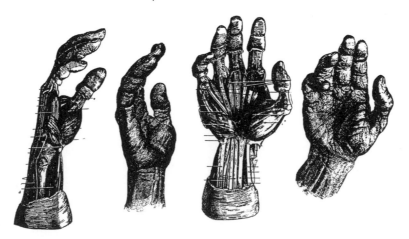

Here is a collection of expressive hands from Disney veteran, Milt Kahl.

And more from the pages of *Mad* magizine.

There're lots more but I don't know how many pages I can staple, so more later. And by the way, when you study hands, study the wrist too — they are partners in any "hand gesture."

24 Plight of a Gesture

Hello. I'm a Gesture. It is my purpose in life to get drawn in a way that brings out not only the basic "story point," but also the subtle nuances of the pose. All my acting ability goes into my poses.

It is relatively easy. First I think of what I want to do, then almost like magic my body just moves into the pose. All the parts of my body know instinctively what to do. It is, of course, a contrived pose, that is, I am not really doing it — I'm just "play-acting." Nevertheless, I sum up all the necessary forces to pull it off.

I realize that when an artist is drawing me, the pen or pencil does not automatically or involuntarily assume the gesture like my body does. The artist has to figure out how my body accomplished the gesture, you might say, intellectually. He has to see (mentally) how I am balanced; the angles various parts of my body have taken; the squashes and stretches; the opposing forces, etc. This is so he can feel those forces I am making use of in expressing the gesture, so that he can guide his pen or pencil correspondingly.

When I first strike a pose, the newness of it is very vivid in my mind and body — it is clear, definite, and well-defined. I usually caricature it enough so there will be no mistake about the story behind it. It is odd that after a while I lose the newness of the feeling, and have to remind myself of the original concept. I realize that the artist has the same problem. When he first looks at my pose he sees the gesture in a sparkle of clarity. He immediately sums it up and forms a "first impression." As he proceeds, he often begins to get involved in drawing problems, and that first impression — which was so crystalline clear-cut, so obvious, so apparent — begins to slip away. So the artist has to constantly renew that first impression in his mind, too.

With me, it's easy to strike a gesture, because I am it. But the artist has to re-create it on paper. I don't envy his task, so I try to make it as easy for him as I can. I can't help it if my clothes don't always cooperate and act as drapery ought to. All too often they don't fully explain what is going on underneath — that is one thing the artist has more control over than I do. And drapery is an important factor in gesture drawing.

Here's a pose where I was acting like I was pushing a boat or raft along with a long pole. The student's drawing (on the left) shows that he did not feel the weight of my body as it pressed down on the pole, and that I was leaning into the "push." The instructor's suggestion (on the right) at least captures some of my efforts.

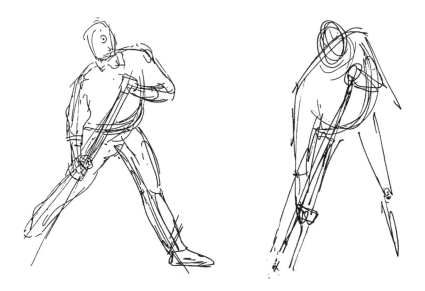

Here's another pose, where I feel kinda' slighted in the student's drawing. I'm hitchhiking, and it's as if a car just went by without stopping for me. My looking off to stage left suggests that. The instructor's drawing has me following the car with my whole upper body as it passes. It hints of a contemptuous backwash of wind as it passes, or perhaps that I leaned toward it to voice some unfriendly comment.

There might even be a suggestion of the middle finger replacing the thumb...

Whenever I pose, I use the space around me to do it in. I form different perimeters that help define the gesture. For instance, if I spread my arms apart, I am increasing the space between them. A good way to think of the tension thus created, is to imagine I am stretching a rubber band — the farther apart my hands — the more tension is suggested. That is what I did in this next pose. I spread the newspaper open and then positioned my head a little closer to the right hand, because I was looking over to the left side of the paper. I had to turn my head (face) toward that page to appear to be reading it. That created a nice tension between my face and the page, just like the outstretched hands. I, the Gesture, used a body to manifest myself, but the body is not me. Likewise the instructor ignored the details of the figure as he went for the essence of the gesture.

There has to be a certain amount of attention paid to the body (anatomy) in acting out a gesture or in drawing one. One student had become frustrated with his attempt to capture this pose. The instructor saw that the student had lost control because he had been copying some of the lines that appeared on the model's body rather than the gesture of the body itself, to express the pose. His suggestion was to draw the torso first, making it easy to see where the arms, legs, and neck are connected. The torso, in effect, becomes the nucleus, or the foundation for drawing.

I hope I haven't bored you with all this analysis, but I feel strongly about having my efforts depicted with all the integrity due a gesture.

25 Concepts for Drawing

I'm planning on taking a few months off so I thought I'd load you down (maybe that should read, load you "up" — for this is all inspirational stuff) with some heavy but basic drawing concepts that you can mull over in my absence. In directing my thoughts mainly to the artists who feel they still need further enlightenment, I sometimes wonder if I am getting too complicated, analytical, and long winded. I don't mean it to be complicated — I just try to approach drawing from as many directions as possible. Being a "crab" (July) it comes natural to me. Ward Kimball once said: "If I can take a thing apart and put it back together again, I can draw it." Well, that sure means seeing it from all angles, doesn't it? So the more you know about any subject the easier it is to deal with it — and the more simple it becomes. In the words of Andrew Wyeth: "When you lose simplicity you lose drama."

It is entirely possible to achieve a convincing drawing by tracing a photograph or copying a model inch by inch onto drawing paper. You could even resort to a plumb line, calipers, charcoal, and stubs to create an acceptable illusion of roundness or third dimension. But the illusion animators are after is of a different nature. It has to be in line alone and it must represent some story point. In that sense, drawing is less a reproduction of nature, and more of an invention of the artist. It has to be a subtle mixture of reality and imagination.

It can be a greatly detailed drawing or it can be a simple cartoon like a *Peanuts* drawing, but it has to state its reason for being; that is, illustrate a story point. For the animator's purposes a special technique of drawing/cartooning has evolved that should be studied by any artist contemplating a career as an animator.

I have developed the habit of transposing facts, theories, and postulations that I hear and read into categories other than what they were intended. It's the Stanchfield "truth is omniscient, omnipresent, and omnipotent and therefore applicable to all things" concept.

So last week I'm at the Solvang Branch Library perusing some *American Artist* magazines, and start reading this article about Herbert Barnett, artist, teacher, and landscape painter, and right away my mind starts metamorphosing everything into the write-up of this handout. Look beyond this stuff as theory, or as someone's private opinion, and try to blend it with your present understanding of drawing. Let it help form a clearer concept — one you can utilize with confidence.

In an article from *American Artist*, October 1990, Barnett is said to have told his students:

> …forget all hopes for a sure-fire formula. He couldn't teach them tricks. He could only recommend one answer: to see something as a whole, to visualize a subject as a complex of shapes, rather than as independent elements, (sound familiar?) to seek out the invisible web of line, shape, and form that lies beneath the apparently unconnected set of objects and creates the rhythm that vitalizes and unifies all parts of the image. Barnett felt that once the student could learn to see in this rhythmical, unifying way, "It's likely that (he or she) would not need to study or to learn anymore.

> Students found this concept elusive. Barnett wrote that most students, looking at a still life or model, would be deluded by the notion that if they can copy the subject accurately enough they will convey to the viewer the same sensation that they've received. But the truth of the matter is quite different. The essence is, "…elusive and lurks under the casual, superficial experience," he noted. "Volume is not a realistic element but an abstract one. We don't see volume, we sense it; we remember it; we feel it in our bones. We can hardly expect to capture it by looking at individual objects.

> Barnett stressed that when we look directly at an object, we miss its relationship to the things around it. (Like drawing a hand or a knee without regarding its relationship to all other parts of the body.) To see a thing well, he advised, "Always see it at the same time as something in another part of the picture (or figure). To paint (or draw) a right hand area, stare at the left. Look at a part of the subject and draw the part required as it is seen out of the corner of the eye. When studying one side of an object, always see the other side. See both ears of a head, both sides of an apple or jug. In a landscape, see the roof, foundation, and the ends of the barn all at once. In a still life, see the front of the table and the background at the same time."

Now if we may return to our own backyard… When I reprint a student's drawing with an accompanying correction, I never use a name, but when printing the outstanding drawings from our classes, I tell who did them. This does not mean I am trying to "sell" the artist. If I print one artist's drawings more often than others, it is only because those drawings fit into my line of thinking. Here is yet another such case. Recently, Richard Oliver modeled for us. He does a lot of poses that are kooky and hard to form a story for. In one pose he stuffed some cloth into the back of a strange looking coat as if he were a humpback. The hump was crooked and just looked like it was something stuffed into a strange looking coat. But Dan Boulos, captured (or created) the essence of this one with quick-witted perception. Here are two versions of the same pose. You can see by the variance in them that *he was not copying, but did them with a generous mixture of imagination and creativity.*

I have always known what motivates Dan in drawing the way he does, but last week I interviewed him to hear it in his own words, and to share those words with you. You might consider some of Dan's views as worthy of adoption. (Perhaps all of them.)

First of all, he has gotten over the fear of making a "bad drawing." He found that in trying to make a "good drawing" there is a tendency to judge every line you draw. This can tighten you up and take your mind off the gesture. Dan doesn't look too long at a pose nor does he refer back to the model over and over. He says the pose gets "frozen" and you begin to see a lot of "stuff." Also in looking too often at the model, you begin to lose the overall pose and find yourself drawing one little section — then one line at a time.

Dan has a hard time holding on to the "first impression" but tries to get the "feeling" and work with that. He works fast because of that. He says, that allows him to do three or four sketches while others are struggling with some worthless details. Each sketch allows him to try to improve on the others. And anyway, looking up and down between model and paper takes too much time — doesn't give you time to think. Those still struggling on the head and shoulders never get the overall feeling.

Here is some good philosophy from Dan: Making a mistake liberates you. You can then get on with the drawing and when something pleasing shows up, which it's more apt to do when you move along, you can say "Hey, that's great." It spurs you on to the next thing — to enlarge or to finish your drawing. And he says doing three or four versions of a gesture is more related to animation.

The way Dan arrived at those sketches above was by having fun drawing. He says you should balance fun with discipline. He thought it was silly for the model to stuff something in his back, so he decided to make it even sillier. Dan stops drawing when he figures he has captured the pose, otherwise, why be there? Get on with it — use the time to learn more.

26 Drawing Appropriate Gestures for Your Characters

Well, the perennial dilettante is back! During my time off I've done some oil painting, some gardening, some piano playing, some carpentry (kitchen cupboards and drawers), and some thinking about how I could inspire my friends at Disney Studios to keep up their enthusiasm for drawing; that is, if and when I should come back. So here I am offering my support to you in your quest to improve your drawing skill.

You are all invited to take advantage of the evening Gesture Class (or classes), which will now be on Monday and Tuesday evenings. And if enough are interested we will have a noon session (possibly two). The classes should be fun, so what better way to improve yourselves and have a nice, relaxing time at it.

The theme will be "gesture" again — as it relates to acting. There may be only one or two handouts a month, but I'll try to pack them with thought-provoking, goal-seeking, inspirational meandering. And between classes I will be available for work-related problems that require some great-grandfatherly counseling.

To start off with, I am reprinting some cartoons from the daily newspaper. I'm sure you enjoy the strips, but have you ever noticed how expertly the characters and their gestures have been developed to fit the story. It's hard to imagine the characters from one strip doing things that are happening in another strip. That's what gesture drawing is — caricaturing your characters and having them do the appropriate gestures (acting) indigenous to that particular character.

Many of the cartoon strips in the daily papers have reached a high degree of characterization. The characters fit so well into the role they have to play; we don't have to struggle with them. We know at a glance what to expect of them, and are satisfied because we usually get what we expect. That makes us, the audience, feel good (even superior) because we foresaw the unfolding of the story or the gag.

The gestures (acting) in *Peanuts* are usually pretty subtle, but where the story or gag doesn't require a flamboyant action, the contemplative style of Schulz's gestures tell the story very well.

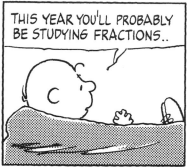

For Better or For Worse has some good drawing in it and also some amusing teen-age "philosophy." The action in the strip is always apropos to the business and to the characters.

For Better or For Worse®   by Lynn Johnston

The Wizard of Id shares his strip with some great actors. He, the Wizard, is "above it all," so assumes gestures that attest to his superior intellect.

Sir Rodney, the inept warrior, is a smart aleck with a sharp tongue, often suffering for it in gestures not of his own choosing.

The King, who takes offense at any remark about his shortness, is very unpopular with his subjects. Speaking of gestures, how about this collective crowd gesture?

Here's the always inebriated court jester's version of Aladdin's lamp as seen in the strip on the next page.

It's a temptation to go on — there's *Beetle Bailey, Calvin and Hobbes, Andy Capp,* etc. All characters who do their thing in a perfect marriage of character, story, and gesture.

When you are going to draw someone — a model, a sketch, a character in a cartoon — you sum up his personality at a glance. Your discerning appraisal tells you instantly how he will deliver his speech, how he will walk, throw a ball, and to what extremes you may push his actions. Usually the face tells you much about his character. The first thing you look for is sincerity. You immediately categorize the person (or animal) as sincere or devious or affected. Either way you have some aids to help you make your drawing.

Part of our individuality in drawing stems from our own personality and training. We have spent all of our lives observing, comparing, and judging the character of others, and generally speaking we all arrive at similar judgments. And though your assessment and mine may be agreeable, our portrayal will be uniquely different.

So when you begin a drawing, don't get bogged down in the anatomy, the outline, and details, but call upon your sense of character judgment and draw accordingly. Usually we have models come as characters, such as a clown, a carpenter, or a cook. It gives us a chance to play-act, which takes the great weight of seriousness off our shoulders and gives us a pleasant theme to work on. We can urge this make believe character to do his thing in our drawing — in the form of appropriate gestures.

When drawing for an audience, we have to make sure we have put all the elements (gestures) of the character into the drawing so they, the audience, are literally coerced into seeing the character the way we want them to; that is, in accordance with the way the character fits into the story.

That is what gesture drawing is all about. We're not studying anatomy or drapery — we're studying acting and the art of persuasion.

Always remember the company may think of the audience as customers, but you have to think of them as fans.

When I was studying singing years ago, a teacher told me to sing to one person in the audience. It could be my mother, wife, or a friend. That applies to drawing also. It's not much fun expressing yourself if you have no one to direct it to or to appreciate it. That is why apprentices work hard and make such strides — they try to do well for their instructors. Athletes try to win for their country, school, or bankbook. And of course everyone wants to please themselves.

The author Kurt Vonnegut said: "Even a successful creative person creates with an audience of one in mind."

The author E. B. White said: "...the true writer always plays to an audience of one."

John Steinbeck said: "Your audience is one single reader. I have found that sometimes it helps to pick out one person — a real person you know, or an imagined person and write to that one."

Here is a good one to apply to drawing when things seem to be especially tough: Nathaniel Hawthorne quipped, "Easy reading is damned hard writing."

(Those quotes are from *Writers on Writing*, by Jon Winokur.)

Nietzsche, that controversial philosopher said: "Even a thought, even a possibility, can...transform us."

That is the spirit with which I print this stuff.

27 Drawings Ain't Just Drawing

A writer of fiction or film scripts must be highly skilled in the art of storytelling; how to develop and further the plot by use of characterization, dialog, action, locale, emotion, etc. All of those things must be interwoven and revealed at the proper time so the reader is whisked along through the story with as little intellectual discomfort as possible. Present day prose must move along at a respectable twentieth (almost twenty-first) century pace. Contemporary writers can't mess around with long and boring (even if well written) explanatory passages, descriptions, and meandering dialog. Every word has to be carefully chosen. One single sentence may have to describe the character, the locale, the reason for being there, and what might happen as a result of all these things.

In the last handout (Chapter 26) I used some cartoon strips as examples of characterization. Here I present still another to illustrate the desirability and benefits of being brief and yet explaining everything. By the use of a simple setting, well-chosen props, the attitudes, and terse, unambiguous dialog of the peasants; the locale is set, the story line is clearly presented, the characters are elegantly described (both by looks and dialog), and the story line moves right along to a definite conclusion — in two frames! It's beautiful, whether you believe in the basic premise or not. Even the horseflies add atmosphere without distracting from the story's progression.

Anyway, it takes an infinite amount of observation and empathy on the part of the writer to make the story interesting but not get too bogged down in superfluous details. The audience has had a life-drama of its own, dramatic and humorous, so the storyteller has but to create a new life-drama, designed so the audience, drawing on its own past experience can enter into the fabricated one with ease and hopefully, pleasure.

I've come to believe that artists and cartoonists must know what the writer knows and perhaps then some. If one picture is going to live up to the old Chinese saying and be "...worth a thousand words," it's sure going to have to be very articulate and expressive. The writer tells his story with words; the artist does the same with drawings. One word can be important in writing, even critical — can change the feeling, the mood, the nuance. So can one drawing, or even a line in a drawing, be important in carrying the story in a forward direction.

One way to create interest in a story is to introduce conflict, and then proceed to resolve the conflict is some unique way. Conflict can be between good and evil, male and female, aggression and peacefulness; man against the elements, man against himself or his neighbor, or against an imagined thing, etc.

Conflict, in the form of tension, also adds interest to a drawing. One arm stretching *up* as the other reaches *down*; a person stooping *down*, picking something *up*; a person's feet wanting to walk to stage *right*, while the face looks to stage *left*, thinking, "Maybe we ought to be going the other way." The hips may be twisted to the *right* while the shoulders twist to the *left*. Sometimes these things happen as the result of decisions (or indecision) on the part of the character. At other times they are the result of personal physical idiosyncrasies, or some outside influence.

A purely spontaneous use of bodily tension occurs when a person stands with their weight on one leg. Almost always, if the right hip is high, the right shoulder will be low. Here are a couple of examples from a recent drawing class to illustrate the point. In the first example the student came very close to making a nice drawing, but there is no tension (conflict). In my "suggestion" drawing, I figured that since the left leg was sort of pushing up from the floor, the left hip would be high, causing the left shoulder to be lower than the right one. The body always attempts to stabilize or balance itself. Here we have a paradox, for it seems that to balance itself and to maintain some stability and symmetry, the body has to establish some kind of conflict or tension. But this is as it should be, and a drawing without tension tends to be rigid and lifeless. Life itself would be boring, even as a story or a drawing without tension would be boring. Maybe that's why we enjoy competitive sports, mystery programs, puzzles, etc. For drawings to reflect real life they must have conflict or tension in them.

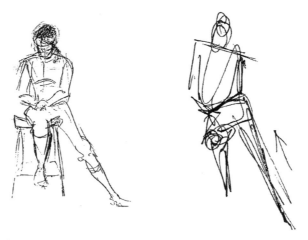

In this next example the pose was a difficult one, so the student was stumped. I suggested using some logic. Since the weight was on the left leg, that hip would be high, so to create balance to this situation, the left shoulder is dropped. We all do it!

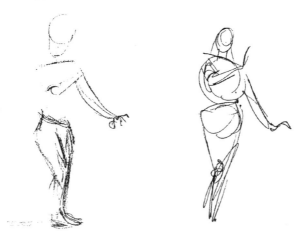

I often suggest in class that we try to feel the pose in our bodies. After all, we won't have a model to look at while struggling with a difficult action at our animation desk. We'll have to rely on our sense of the pose — kinesthesia, the sensation of position, movement, tension, etc., of parts of the body. That is what I mean by "play-acting." To draw it faithfully and expressively, the artist has to be passionate about the gesture. He has to feel as if he were performing the action himself. To sit back and suppose that the model has done all the work and all we have to do is copy what's before us is folly. That is not the purpose of drawing from life. The purpose of drawing from life is to transmute the essence of the gesture into our chosen medium, drawing. Not a copy of the model, but a "paraphrase" of it — a caricature — after it has been filtered through our individual creative process. If we really saw what we were looking for, we could go into an adjoining room and draw it. Otherwise we have to stay before the model and work at weaning ourselves from the habit of copying.

Now, there are probably almost always exceptions to almost all rules (I almost, nearly pinned that statement down) and here's a good example, where both the left hip and the left shoulder are raised. It happens! Rules are tools that help us, but like traffic laws, sometimes you have to break them to avoid an accident. This drawing is by Dan Boulos and is an excellent example of twisting the body to attain maximum tension.

How does one "play-act" while drawing from the model? Well, in this pose you could surmise the girl was walking a bit to stage right when something or someone at stage left attracted her attention. She stops in mid-step and pulls her left shoulder abruptly back to make a clear path for her look over there. It's a nice drawing and there is lots of tension generated to create an exciting play-act situation. Many such story situations could be invented to "cover" the gesture. But whatever it is, it should include the artist's passion for storytelling.

On the following week we had a male model. Toward the end of session we worked on heads. Here are two views of a subtle bit of conflict going on between the hand pulling forward on the hat brim, while the neck does its part by resisting the pull. The students got all the essential components, but missed the "conflict." If you glance from the student's drawing to mine several times you will see the pull was accomplished by changing the shapes of the hand, hat, etc. Check again and notice changes in the negative shapes. It's the difference between saying, "Look, I'm holding the brim of my hat," or saying, "I want my hat set at a cocky angle, and knowing how it feels at that angle, I'm shifting it around till I get that feeling."

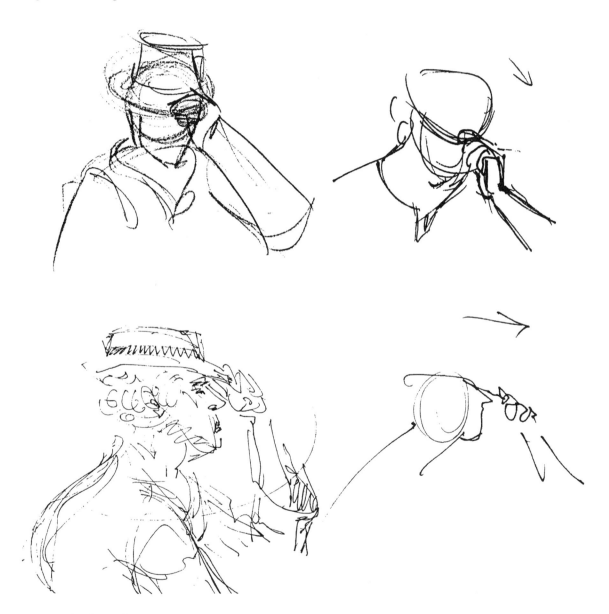

I recently clipped a quotation by Jules Henri Poincaré from the *Santa Barbara News-Press* which went, "Science is built up with facts, as a house is with stones. But a collection of facts is no more a science than a heap of stones is a house." Well, this will never make the *News-Press*, but I tinkered with that quote and came up poetic:

Hats and hands and faces
Do not a drawing make.
They'll need a bit of tension
For entertainment's sake.

I must say that there were some nice drawings made that night. Here are a few excellent examples of caricature and character portrayal. Each one has a flavor and charm of its own, and in each you can sense the churning of thought that took place as each artist rendered his or her interpretation. The first two are by Ellen Woodbury, and Mark Kausler. The next two are by Terri Martin, and Ed Gutierrez, who added a festive touch — a toy balloon — to an otherwise rather melancholic pose. Oh, I tell you, the gratification of drawing and acting. The ability to portray these things, to arouse an audience emotionally, and to make them laugh or cry is a wondrous thing.

28 The Importance of Sketching

Sketching is a way of awakening and sharpening our awareness. If our awareness is sluggish, some of the impressions we receive through our senses, which are so important to drawing, will be overlooked. Like watching a sunset with dark glasses on. While we are sketching, our sensibilities should be honed in on the meaning of, the story behind the pose. Sensibility means, in part, *"The power of responding to stimuli; the ability to feel. The capacity for being affected emotionally or intellectually...receptiveness to impression,"* especially first impressions.

If you find yourself overly absorbed in details and small isolated sections of the figure, neglecting the real objective of drawing, you might try imagining you are a creature from some distant planet... one that has a different form of life. So everything you see here on earth is new to you. You can't name anything...that is a button, this is a collar, etc. You join a drawing class, and the model assumes a pose and all you are aware of is the broad shapes. So you start drawing these shapes. All your senses reveal to you are the bare essentials, while the earth student next to you is struggling with the "recognition syndrome," seeing all the hairs on the eyebrow, the clasp on the belt, the bumps and wrinkles on the cloth, the etceteras ad infinitum. If he had had a scientific background he might be looking for cells and atoms and other minutiae. Granted, the details of a subject are a part of it, but without that solid foundation, the essence of the pose, the details mean nothing. It's like the ingredients that go into a chocolate chip cookie, by themselves they are merely details. Only after the proper amount of each are mixed together and baked can they be called, "cookies."

I recently attended a lecture by a local artist, Ted Goerschner. He said he had a painting in one of his exhibits of a basket of eggs, one of which had fallen out and was broken in two. A scientist from Vandenberg Airforce Base was studying it at great length. Asked why, he replied, "Those two egg shell halves would never fit together." If there was any artistic or esthetic beauty in the painting, he missed it because of the information he allowed his senses to accept. That's not to say that the things you draw needn't "work", but it's the gesture you're after, not scientific accuracy. Otherwise we would never have had flying elephants, talking mirrors, and singing teapots.

You might also try imagining your audience being right there watching over your shoulder as you draw. Don't make them wait through a lot of laborious copying of lines and details...they want to see the action right now. I used to do chalk-talks for the studio and was at Disneyland on the opening day drawing Disney characters for the kids. If I took too long on a sketch, they would moan and groan or leave for something more exciting.

If you are auditioning (I've done this, too) for a part in a stage play or a musical, the director will probably have made his judgement in the first 10 bars of your song. So it is with drawing. The first 10 lines in a drawing are crucial. So be bold and venturesome with your first impressions – pack them with action and expression.

When you are drawing, you might also imagine you are a performer in a variety show and you want to be more spectacular, funny, or impressive than any act that went before you (I've done that, also). It requires a little extra energy to "top" a good act. You will have to psyche yourself up, energize yourself, for complacency or hesitancy will spill over into your drawing.

Remember, real life is your source, and it's everywhere. So carry a sketchbook at least some of the time. Make it a habit of sketching in the variety of places you may find yourself: restaurants, grocery stores, ball games, and while watching television. Try to get the flavor of the locale, the people (characters) and their activities. And stay loose! The time to get tight and meticulous is when you are doing a blueprint for some delicate machine part, and, of course, in final cleanup.

On Tuesday and Wednesday, February 18 and 19, Bobby Ruth Mann will be modeling in the evening classes. She will be wearing her stimulating "Hobo" costume. Here is an opportunity to have some fun, to stay loose, and though she will give you some terrific poses to work with, you might take off on your own and to a little farther with the gesture.

Below are some drawings that James Fujii did of this costume many months ago. Notice there is some detail, but it is handled quite casually – just enough of it to add texture to the drawing, but not involved enough to take his mind off the purpose of the drawing, which was, of course, capture the gesture. Study these drawings (but don't try to copy them). See how simple everything is drawn. The eyes are just slits, the nose is just a blob, the hands, though very expressive are merely suggestions.

29 Getting Emotionally Involved

I was sitting at my desk wondering what to put in my next "handout," which from now on appears in the *BARK*. I looked up, and pinned on the windowsill is a quote I copied from I don't remember where, "*It doesn't really wash unless you get into it emotionally.*"

Isn't that the way it is? Whether you're talking about sports, religion, marriage, or career, it won't "wash" unless you get into it emotionally. There is a large following of the cult of mediocrity these days. Even one of my favorite cartoon strips, "Calvin and Hobbs," jokes about surrendering to the hopelessness of attempting to improve oneself (see drawing #1 on illustration page). I forgive Will Watterson because it's a humorist's prerogative to poke fun at some of our shortcomings and the excuses we use for the way we are. But shortcomings and the way we are, are as changeable as the amount of emotion we agree to expend on change...on improvement. Many people feel helplessly trapped in our sociological maze; our economical/educational/moral/ethical jungle. What can they do, without some emotional incentive, but to join the ranks of mediocrity.

On the lighter side, here, pinned to my desk, is a quote by Robert Burne, "*To err is human, and stupid.*" Here's one from today's paper, by Tallulah Bankhead. "*If I had to live my life again, I'd make the same mistakes, only sooner.*" And here's a good quote if you need some extra impetus for continuing sketching. Rebecca West, author, said, "*I write to find out about things.*" We could apply that to sketching, couldn't we? Read this excerpt from one of her books. She is writing about a lynch trial, but includes this little gem for color. "*The Bible belonging to Greenville Country Court House is in terrible shape. Like many Bibles, it has a flounce, or valance, of leather protecting its edges, and this is torn and crumbling, while its boards are cracked, and no small wonder. Its quietest hours are when it is being sworn upon; at any other time it is likely to be snatched up from the small stand on which it rests, which is like that used for potted plants in some homes, and waved in the air, held to an attorney's breast, thrust out over the jury box, and hurled to its resting place in a convulsion of religious ecstasy.*"

How beautifully and descriptively she creates a little "story" about this book. That's what I mean when I speak of creating a story around a model's pose before you being to sketch. And notice how in just describing a book, Rebecca West uses action words like, "torn and crumbling," "cracked," "hurled back," "in a convulsion..." All that, what could be called, "story telling," about a mere book! Should we not then also find ways to make out drawings come to life...tell a story?

In a charming little book entitled, " A Life In Hand," a book suggesting ways to start an illustrated journal, Hannah Hinchman, aptly says about gesture drawing:

> Another exercise involves a way of drawing that will sharpen your ability to see and glean essentials quickly, a useful skill in the field where animals and light conditions change. The term is gesture drawing, and applies to you making the gestures of drawing as well as the gestures made by whatever you are looking at.
>
> Everything has its own unique gesture: the table's "tableness", the crow's "crowness." When you get to people or animals or things you know well as individuals, the quality gets even more specific, belong only to him, her or it. Drawing can find and record the gestures: in fact, such recognition is at the heart of all truly great drawing.
>
> As you start to learn gesture drawing, speed it essential because it is so easy to be led astray by peripheral details. Later, you will be able to get at the same gesture in a more deliberate way, but for now speed will help you cut through the essential.

On the illustration page are a couple of correction/suggestion sketches made in the last gesture class. See if you can see the thinking behind my corrections. If I may borrow Hannah's "tableness," and "crowness," in describing a thing's essence, these then are a character's, "lookness," and "leaning-forwardness," (drawing #2 and 3). Then there is a drawing where the student spent too much time and energy on the head, missing out on the benefits found in the overall gesture. After all, the head shape and head attitude work in unison with the body – you can't draw one without knowing what the other is doing (see drawing #4).

Now for the last drawing. This is by Cynthia Overman. A very nice drawing. It is simple, expressive, loose; it has lots of twist, tension, weight, clarity, and a light touch to boot.

It really pays to get emotionally involved!

30 Gesture Further Pursued

I don't think it's too early to mention an upcoming picture with lots of animals in it — *King of the Jungle.* Studying and sketching animals is in line, even as you work on *Aladdin,* or any other project. So keep up your sketching of people, but also let a little animal sketching overlap, so to speak. There will be an attempt to bring in some jungle-type animals for study so keep a supply of adrenaline handy. And to pique your creative craving, I am printing some delightful animal sketches by Dan Boulos, James Fujii, and Terri Martin (order is according to alphabet, not skill - see the drawing section.)

In the gesture class on March 3 & 4, we had Wendy Werner and her charming dog, Abbey, pose for us. It was a delight! The dog is a Lhasa Apso, a Tibetan guard dog. Its ancestors were stationed on the towers, where with their acute hearing, they would detect approaching intruders and bark - waking up the larger and more capable guard dogs. I apologize for not knowing this at class time, for an artist should know everything possible about whatever or whoever he draws. I asked the class to forego trying to draw a girl and a dog, but rather to draw the relationship between the two. I suggested they try for just the essential inter-relationship that, in effect, amounted to one pose. I suggested they think of it as an assignment where they were to capture the gesture only - then there would be enough information there to finish up the drawing at some later date. I reasoned that getting their minds off drawing "things," i.e., heads, arms, etc., they would then go straight for the gesture - and that is exactly what they did.

I was so proud of Grant Hiestand, I am reproducing 1 2/3 pages of his sketches. Keep in mind, these were constantly moving targets. The artists had to employ their short term memories to grasp the whole picture and get it down before some new pose, that seemed more interesting, caught their fancy. The adrenaline flowed or you got nothing. This is one reason why I keep harping on carrying a sketch book with you. It develops a quickness of hand and eye. And this is most important, it will help you envision poses and actions when there is no model to work from - which is the normal state of affairs at Disney.

And of course I can't pass up an opportunity to share a critique with you. Here's a student's drawing of Wendy and Abbey relaxing in a chair. The "story" behind the pose is, "*Wendy and Abbey relaxing in a chair.*" Does this suggest anything to you? Of course it does. And if you had thought of it as you began to draw, you no doubt would have tried to portray that very thing. If on the other hand you somehow get involved in drawing things, i.e., heads, arms, chairs, etc., you would have lost the basic purpose of the drawing. Next to the student's drawing is my suggestion for *"Wendy and Abbey relaxing,"* (last drawing in drawing section.)

I left out the chair in my sketch, but explained later that even a chair is part of the gesture as is any prop. A chair will either resist or submit to a sitter depending on the story point. In animation there is no such thing as an inanimate object - everything contributes to the story. To carry the thought a step beyond, consider the chair designers and manufacturers - they produce chairs to either relax in or to make a person sit up and remain alert. Even so, in animation an object like a chair can change its function at will. As Shakespeare might have said, *"The story's the thing."*

Remember, whenever a prop like a chair is used in connection with a character, there is a relationship formed. As in the case of Wendy and Abbey, you might say that the relationship has gone beyond just a prop and has become a personal attachment - a bond. In such a case, you search for ways to portray that bond. But whether personal or impersonal, the prop becomes a part of the gesture. There are two actors, but just one pose.

I contend that it is infinitely easier to make a drawing if there is a story established in your mind. The verbal description of the gesture always suggests ways to bring about the drawing. Even as you inwardly voice the components of the pose, the very words will evoke the kind of line or the positioning of the parts that is best suited to your interpretation. Especially is this true when you emphasize the verbs: the model is bending, twisting, leaning, sitting, reading, etc. It is all compounded when you say: bending in an epileptic convulsion, a sudden twisting motion, leaning precariously, or sitting attentively.

Even subtle gestures deserve full attention: a person gracefully bends forward, a barely discernible twist to her body, leaning almost imperceptibly, sitting as if a part of the chair, etc.

Famous Amos, one of my inspirational idols, was not thinking of drawing when he said, "When you begin to examine life more by taking time to see and feel what is happening, your imagination will begin to expand." But for our purposes - it can be applied to drawing. As a matter of fact, seeing and feeling is the very heart of gesture drawing. So maybe xerox that quote 10 times larger and pin it on your desk...

Dan Boulos

James Fujii

Terri Martin

Grant Hiestand

31 Caricature

I have been anxious to do a handout on caricature. I realize it is such a broad and nebulous subject that it can hardly be pinned down to a teachable art. So being inadequately prepared, but loving a challenge — here goes!

In the first place, caricature has lost a lot of its meaning by having been identified almost exclusively with the drawing of funny likenesses. I recently went to my local library in Solvang to check out a book on the subject. In it there were no drawings below the neck. Yet actually, caricaturing the face is but one small facet of the art. The word *caricature* was derived from the Italian or French word, *caricatura*, meaning satirical picture, literally an overloading; or *caricare*, to load, exaggerate, i.e., greatly distort. The exaggeration can be humorous or corny or weird. At any rate it does not just apply to the face. Therefore, we who are interested in gesture, apply the meaning to the whole body or the relationship between two or more bodies. Regardless of the origin of the word, the important thing is the idea of exaggeration. Not just for the sake of exaggeration, but to extract every bit of personality or action from a gesture that will best portray your character's special traits, whether it's Beauty of *Beauty and the Beast*, or Roger Rabbit.

One of the most obvious geniuses of caricature is Al Hirschfeld. But even he can't tell how he captures likeness. When asked how he does it, he said he is "...reduced to blubbering nonsense."

Hirschfeld was influenced by having lived in Bali, where everything seemed to suggest itself in line and where he suddenly discovered that there's a kind of *magic* to line. He was influenced by Harunobu, Utamaro, and Hokusai. (See Hokusai drawings below.) An interesting thought by Hirschfeld: "A painting or drawing that doesn't help the next fellow is of no use. It ceases to be a work of art." He said, "Javanese shadow puppets impressed me enormously as well. They just throw shadows onto a screen; the black and white design is exaggerated, almost caricatured, whatever that means."

So from the "horse's mouth" you get nothing by the way of intellectual explanation — only perhaps inspiration. I like this statement of his: "I have always loved to draw the explosive kind of actor, the ones who never closed the door. They *slammed* it." And, "I have never been able to convince anyone of the simple fact that *caricature* and *beauty* are the same to a caricaturist."

One of the things that helped Hirschfeld in caricature was to liken a person's features or appearance or expression to something that sparked an association, for instance, his nose looks like a sausage, or his hair looks like spaghetti. For some of Hirschfeld's drawings see below.

We have some extremely skilled caricaturists in our midst here at the studio. I hesitate to mention any names, but the only ones I talked to about it, and then only briefly, were Eric Goldberg and Glen Keane. They, like Hirschfeld, could not pin down the process, but suggested that there has to be an emotional involvement. This is akin to my suggestion in the gesture class to talk to yourself as you draw, saying, "This is doing such and such; and the heart of this pose is..." You simply have to involve your deepest feelings — or there will be no depth to your efforts.

As you might surmise, there is no sure way of learning caricature. I think it has to do with the desire to entertain. A caricaturist (my definition is one who is good at gesture drawing) merely "overloads" his drawing so it stands out as the epitome of whatever he is portraying. Especially for the cartoonist — and after all we are all cartoonists. We are dispensers of joy, happiness, entertainment, amusement, pleasure, etc. You, in a word, have a mission as a cartoonist/artist to entertain your audience. This is a serious calling. Not one that requires a long face and grave attitude, but one that requires you to see and draw the light side of life (or whatever the script calls for). We can't all be a Goya or a Kollwitz's. So for heaven's sake lighten up! Enjoy drawing! Assume the role of entertainer! Relax and get out of yourself and inside your characters! Transport them from the mundane into the odd, bizarre, ridiculous, farfetched, romantic, visionary, fanciful — whatever! That is caricature — that is drawing!

Another great contemporary caricaturist is Ronald Searle, some of whose drawings are reproduced below. It seems that his ability to caricature stems from his outlandish "British" sense of humor, and his either sympathetic or merciless views of his fellow man. Maybe neither — maybe his view is *truth*, or at least one extremely perceptive interpretation of it. After all, when you are caricaturing or telling a story, you have to stick to character. The characters in our cartoons have to remain incorruptible, so that, good or bad, we can believe in them. In Searle's case, his characters are having something revealed about themselves — not always (perhaps never) flattering. Although from the viewer's standpoint, they are often not only humorous, but also poignant, pathetic, sad, even heart-rending. Whichever, his drawings are always very incisive.

Notice especially that Searle's caricatures are not of famous people or celebrities, so the likenesses in that respect do not matter. Faces, bodies, props, personalities, and attitudes are the subject. He is making a statement — a caricatured statement about the people he is drawing. Notice too, that the settings, the props, the gestures, all contribute to the subject's character (the story).

In our gesture class (and in our regular studio work) we have the opportunity to use such masters as Hokusai, Hirschfeld, and Searle as a kind of technical and inspirational guide. Not to copy their techniques but to reassure ourselves of the importance of caricature, as opposed to copying the model in class or tracing live action in animation.

In the last noontime drawing session there were many drawings made that impressed me as much as the pros I spoke about earlier. I confiscated a few from James Fujii, Francis Glebas, and Jane Krupka to share with you. In my crusade to suggest that caricature is synonymous with gesture, I would have you view these drawings as perfect examples of caricature. They go beyond just caricaturing someone's face, they accomplish what every animator must do daily — caricature of action.

32   Perspective

You may recall me mentioning a tendency to straighten everything up in a drawing. You know, the crooked-picture-on-the-wall phobia. This tendency goes beyond straightening things up horizontally and vertically, but also depth-wise. That would be like taking the lines in Plate 1a and straightening them up like Plate 1b, which you can see, destroys all illusion of depth.

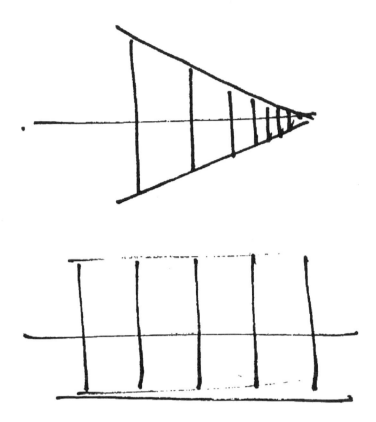

I am relentless in my crusade against this kind of seeing and drawing. You all have at least some knowledge of perspective, but sometimes the mind wanders and you fail to make use of what you do know. To further complicate matters — beyond just knowing the rules, you have to carefully observe (and feel) the pose so that you can fit the two together. So much depends on perspective — not just what is called linear perspective (see Plate 3), which is a system for linear depiction of three dimensions, but also what I will call *Spatial Perspective*. (There may be a more specific term, but I am not aware of one.) In drawing human or animal figures, which are loaded with complicated planes, there would be so many vanishing points you would need a computer to keep track of them. But take heart, there is a simpler method, thanks to Bruce McIntyre, former Disney Studios artist and subsequent drawing instructor. This method involves a few very simple rules which, once understood, are easy to apply, effective, and fun to use. I refer to one or more of them often in the evening gesture class critiques. (If you'd like a more in-depth analysis of these rules, let me know — I'll make an effort to work something up.) Here in Plate 2 are the six principles perspective.

SURFACE   DIMINISHING SIZE   SURFACE PLUS DIMINISHING SIZE   OVERLAP   SURFACE LINES   FORE-SHORTENING

Three of those rules are illustrated in Plate 4.

Plate 4a   Plate 4b

Take the hands first. They illustrate the second rule (see Plate 2), *Diminishing Size*. The hand farthest away being the smallest. Next, the left hand overlapping the forearm, the forearm overlapping the upper arm, the shoulder overlapping the chest area, the front of the neck overlapping the far shoulder — all illustrate the fourth rule, *Overlap*. The way the forearm delineates the contour of the arm as it overlaps the upper arm, and the left shoulder follows the contour as it overlaps at the trapezius muscle, illustrates the fifth rule, *Surface Lines*. Plate 4b further explains the *Surface Lines* rule.

The last rule, *Foreshortening*, is present everywhere in every third dimensional drawing. It should be felt rather than diagrammed, although at times, a few perspective lines may help. Here Donald demonstrates how that particular perspective rule has been pushed to great extremes. This is called *forced perspective*, and is universally accepted as normal.

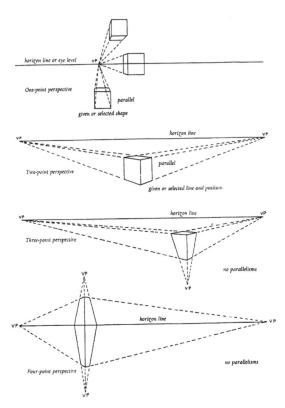

horizon line or eye level ···· VP

One-point perspective

parallel

given or selected shape

VP ···· *horizon line* ···· VP

Two-point perspective

parallel

given or selected line and position

VP ···· *horizon line* ···· VP

Three-point perspective

no parallelisms

VP

VP

horizon line ···· VP

VP ···· VP

Four-point perspective

no parallelisms

VP

Okay, now for the drawing that instigated all this. In Plate 6a is a student's drawing which is about 98% two-dimensional. Next to it in Plate 6b, I show how the artist must have envisioned himself on a crane which lifted him up and down so he could get a straight-on view of everything.

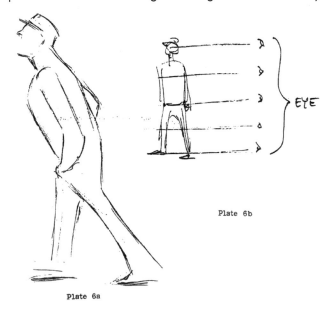

EYE

Plate 6b

Plate 6a

This approach to drawing either displays an ignorance of the rules of perspective, or a lazy approach to drawing. The thing is, perspective is so much a part of drawing that an artist cannot neglect mastering it. Putting off learning it only prolongs the agony. Then of course, once you have it, you will joyfully exclaim, "Oh, how sweet it is."

Here is my correction sketch of that drawing (Plate 7a). Next to it is a chart which shows how the eye saw it from a waist high vantage point — no cranes (Plate 7b). Then in Plate 7c, I have translated what the eye sees into the rule of perspective, *Foreshortening*.

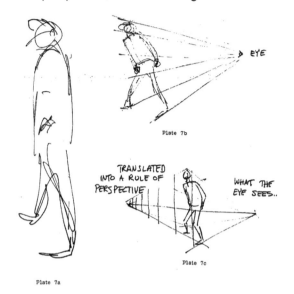

Plate 7a

Plate 7b

Plate 7c

So many things to think about! (Pity poor me who has so few brain cells left.) Anyway, we wouldn't have half as much fun if we could just sit back and draw by the numbers, as my cartoon, Plate 8 postulates.

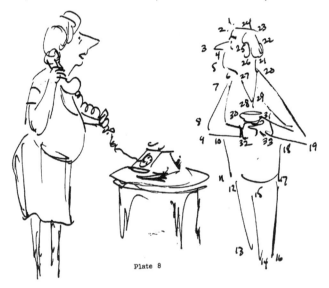

Plate 8

It's Mr. Stanchfield at the Disney Studios. He wants to know if you will pose for his gesture class...

33 Have Something to Say and Keep It Simple

My friends, today's suggestion is to adopt a simple approach when drawing from a model. Especially now during the annual "push" when you have so many work related things on your mind. I'm proud of you who come to the evening gesture class in spite of your tight schedule. Anyway, the more complicated you draw, the more tense and bogged down you become. There's nothing wrong with capturing a pose with a simple drawing. How about trying something as simple as this.

There should be no problem applying whatever costume the model happens to be wearing.

With a simple drawing, you can get the gesture in seconds, and being simple, you can adjust it easily, "nudging" the drawing here and there to strengthen the action of the pose. And you can draw fairly complicated gestures with that simple a figure.

It would be extremely difficult to draw any gesture in a realistic style if, for you, the pose is hard to understand or the meaning (the story) is murky. The best of models often strike unclear or puzzling poses. I'm not saying, don't strive for that "perfect" drawing — it will come. But in the meantime prepare yourself in the art of gesture so that when that perfect drawing does come, it (they) will be more than just photographic likenesses — it will be a vehicle of communication between you (the artist/storyteller) and viewer (the audience).

I don't mean to suggest that you reduce drawing to a formula, but it will greatly help to reduce the complicated figure and drapery to a manageable minimum. After all, any drawing, no matter how realistic, is not the real thing — it is just a symbol of the real. So, if some simple symbols are used, a reasonably good drawing will still be possible. It's likely too, that the simpler the drawing — the clearer the gesture.

Certainly, it will be easier for the artist to accomplish a good gesture drawing if he does not get captivated by the complications of the parts and the details. A big part of an artist's skill is leaving out what doesn't matter and accenting what does matter.

My theory is that when you draw simply, but capture a good gesture, you can use that gesture at a future date for a final drawing. But if you copy some of the details of the figure but miss the gesture — you cannot reconstruct the missing gesture at some future date.

Remember you are not just making a drawing — you are making a drawing of an action, by a particular character that is performing that action. Like a few weeks ago in the gesture class, we had Craig Howell, a great model, as a "waiter." But not just any waiter, this one was slightly portly, stoop-shouldered, double-chinned, and spindly-legged. (Doesn't that help form a picture in your mind and make you want to draw him?)

But there is more! He was very professional in manner, proud of his calling and his expertise — proud to the point of arrogance — even disdain. You who were there may recall he was rather overbearing to one of the students who posed with him.

He was easy to caricature because he was obviously trying to be the typical waiter.

Those are some of the things that are good to have in mind as you draw a character doing something. Just relying on "inspiration" won't always work. That would be like trying to drive to some unknown (to you) address in New York by inspiration alone.

So remember today's suggestion: Have something to say, and keep it simple.

Here is one student's drawing with my correction from that evening. The waiter was holding a menu and suggesting something delectable to the customer. The student began to draw the elements before him — the head, torso, arms, and menu. They are all there and there is no doubt about what they are.

But, the story is the waiter is making contact with the customer, and though unseen, you should feel that there is a customer present. In my correction sketch, I pulled the menu out of the way of the look, so you could feel the "contact." Actually, it's not just a "feeling," it's an actuality taking place. The spotting of such a fact should help to mobilize all your drawing skills to put over the story, i.e., act out the story in drawing form.

Here is a drawing problem from a couple of weeks ago. It brings to light the need to "experience" the pose personally. I have used a simplified drawing, necessarily, for I do these in about 5 or 10 seconds, but as you can see I was therefore not hindered by details and was able to express my ideas in a free manner. The model had a box, which he has indicated is extremely heavy. To emphasize (caricature) this he is supporting the weight on his midsection, which is suspended between his left arm and his right knee. The student not only did not "experience" the weight of the heavy box — he didn't even show it (the whole idea of the pose!). I'm saying, rather than back off on a pose, push it farther. Caricature it so it will read. Your audience, unless they are students of anatomy, are not interested in muscles, they are interested in story and action. Am I too rough on you?

Writing is another form of communication which like drawing should be simple and to the point. I recently came across this example of gobbledygook (unintelligible jargon) in *The Writer's Art*, by James Kilpatrick. This was a message from a high school principle to the student's parents:

Our school's cross-graded, multi-ethnic, individualized learning program is designed to enhance the concept of an open-ended learning program with emphasis on a continuum of multi-ethnic enriched learning using the identified intellectually gifted child as the agent or director of his own learning. Major emphasis is on cross-graded, multi-ethnic learning with the main objective being to learn respect for the uniqueness of a person.

You still there?
I want to go on and on but must keep these handouts to somewhat reasonable lengths, so until the next one — HAVE SOMETHING TO SAY and KEEP IT SIMPLE!

34 Keeping Flexibility in Your Drawing

I hope a lot of you have taken advantage of the anatomy classes with Steve Huston. Furthering your knowledge of this important essential in drawing is to your lifelong advantage. Anatomy is fascinating. It is wonderfully complicated, yet incredibly simple if, when you draw, you concentrate on character and gesture rather than muscles and bones. Study muscles from all different angles and learn how they adjust to each action. You don't want your drawings to look like they just came from the freezer — all muscles frozen and unable to adjust themselves to each action. Fortunately (or mercifully) those stringy muscle fibers have been coated with layers of drawable fat, flesh, and skin.

When drawing from the model it is easy to misinterpret the pose and see it as inactive or static, even lifeless. So you must keep reminding yourself that it is an action — an action held long enough for you to draw. If it were possible we would have the model high jumping or turning somersaults, but due to gravity we have to limit the poses to less active action, but nevertheless, action.

For instance, if you are drawing a person stretching both arms forward, you have to look at it from the standpoint of an action, not just a "still life."

Let 's go to the other extreme so we can see the action happening. Here is the same guy with arms stretched backwards. Notice how the stomach protrudes, which is a natural and necessary move for the action.

If you will look from one drawing to the other you will see the action (animation) take place. Looking down at this action, it would appear something like this.

So when you see a gesture, try to imagine where the action came from, so you can feel which muscles are being stretched and how the parts of the body around them are affected; that is, how they take part in the action. Again, look from drawing to drawing and see how pliable those parts are. They are not rigid and unyielding (though the model is still for the pose) but are very elastic, supple, and limber.

If you get too tied up in construction, muscles, bones, and drapery (necessary though they are), you might end up with a stiff drawing as if of a wooden puppet.

It may move but it has no life in it, and what we are after is life.

Every action has some kind of opposing action, or opposing force in it, as you saw in the very first illustration. For instance if one arm was pointing, the other arm would counter it in some way. Or even the body might lean forward or backward for emphasis.

The action would not be so strong if both arms came forward or if the body didn't react.

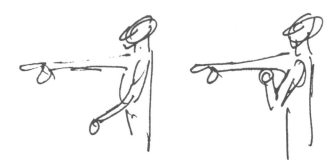

Walking is an obvious example of opposing forces. As the left arm stretches forward, the right arm stretches back. This is not a mechanical thing — it's a very flexible move — the arms bend and tilt, the legs bend and stretch, and the body leans and twists.

So by all means, study anatomy. It is the basis for all drawing. But keep in mind how the bones and muscles contribute to the hundreds of possible nuances of motion. Even the head, which is mostly bone, is treated like soft clay in cartooning.

Recently we had R. C. Bates pose for us. What a great model! He did a WWII pilot and a pros-
pector. He set the stage for many a stimulating story vignette. I saved one correction drawing, one that
points up an oft missed opportunity; that is, when a character assumes an attitude that requires his stomach to protrude. So many times the artist gets the upper body angle, but when drawing the lower body
he seems to forget the pose and comes straight down with the legs, overlooking the stomach's gestural
capabilities. In my sketch can you see an arrogance, pompousness, or maybe just a little swaggering or
maybe a Hitler-like contemptuousness? That's what gesture drawing is all about!

There were many excellent drawings made that night, but in my estimation, Mark Kausler seemed to
be especially sensitive to R.C.'s poses. Here are several of his drawings.

And here is an excellent drawing by Jane Krupka.

35 Seeing and Drawing the Figure in Space

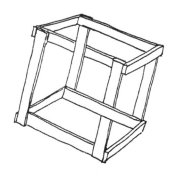

Isn't this a beauty! Of course, you'd have to go out of your way to draw something so third dimensionally screwed up. Even a non-artist could come closer to reality than that, because a box is a relatively simple form. A box takes place in space, and as we draw it, it's easy to think of it as occupying space, especially with the help of some elementary perspective.

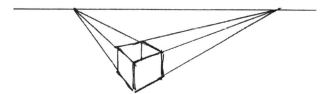

The human (or animal) shape exists also in space, and though much more complicated, the idea of it displacing space is the same. However, quite often when drawing from a model (or from real life) we switch into a different mode than when drawing a box. With a box, it's easy to see the space inside and around the shape, but with the more complicated human figure that aspect is not so obvious.

Let's try to establish a clear concept of seeing the figure in space by using what might be called the "shock" treatment. Here is a screen with a two-dimensional shadow of a figure cast on it.

Now the screen is suddenly pulled away and there before us, without 3D glasses, is the same figure in glorious 3D. (Drawing by 3D advocate, Mike Swofford; modeled by third dimensional Allison Mosa.)

Look from drawing to drawing and you can see it happen. That gratifying and fascinating realization of 3D that overwhelms you — which should be your normal realization at all times while drawing. Superimposing the box onto the figure illustrates how they both relate to space in a similar way.

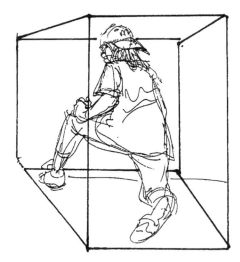

Actually this can be done in the mind's eye, so that you are drawing the figure in that imagined space. One thing that is imperative when drawing a figure or a cartoon in a scene of animation is to be aware of the "grid" that the layout department has established. That grid is like a vinyl tile floor, whose lines all proceed to one of two vanishing points. Not checking the layout for that perspective before starting to *animate, cleanup, or inbetween* a scene is one of the cardinal sins of animation. Putting it in a more positive way, that grid (perspective) is one of the principle means of laying in or establishing the foundation for a background. "Follow the Yellow Brick Road" when you have time to dream — but while drawing — follow the "grid."

It may help to think of a figure as enclosed in an invisible box, subject, of course, to your viewpoint.

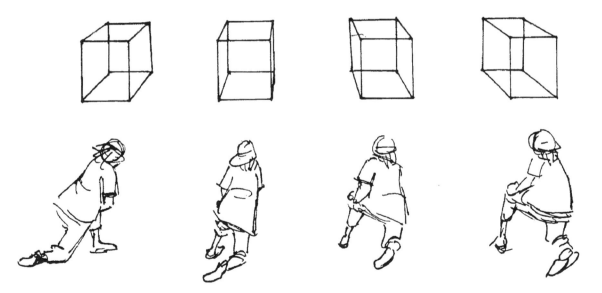

This is not to be thought of as a prop, but as a concept that will aid you in any third dimensional drawing you will ever make. It's a kind of drawing grammar. In writing, grammar deals with the forms and structures of words and their arrangement in phrases and sentences (syntax). So "drawing grammar" deals with forms and structures and their arrangement, not in phrases and sentences, but in third dimensional space.

Circles, incidentally, although good for locating things on the page, are not much help in revealing the illusion of 3D. Here are four views of a tennis ball.

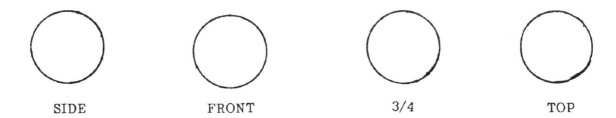

SIDE   FRONT   3/4   TOP

Next is an attempt to illustrate how important seeing things in space is by using the box symbol. These are some old drawings that were used for other reasons but will work for this demonstration. There will be a student's drawing, accompanied by a "box" drawing, showing his perspective. Then there will be my correction drawing with a "box" drawing to show how perspective can enhance the illusion of space.

Granted, it's easy to analyze another person's drawing, but by the same token it is extremely difficult to analyze one's own drawing. That is why we must form some useable concepts of gesture, proportion, balance, etc., in space, so that we can see those good things as we draw. Just moving the pen or pencil around the surface of the paper, no matter how intense our desire for a good drawing, is simply not enough.

36 Don't Let the Facts Get in the Way of a Good Drawing

On the Channel 5 morning newscast, weatherman Mark Cristi related an amusing story, but couldn't remember the name of the person he was quoting. Barbara Beck, anchor woman, said, "Mark never lets the facts get in the way of a good story." It was a good story and whether the person quoted was Rodney Dangerfield or Prince Charles, it wouldn't have added or taken away from the comical twist. (The story was about some older man who had gotten his much younger wife pregnant so she would have a playmate.)

Here is a paraphrase of that line: "…don't let the facts get in the way of a good drawing." All the facts in the world are only "grist" waiting for a good story. Or to look at it from another angle, "A good story just needs enough facts to give it a vehicle for expression."

In other words, when you draw, draw the story (or the gesture) and allow just enough facts to creep in to give your pen something to do. It's something like the guy who was photographing with no film in his camera. He didn't need factual proof that he was taking beautiful pictures — he could see what he was getting in his view finder.

Many years ago Stan Green stepped into Milt Kahl's room and said: "Such-and-such-a-scene has come back from camera — it's on the Moviola, do you want to see it?" Milt said, "Hell, no. I animated it. I know what it looks like." Well… it may be a long time before some of us will be that confident (or that conceited), but you might take a hint from one of the "masters"; that is, know what your drawing looks like before you start detracting from the story with too many facts. You know what a lot of floundering and superfluous words can do to a joke's punch line.

Ruth Rendell, British detective story writer, said she doesn't research the mechanics of policedom for her stories, "I find if you do it consciously (rely on facts) it doesn't work." Well, in drawing you do have to be conscious of the gesture and the story. Most other conscious effort should be done in an anatomy class or curled up with a good anatomy book, remembering always that what a muscle does (verb) is more important than its construction (noun).

Keep your drawings vital, zestful, and entertaining by drawing verbs not nouns. A list of verbs should be enough to convince you of their importance: twist, bend, stretch, run, jump; look, stare, be surprised, be mad, be coy; sit, lay, lean — the list goes on and on and encompasses all the activities that a story might require. Nouns are facts: a belt buckle, a shirt, a hairdo, eyes, or a mouth. Writer Josephine Tey recognized the principle of facts versus content (story). In her book *The Daughters of Time*, she has one of her characters comment on a portrait of Richard III, "Whatever it is, it is a face, isn't it! Not just a collection of organs for seeing, breathing, and eating with…."

A couple of weeks ago Tom Sito, one of our favorite people and certainly one of our best models, posed for the evening classes. As a civil war officer, he amused us with lines like (through clenched teeth that held a cigar), "Forget it General. I'm not going up that hill — it's too dangerous." Anyway, Tina Price, who has renewed her interest in drawing and possibly animation, did some nice drawing those evenings. She has been attending the gesture classes for quite a time now, and has, in my mind, recently made a quantum leap in her drawing ability. She has been concentrating on the story behind the pose, and as you can see by these reproductions of her recent work — she is right on track.

Allow me to present a couple of critiques, which were designed to open up some revealing vistas of creative prowess. One student began his drawing with something that obviously fascinated him — the box that the model was holding out in front of her body. I suggested that perhaps if he drew the body attitude first, he would then be free to manipulate the arms and box to the greatest possible advantage (staging). Stare at my suggestion of a figure and let your imagination play with various possibilities for the arms and box. You can extend them, hold them close to the body, tip the box to show the audience what's in it or hold it up high as an offering to some deity. On the other hand, look at student's drawing and try to do the same with the body. The choices for variations are few.

Here is another one where the model was about to pick up the box. In the student's drawing, the twinning of the arms is rather static and leads nowhere. In my suggestion sketch, I angled the arms and hands in a way that suggests a movement toward the box. All the elements are arranged to concentrate your attention on the action, which is — preparing to pick up the box.

Here is Tom Sito as a Russian — with one of those black cossack hats on and a sword close at hand, looking for the enemy — but according to James Fujii, finding something much more welcome than some opposing military force.

37 Hey, Look at Me ... Look at Me!

How excited children get when they strike a pose, perform some feat, or do anything that seems worth sharing or bragging about. If you don't look, they scream louder, "LOOK AT ME... LOOK AT ME!" It's some rare or special moment that will last for only a few seconds and it's just got to be savored, and the onlooker plays a vital part in the excitement of the occasion by experiencing it, too.

I think when a model comes to our drawing class to pose they are, in effect, saying "Look at me... look at me!" (Or perhaps, "Draw me, draw me!") So we look at them, and we experience the excitement of the moment, and we attempt to record it for still others to see, and our senses are sharpened by the responsibility to convey the gesture in its fullest measure.

Here are some words that cover the whole process — *exciting, breathtaking, spine-tingling, impelling, stimulating, thrilling* — and furthermore, when one gets excited, one is *aroused, energized, fired-up,* and *inspired.* Now this is not to say that you have to turn into a human tornado as you draw — but it does mean that if you are not experiencing these things, in some measure — you are missing out on something. (And so are your drawings, probably.). Let me try to convey that premise by presenting some critiques wherein you may see where the excitement I experienced over the poses helped to create the illusion that the model was indeed saying, "Look at me... look at me!"

In this first example, the student's drawing indecisively shows the model (Kevin Smith — a great model) pulling his leg into a folded position. But actually, his leg was already folded and he was stretched back, relaxing — as you can see in my sketch. The exciting thing was, if his hands slipped off his ankles, he would have fallen over backwards. That is exciting! It is suspenseful — there is a kind of iffy tension there. I projected his nose (head) forward for counterbalance, and also, to suggest his inner concern — his body enjoying the precariously relaxed position, but Kevin thinking, "Boy, I hope my hands don't slip." Whatever story you decide to fabricate, try to make it a "Look at me!" pose.

Some days you wish you'd stayed in bed. In the drawing below, the student, who ordinarily draws quite well, was searching desperately for some "handle" to grab on to. I suggested, as always, to first form some kind of a story — there could be any number of them for each pose — and go for it. In my critique sketch, I chose to create a stage where the arms form the right and left extremes, with all the action taking place on center stage. The action was looking intently at his hands holding on to his ankles, which in turn creates the impression that he is in deep thought. You can feel a three-dimensional area (arena) of "charged" space there. I call that the "stage." Stages are exciting — look for them in all poses and gestures.

Talk about excitement. You can imagine the excitement I was enjoying while drawing this next correction sketch. The sketch took about 10 or 15 seconds. You can't sustain that pitch of excitement much longer than that. I'm kidding. You can. Ask any animator and they will assure you that when they get involved and excited while working on a scene, every drawing produces a "high," and time seems to disappear as they translate story into drawing.

Look at these drawing below and try to imagine the story behind each of them. My interpretation of the student's drawing is "Let's see, shall I go farther forward… or back up a bit… or maybe I had better stay right here." The thought behind my sketch is "Hey, this pose has been done before — but I'm going to do it better — with more stretch, with more pizzazz. If there is an ultimate to this pose — I'm going to make a daring attempt to reach it. I want my drawing to look like it's saying, "Hey, look at me… look at me!"

You should always keep in mind that the model's presentation of the pose is not sacred — it's only a suggestion for you to do with as you see fit. *What you get out of the pose is what you put into it.* That means that if you're satisfied with it as is, you can go ahead and make a photographic copy of it. But if you get your actor/self emotionally involved, you are then free to carry the pose to a more dramatic expression.

On the following page is another high-level-excitement pose. The student has made a fairly powerful looking drawing — parts of which are very well done. But the character seems to be saying, "Hurry up and change the pose. My shoulders are killing me." In my sketch you can see that I put myself in the model's place and was attempting to push to a "Hey, look at me!" type pose. It just requires a little touch of exhibitionism — a bit of childlike abandon. Sometimes we may be tired or feel a little sedate or mellow or reserved, so it may require a little mental goose to bring ourselves up to a more exciting, feel-good-about-yourself-hey-look-at-me level.

In the *Illusion of Life*, by Frank Thomas and Ollie Johnston, there are many references to faithfully drawing the thoughts or emotions of the characters. Some suggest that no matter how good a drawing is, if it doesn't faithfully portray the emotions of the character it is worthless. "One young animator," they suggest, "was quite shaken by the criticism of his scenes. The best drawing in the world wouldn't have helped because it would still be empty; it was because of the emptiness in the business that they criticized the scenes." He went on to explain, "I can't make a drawing until I know what I'm trying to draw."

A pertinent suggestion in the book is "Resist the temptation to tell too much in one drawing. The important thing is that the drawing be quickly read. No matter how beautifully it may be drawn, it should not be forced into a scene if it does not animate properly. Do not be afraid to discard your best drawing if it does not fit your action. It is the *idea* that is important (emphasis mine)."

Walt Disney was keen on getting the appropriate graphic portrayal of the character's emotion. When someone is lifting a heavy weight, what do you feel? Do you feel something is liable to crack any minute and drop down? Do you feel that because of the pressure he's going to blow up? That his face is going to turn purple? That his eyes are going to bulge out of their sockets? That the tension in the arm is so terrific that he's going to snap?

Do you feel that same intensity of concern for your drawings? (All of them?) Can you imagine Laurence Olivier or Bette Midler rendering only an unthinking, aimless, or lackadaisical performance? Well, you are a performer just as they are. Think about it...

A gesture may be subtle, such as someone in peaceful relaxation, but that does not mean the drawing has to be lifeless — without tension or balance and counterbalance. The drawing must look like the character is alive and thinking, and the only way to accomplish that is for you, the artist, to think about what you want the character to appear to be thinking.

In this next example, the student's drawing is *inactive but not relaxed*. In my correction sketch, he is *active but relaxed*. I have the character bending forward (action), stretching his arms forward (action), gently leaning on his knees (action), and his neck stretched forward, while his face is angled up to see forward (actions). You might say he is actively relaxed — another "Hey, look at me!" action.

Here is a quote from one of my favorite authors, E. B. White. See if you can feel the anticipated excitement he felt in creating a story (in our case it would be a drawing) out of nothing but a blank page. (And of course, a lot of mental gymnastics.) It's really an awesome thing, creating a story, and illustrating it in an appealing, entertaining, and exciting way, even when the story is only one drawing long. Here is what he said: "... a blank sheet of paper holds the greatest excitement there is for me — more promising than a silver cloud, and prettier than a red wagon."

38 Learn From the Mistakes of Others

One good excuse for doing these "handouts" is, if you can't make it to the gesture class, the gesture class can be brought to you. Or as some obscure philosopher said: "Learn from the mistakes of others, you can't live long enough to make them all yourself." Actually, these critiques are not presented as corrections of mistakes — they are just other ways of seeing things. Another instructor may come up with an entirely different set of suggestions that might send you into wild and riotous states of creativity. A critique should broaden ways of seeing things. It is not saying this is how to draw this thing or this action. It's saying, hey, if you think things out, you can make a more exciting drawing — and who doesn't want to do that?

Drawing is a breaking away from copying, thus adding life to your characters. It expresses some emotion or story point. In animation it is both of those things. If the student of drawing gets too preoccupied with the building blocks — he is apt to forget the life that is lived in the building after it is built, bought, and lived in.

So I present to you some critiques. Not so you will draw like me, but so you will look...and see... and draw in an inventive, inspired, and innovative way — having a plan in mind before you make even one line.

Here is a model, David Roon, sitting on a stool with his left hand grasping the seat, right elbow leaning on his leg.

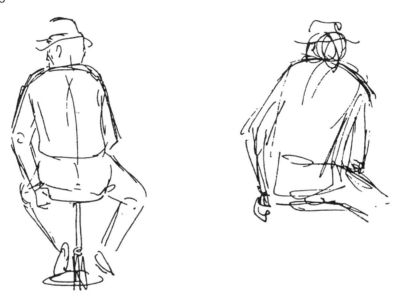

Logically, for the elbow to get down that far, the character would have to bend forward. How does one draw someone bending over from a back view? Cheat! Yes, cheat. By turning your figure a bit, you can show a slight bend. You can round off the shoulders. Actually, it isn't the shoulders you're seeing, it's the upper back. If you insist on showing the shoulders, you in effect straighten up the bend. Here is a side view of that pose showing how you are looking at the back, not the shoulders.

Here's an interesting pose where I picture the sides of the torso as if they were suspension cables on a bridge with the left arm being one of the superstructures, and the knee being another one.

I imagined myself in that pose and I could feel my left side sagging between the shoulder and the hip. I visualized my body sitting on the floor, completely relaxed and not in the stiff manner of the student's drawing — nice drawing though it be.

Here's a pose where the model was reaching up with the right arm. I stood up before the student and reached up showing what takes place in the body: the slight lean to the left, the right hip protruding, plus getting the arms in the clear so their actions can clearly be seen. You have to form a story, and rehearse

it constantly as you are drawing. Just putting marks, which have no meaning, onto the paper, is really courting failure. Drawing is a thinking/feeling pastime. If you want to earn a living at chance go to Las Vegas and pull on those slot machine levers. After a hundred or so pulls you may come up with some cherries, lemons, or oranges that will form a profitable configuration. But successes there are rare, and so are they rare in drawing when you just start putting marks down (pulling levers) without some plan (story).

The human figure is amazingly supple — capitalize on that fact and your drawing will have a persuasive vitality. You do *not* want your characters to look like rigor mortis has set in. Cartoons have even more anatomical leeway and you being essentially cartoonists — well, lee away!

Next is a fairly nice drawing by a student who is an excellent artist. In this drawing, though, she ended up with some tangents that caused some confusion in one area of the drawing. You can see where the hand, the wrist, the cheek, and the shoulder all meet at one point. It destroys all sense of space there. The solution was simple, as you can see in my accompanying sketch. The parts were simply separated in a way that created a more pleasing third dimensional space around the parts. It sets that part of the action in a kind of "stage." A good set designer or layout person will form such a stage to set off the action, and focus the eye on the main story point.

In this following pose, the model held a long pole behind his head. Now whether you have ever done this or not, surely, you can imagine the strain it would put on the back of your neck, and how it would force your head forward. It's a piece of business that you have to feel to accurately draw. Even when the model doesn't give you such a definite piece of business — make something up. Give your poor drawing a story to tell so it has some reason for being. Mull over this quotation from Frank and Ollie's book, *The Illusion of Life*. "If you don't have a positive statement to make, you should never pick up the paintbrush or pencil. More than a positive statement, it must have enough importance to be worth communicating — to be worth the work and the effort that will be required to put it on the screen. It must be interesting, provocative, spellbinding; it must be a story." Sound familiar?

Here are two views of the same pose, both of which needed a little more pizzazz (a more gripping statement). In the first correction sketch, I realized I hadn't gone far enough, so sketched a second one with the head farther forward. In the next one, having learned a lesson, I drew what I thought would give the viewer a sense, or better yet, the sensation of the strain one would feel when assuming this pose.

I left some of the body on the student's drawing so you could compare it to mine, where the whole body is learning forward — to ease its pain.

39 Quest and Fulfillment

QUEST ———➤ *The purpose of learning to draw is to be able to express yourself in drawing.* Fact: Limited drawing ability equals limited self-expression.

FULFILLMENT

The trouble is, it's hard to face the fact that learning to draw ends up being a lifelong struggle. We (some of us) start off with a bang, attending drawing classes and carrying a sketchbook. Then we get a job as an artist and somehow that seems to fulfill our goal, so we begin to taper off on the study and the sketching. But finding employment as an artist is only one step in a more far reaching and richer goal — one that can be reached only by continued effort, devotion to the art of drawing, a resolve to self-improvement, and some good old-fashioned perseverance.

It might help to realize that everyone is in the same boat. We all have to fight discouragement. We are all susceptible to negativity, and the seductive temptation to settle for "adequate" when with a little more effort we could be "outstanding."

One comforting thing: you don't have to expend a lot of energy and effort all at once. Remember it's a lifelong journey, and a good steady little-bit-more-effort will do the trick nicely. An occasional anatomy class, some periodic study from an anatomy book, and of course, the habit of carrying and using a sketchbook. Ah ha! Sketching! What a sneaky way to bring up sketching. "So," you may be asking, "I suppose this is part of your ongoing effort to have us carry a sketchbook wherever we go and to actually use it?" Well, now that you pin me down... yes! I think a sketchbook should be standard, everyday equipment for every artist. *Sketching is an Artist's Ultimate Enlightenment..* And read it again!

I probably learned the importance of sketching from a cartoonist in the 1940s. In his book, *Cartooning for Everybody*, Lawrence Lariar astutely counseled, "Sketching is sketching. It involves a model, usually, whether the model is a buxom nude or an old tomato can. It is copying, after a fashion. The cartoonist, when he sketches, is going through a process of study. He concentrates upon the model, plumbs its movement, bulk, the 'guts' of the thing he's after. He puts into his drawing (though it may be as big as your thumbnail) all his experience. He simplifies. He plays with his line. He experiments. He isn't concerned with anatomy, chiaroscuro, or the symmetry of 'flowing line.' There's nothing highbrow about his approach to the sketch pad. He is drawing because he likes to draw!"

Even Tony Bennett does it! In his book *Painting More Than the Eye Can See*, the author, Robert Wade, slips in this bit of trivia: "Tony Bennett, the fine American vocalist, visited my studio during his recent Australian concert tour. Tony is one of the world's greatest artists in modern music, and I'm a long-time fan. Tony sketches and draws everywhere he goes and is never without his sketchbook and pens."

One of the great rewards of sketching is that you are drawing people doing different things, and you find yourself forming a little story about what you're drawing and directing it to: a gal looking at herself in a mirror as she tries on dresses; a guy leaning against a building looking bored. As writer/director you can place a cigarette in his mouth, and have him look at his watch. You don't just draw anyone — you draw someone who is doing something that is interesting enough to record, even if you have to add a little of your own theatrics. In any case, your thinking process should always be several steps ahead of your pen.

Being fluent in speech means you're able to speak readily, articulately, and facilely. That is what constant sketching will do for you, allow you to draw readily, articulately, and facilely.

The painter Robert Wade, speaking about thinking through problems in painting, said, "...the artist is the director of the show, so I did it my way!" In gesture drawing, you are director, and if you know anything about directors, it'll be that they think things through pretty thoroughly. Sketching will develop that skill. Hey, I kid you not!

Veteran animator, Ron Husband, inveterate sketcher, has been carrying sketch books for years — we are talking hundreds of them, and it's a privilege to reprint a few of those sketches here. I hope they will be an inspiration to you.

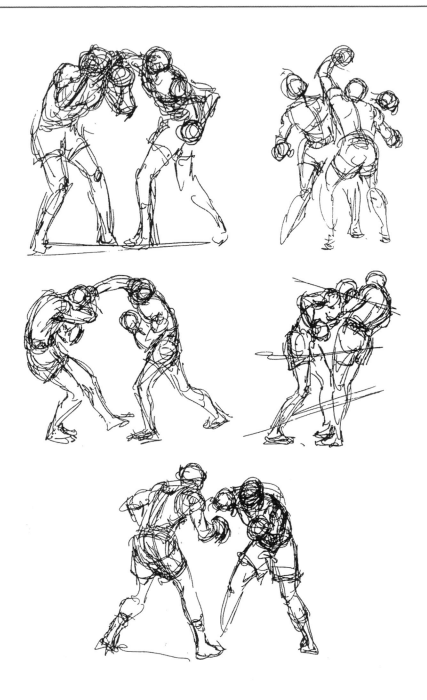

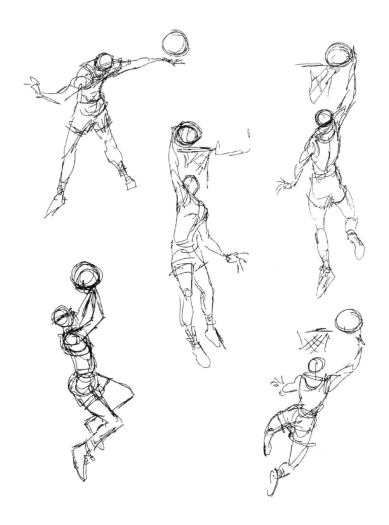

40 Getting Adjusted to New Production

I remember those exciting days when we started on a new picture. All the previous production's model sheets and inspirational material was put aside, and we began to gather research for the next film. We ordered books from the library, delved into our personal morgue, and shared our findings with each other. It was (and is) a necessary transitional period of gathering material pertinent to the new project. Footage on animals, birds, and humans; or new footage shot if none was available. The film was practically worn out from running it over and over, studying it sometimes frame by frame. Helpful studies were copied and distributed to other artists. It was a period of changeover — a new way of thinking.

Now comes another "changeover." *The King of the Jungle* is on the line (editor note: this was the early name for *The Lion King*). Who is not anxious to make the transition by familiarizing themselves with the physical, mental, and personality makeup of the jungle creatures that comprise the cast of characters? You may be thinking, "Oh, sure, I'm going to study animal anatomy, but what's with the mental and personality bit?" Well, I'm glad you asked!

Since time immemorial man has attempted to understand the minds of animals — and animals to understand the minds of man. There is a wealth of lore, from whole civilizations to individual tribes, where animals and birds have assumed roles of stewardship or have influenced significantly the daily lives of the believers. Fairy tales are rife with animals and birds talking, thinking, and acting like man. Occasionally, man becomes animal-like. We think of people as being foxy, or stubborn as a mule; cowardly people are called "chicken," or they move like snails, run like deer, or swim like fish.

The Disney Studios has always given animals the attributes of man, having them perform human feats and think human thoughts. Remember King Louie, who in song expressed the desire to be like man?

Now I'm the king of the swingers
Oh, the jungle V.I.P.
I've reached the top and had to stop
And that's what's botherin' me.
I wanna be a man, Mancub,
And stroll right into town,
And be just like the other men,
I'm tired of monkeyin' around.

Oh, ooh be do, I want to be like you hoo,
I wanna walk like you, talk like you, too hoo hoo,
You see it's true hoo hoo
An ape like me hee bee
Can learn to be a hu-hu-human, too boo hoo.

Our dog Bonnie, a blonde cocker spaniel, wanted to be like humans, too. When my wife, Dee, and I would talk together or with a group of friends, Bonnie would try to join in with an uncanny likeness to human talk. (Quiet, Bonnie, you're just a dog...we think!)

We have a huge Himalayan cat that Dee talks to. It's like they're both trying to enter the other's realm. (They've got me convinced that something is going on between them, the "Meows" are so conversational.)

A guy named Fred Kimball, *The Man Who Speaks to Animals,* actually did converse with animals. At a demonstration I was privileged to witness, people in the audience brought their pets (hamsters, canaries, dogs, cats, ducks, etc.) onto the stage (one at a time), where Fred would ask questions of them telepathically. Then he would tell the owners what the animals said — for verification. The owners would burst into laughter and say, "Yes, that's exactly what happened."

I'll relate only a couple of exchanges — a duck told him that he had two bodies of water in his yard. "That's right," explained the owner, "One of them is for drinking, the other is for swimming."

"He keeps telling me that his yard looks like a garden — what does he mean by 'looks like' a garden?" The owner laughed and explained, "It used to be a garden, but the duck ate or otherwise destroyed all the plants, so we put in some plastic flowers."

Kimball used his psychic powers to diagnose animal illnesses — somewhat resembling Dr. Dolittle. Ah, yes, Dr. Dolittle! How about Rex Harrison's delightful rendition of Dr. Dolittle as he sang, *If I Could Talk to the Animals.*

If I could walk with the animals, Talk with the animals
Grunt and squawk And squeak with the animals, And they could talk to me.

In the introduction to the tenth printing of Dr. Dolittle, by Hugh Lofting, Hugh Walpole said a very pertinent thing: "John Dolittle's friends are convincing because their creator never forces them to desert their own characteristics. For instance," Hugh continues, "Polynesia the parrot, really does care about the Doctor but she cares as a bird would care."

Here is a typical exchange of thought between the parrot and the Doctor.

"But animals don't always speak with their mouths," said the parrot in a high voice, raising her eyebrows. "They talk with their ears, with their feet, with their tails — with everything. Sometimes they don't want to make a noise. Do you see now the way he's twitching up one side of his nose?"

"What's that mean?" asked the Doctor.

"That means, 'can't you see that it has stopped raining?'" Polynesia answered. "He's asking you a question. Dogs nearly always use their noses for asking questions."

Bet you're dying to get home and check that out with your dog.

I don't want to stretch this psychic connection or relationship between man and beast too far, but in the *Los Angeles Times* (Wednesday 8/12/92) there was an article on Winn Bundy, who runs a bookstore on a remote ranch called The Singing Wind, in Arizona. One day she was down by the San Pedro River inspecting her wells when she spotted a bobcat on the opposite bank. She sat down and watched it.

The bobcat seemed to like the attention, and began puffing out its chest and growling. Bundy was having a good time, too. She eyeballed the preening cat and said, "Yes sir, you are beautiful." The conversation went on like that, two denizens of the Singing Wind chatting across the river like old friends.

Well, the animation staff is even now immersing themselves into animal life as they prepare for the *King of the Jungle* (editor note: *King of the Jungle* was an early name for *The Lion King*), with animals that will be speaking English and acting American. We trust that none will carry this "merging" with the animals too far, ending up in a kind of "Twilight Zone." You've heard of how some actors have immersed themselves so deeply into their roles that it was difficult to adjust back to their normal relationships after the makeup was removed. So be cautious, and in the words of our cat, Casey, "Meow.. ..meeeow!"

Veteran animator, Andreas Deja, has been sketching at the Griffith Park Zoo (as have others) for some time now, preparing for a walk with and a talk with, the animals. He tells me he is going to spend about a week with the animals of the San Diego Zoo — how did he put it — getting acquainted with, or getting close to, or was it something like blending with their personalities — I can't remember exactly, but it reminded me immediately of Dr. Dolittle's song. I asked Andreas to write a paragraph for this handout, so here is a very brief view of his otherwise vast knowledge and understanding of drawing.

As we observe these lions and study how they walk, run, sit down, etc., we must remember the individual type and character of each animal.

If we only concentrate on the technical aspects of movement we'll end up with dry academic studies on the screen. I feel all analysis should start with the personality which will dictate what the character is going to do, and then we worry about how he is going to do it technically.

And finally, for your viewing pleasure and inspiration, here are some quick sketches of animals from Andreas's latest sketch books.

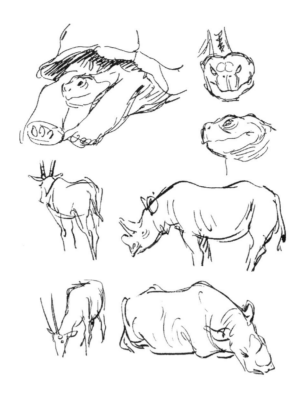

41   More Animal Talk

Recently I had fun doing a handout on animals. It was a blatant attempt to suggest that man and animals do communicate on certain levels. Who knows how much communication of this nature is needed for good animation? We can be sure, though, that the more understanding we have of animal personality — and we will all agree they have character, temperament, and individuality — the better we can draw them.

In that last handout (Chapter 40), Polynesia told Dr. Dolittle that animals talked with their ears, tails, etc. How about smell? Well, Fred Kimball, *The Man Who Talks to Animals*, during that demonstration I told you about, had a hamster tell him (telepathically) that he hid from his owners. "Yes," they admitted, "We had everyone in the apartment complex looking for him." Fred then said the hamster kept "beaming" him the smell of leather. "Yes, we finally found him hiding in a leather slipper in the closet."

Last week I only scratched the surface of this fascinating subject, so this week will carry it a bit further. (Incidentally, the sensitive cat drawings adorning these pages were done by Andreas Deja.)

I suggested that there is a telepathic link between man and animal. You've all no doubt heard of the experiments in communication between man and porpoise, man and chimpanzee, etc. Barbara Woodhouse, the famous trainer of dogs, tells some delightful tales of her experiences along those lines. In *Just Barbara*, an autobiography, she writes:

The importance of your tone of voice when speaking to animals (or human beings for that matter) was made very clear to me when I was in Gambia a few years back. I went to the Abuko rainforests where the nature reserves are. In a cage, was a hyena which had continued, ever since its captivity to throw itself from one end of it to another hoping to escape. It did this twelve hours a day. Nothing could persuade it to stop, in its misery and fear. I asked the keeper who was there if he would allow me to go and talk to the hyena. He said I could, so I went over to it and in what I call my 'little voice' (which is a fairly soft high-pitched tone) I said, 'Come along, come along.' It stopped throwing itself against the cage and came up to me. It raised its nose to mine, put its ears flat against its face in what I call the 'soft look' which means that the animal welcomes you, and actually wriggled as it came up to me, laid its head against my chest and breathed up my nose. Then it lay down at my feet. I was so amazed at the reaction of this animal that I asked the keeper if I could go out to the reserve where there were many more hyenas and he said I could. I was not allowed in with them, so I stayed outside the wire, and again used my 'little voice' to call them which, incidentally, my mother always asked me to use in the old days if there was any unhappy dog in the boarding kennels. She would say, Go and talk to the dog, Barbara, in your 'little voice' — it always makes them happy." Well, I called the hyenas, and one by one, they all came up to me, laying their heads as near to mine as they could and breathing up my nose. One got near enough to push up the wire and lay its head on my chest, and then the whole lot came up, breathed up my nose and laid down at my feet.

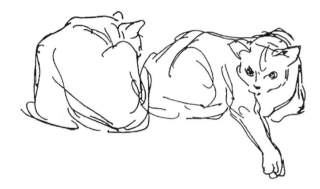

Barbara also tells of some far out experiences with a praying mantis, a family of swans, horses, and of course, dogs, which is how we know of her.

The English cartoonist Thelwell lends his expertise along these lines.

Poet W. B. Yeats writes touchingly of a yearning to communicate with a squirrel in his, "To a Squirrel at Kyle-Na-No."

Come play with me;
Why should you run
Through the shaking tree
As though I'd a gun
To strike you dead?
When all I would do
Is to scratch your head
And let you go.

Poet Tom Robinson doesn't write about communicating with animals, but about running like one. Here is his "Rabbit."

I'd like to run like a rabbit in hops
With occasional intermediate stops.
He is so cute when he lifts his ears
And looks around to see what he hears.

My uncle Rollie, in the 1920s and the 1930s, hauled hay from Lancaster to Gardena, then a dairy town. One day a drunken driver crashed into the side of his truck, igniting the gas tank. My uncle died at the scene from burns. At his home in Los Angeles his dog, Rex, a German shepherd, at that very moment began howling (crying) and would not stop for hours.

In the last handout I somewhat jokingly warned the animators to be careful about getting too far into the animal's roles. This reinforcement of that caution comes from the *Santa Barbara News-Press*: "Bruce Dern says he's paid a price for playing psychos all these years. "It changes your life. It makes you look for the darkness in everybody you see," he tells *The New York Times*. He says his roles have touched his family." See!!!!

Woolie Reitherman, that great animator/director for so many years, and of so many successful Disney films, in 1973 gave an analysis/ lecture on "The Jungle Cat." He prefaced the session with, "How do you capture an action?" (You will note that Woolie was a much more down to earth person than I could ever hope to be — or even care to be.) He said:

I would like to start with, "You're capturing it all the time, because you are watching action all the time during the day. "When you go out to the races you see horses walking and running, you see people moving about, and first, before you get analytical, I think you have to pick up and take note of what you are seeing. I am talking about the sensation you get from seeing something. I am not talking about analyzing it at this point. You get a sensation out of something that moves beautifully. You can say it's the grace of the animal — but more than that, it's the personality of the animal, the feel of that living thing that is after something, or is afraid of something. That's what you pick up first — and that's what you always want to remember — that visual sensation! It's usually more than just the action because there is a real inner meaning to action — there is a life to it, there is a purpose to it.

A little later he said, "I would like to say one more thing — why do we want to analyze action? I guess the reason for that is that really (at least we feel this way), if you know the reality of things you can create a fantasy or an illusion or a caricature much more convincingly than if you try to knock it off the top of your head."

Well, there's no way I can import some jungle animals for the Gesture Classes (oh me of little faith), but a couple of weeks ago David Zabosky brought his young super pup, Oberon, an 11-week-old yellow Labrador to "pose" for us. Oby, as any spirited, young pup would, decided that five-minute poses were boring, informed us in his not too subtle form of animal/human communication that he would just as soon do nine thousand one-second poses. The result was an exciting hour of quick sketching and a worn-to-a-frazzle group of artists. Oby seemed to be constantly recharged — tiring not. (Makes you wonder what's in those dog biscuits.)

Sketches from that class start below, but the need to get those images down in a hurry reminded me of a cartoon I did some years ago.

"Boy, using a "flasher" for quick sketching
sure keeps you on your toes."

Seems like Ron Westlund started a sketch just when Oby decided to move on. You get the feeling of perpetual motion here.

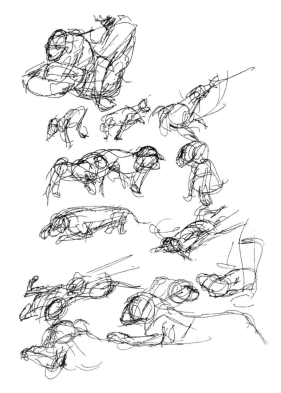

Tapping her reserve supply of adrenaline, Terri Martin captured these.

Here are some warm, touching, soul-stirring pups that I would make room in my household for. These are by Christine Harding.

Carl Bell chose to depict a bit of reality — playing hard, tiring, and finally… resting.

42 In Further Praise of Quick Sketching

The last handout (Chapter 41) brought you some extremely skillful quick sketches of Oby, the yellow Labrador pup. It was a thrill for me to prowl around behind the artists while they sketched and to watch those sketches take form.

Quick sketching is beneficial because it bypasses the temptation to analyze or copy — there is only time to get "that visual sensation," and hastening it onto the paper. You will find that quick sketches retain the vigor and spirit of the impression you get more than longer poses where you have time to copy or duplicate photographically what is before you. There's a big difference between copying and caricaturing. This is not to say that you shouldn't study anatomy and drapery — just don't copy it. Woolie Reitherman also stated, "...if you know the reality of things (anatomy, perspective, weight distribution, squash and stretch, tension, etc.), you can create a fantasy or an illusion or caricature much more convincingly than if you try to knock it off the top of your head."

In terms of right and left brain activity — when sketching, the left brain will want you to dabble and analyze, spend a great deal of time on each part, naming them and getting them just so (the so-called reality of things). In contrast, the right brain wants you to get the whole thing down at once — assembling whatever parts it deems necessary to produce a meaningful statement. To the right brain, third dimensional negative space becomes a stage on which to tell a story. The left brain has no concept of space. It sees only the physical, nameable facts. Space would have to be broken down into gases and atoms to be fathomed. The right brain glories in space — space is the matrix in which all life takes place. It is the stage on which all action and drama are expressed.

For about a half hour one evening in the Gesture Class recently, we had the model move very slowly, and constantly, so there would be no time to copy any lines on the model. The result was very gratifying. Woolie might have said we were drawing the visual sensation, which I sometimes refer to as the essence of the pose. Notice the feeling of space in the following sketches. There was no time to dabble and analyze — the right brain stepped in and got it all together at once, so to speak.

Here is a page of James Fujii's so full of life and spirit quick sketches. Bear in mind these were constantly moving targets.

Mike Swofford's sketches come alive with a few well-drawn lines.

Tina Price's sketches are so full of life they seem to still be moving.

Remember the formula I put in a handout several years ago? Impression − Expression = Depression.

43 Impression – Expression = Depression

As Woolie said in his lecture, "You're capturing action all the time, because you are watching action all the time during the day... I am talking about the sensation (impression) you get from seeing something that moves beautifully."

No artist worth his weight in graphite can go through life gathering impressions without expressing them in drawing, painting, or story. Those "sensations" have got to find an outlet or they will coagulate and bring on depression. You'll get that "Terrible Turquoise Tangle," or perhaps you might even terminate in a "Turmoil of Tintinnabulation," or maybe just fade away in a "Tearful Tedium of Tepidity."

Speaking of quick sketching, some of you already know that when my wife Dee and I go on vacation she drives while I sketch. I have even painted water color sketches while on the move. To paint in watercolors or even in pen and ink at 65 mph (50 or 60 around mountain roads) requires an accelerated awareness and a swift pen or brush. Traveling at those speeds there are simply no lines to copy. And since you don't want to end up with a sketchbook full of roads (looking ahead things don't move so fast), you have to sketch out the side window — which at 65 mph is like fast forward on your VCR.

Here are some of my landscape sketches (the principle of going for the "sensation" is the same as in figure drawing). I'm sorry I can't reproduce my rapid-fire watercolors, but will show them to anyone on request. These sketches were drawn in and around London, where I conducted drawing sessions for the artists on *Roger Rabbit*. Some were done from buses and some from trains.

Writing, drawing, and painting are all a means of expressing one's impressions, which as Woolie said "...are collected whenever and wherever we are looking." Artists are not privy to these impressions alone, but they are stuck with the need to express them.

Years ago when I worked on production, I did research, too. In preparing for the character Hen Wen in *The Black Cauldron*, Ruben Procopio and I visited a pig farm in Buellton to study pigs. Here are a few of those (quick at times) sketches.

3

Expression

44 Drawing a Clear Portrayal of Your Idea

Let's talk a little more about what a gesture drawing is and what it is not. You can think of a good gesture drawing like an expressive bit of body language in real life. We dislike it when people muddle
their speech or make unclear gestures, so that their expressions are not clear to us. We hate to misread
another's intentions — it could lead to misunderstanding (or worse). It is the same in drawing.

Behind every gesture drawing is an idea or story. It's like when you are conversing with someone,
you search for the proper words and body language to get your ideas across. You don't like finishing
your story and then having your bewildered listener say, "Huh?" So like your conversation, your drawing starts with an idea and is stated as clearly as possible so there are no "Huh's?" in your audience.

With that in mind, here are a few examples from the Gesture Class where I made some suggestions
to try to clarify the idea — then to get that idea into the drawing. This first one is model, Little Bird, a
Sioux Indian, looking into his leather pouch. Whether or not a model is clear in his or her gesture, you
the artist have to take it from there, form an idea in your mind, and draw it thusly — making "Huh's?"
unnecessary.

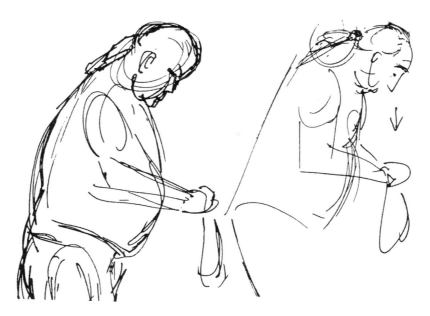

Here's another one that is similar, except in this one the thing he is looking at is off stage. Perhaps
he is sitting on a cliff watching a wagon train invading his territory. Perhaps he's watching the moves of
a band of wild horses — planning how best to capture one of them. Maybe something less dramatic.
Whatever it is, everything in the gesture should point toward that object — no "Huh's?"

In my suggestion sketch I arranged all the parts of the body so that the viewer would be aware of
something off stage. I rounded the shoulders to indicate that he was leaning toward the object of his
interest. I extended his right leg, which also helps to send the attention forward. I lowered his left knee
which also helps point toward that off stage attraction, and lastly, pushed his head forward, creating the
illusion that he is very interested in that out of sight mystery (at least it's a mystery to us). I once painted

a picture of a railroad track. Not a very exciting subject, right? But this track went around a bend and disappeared behind some brush and trees. What attracted the viewer was not the track but the mysterious "Somewhere" off stage. I could have sold that painting ten times over. So anyway, here is Little Bird acting out this mini scenario.

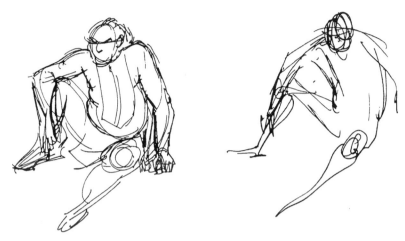

Necks are very expressive, and very difficult to draw. In these following three examples the students allowed the Indian vest to get in the way of a clear statement. Whenever a neck problem arises in class, I usually sketch an ill-constructed neck which generally expresses the problem (the first drawing). Then I do a "Stanchfield" neck (which varies from week to week) showing how the back of the neck very soon becomes the person's back, while the front of the neck goes way down to the sternum bone in the chest area (the second drawing). This helps to project the neck forward, as it does in real life — the forwardness increasing with years of carrying that heavy head around. Then I sketch a possible solution to the problem (the third drawing).

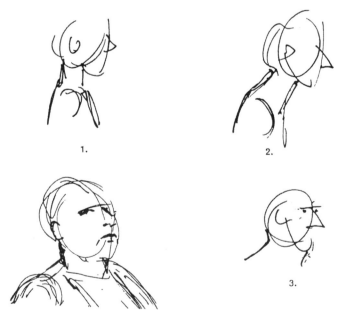

Again, and this is the theme of this handout, don't allow some detail (such as the vest on the Indian) to interfere with a *"clean portrayal of your idea."* Little Bird has a huge muscular neck which suggests masculinity and power. To underplay that feature in favor of a more mechanical and impersonal symbol of power — the breast plate — is to give up a source of intrinsic personal power and expression. I agree a neck is not easy to draw, yet every gesture of the head depends on it. The head can't make a move without it.

Sorry for all the palaver above, but I'm just trying desperately to say, drawing is not making a photographic copy of a pose — it is extracting the idea or story inside (or behind) the pose and then using whatever right brain input you can muster to *"...portray your idea."*

Naturally, all drawings made in this class do not require a critique. There were a number of first-rate drawings made that evening, and I managed to confiscate a few of them to reproduce for you. Here is one by Cheryl Polakow Knight.

Here are some by Terri Martin, who always comes up with some well-drawn and expressive sketches.

Here's an excellent drawing by Bette Holmquist.

Ruben Aquino shows his ability to be serious and lighthearted at will. Below are some really great sketches.

Rej Bourdages did some fine sketches that evening. Toward the end of the session when Little Bird changed into his "civvies," Rej did this very sensitive sketch of him.

There is no way in the world anyone will acquire this kind of expertise other than practice, practice, and more practice. For the devoted artist that means sketch, sketch, sketch. And quick sketching is, if you will excuse the expression, the quickest way to get there.

In *The Seascape Painter's Problem Book* by E. John Robinson, he says (I take the liberty to substitute the word "paint" for "drawing"), "Your ability to draw will be no stronger than your determination to learn."

45 Think Caricature

Walt Disney in his memo to Don Graham, that great drawing teacher, talked about studying sensation and being able to feel the force behind that sensation. I get more complicated and call it kinesthesia, the sensation of position, movement, tension, etc., of parts of the body, perceived through nerve end organs, in muscles, tendons, and joints. It's the sensation of movement when a person performs or images an action. It's a feeling (sensation) that runs throughout the whole body, not just a finger or an arm. Your mind requires the whole body to take part in an action.

In the same memo, Walt wrote, "Without the whole body entering into the animation, the other things are lost immediately. Examples: an arm hung on to a body it doesn't belong to or an arm working and thinking all by itself."

Often, in the gesture class, I find an artist drawing a sleeve before they draw the arm — as if the sleeve has thought itself into that position. Then sometime later they stick in an arm and hand just to complete the parts. It's not a question of which came first the chicken or the egg — it is a question of which comes first, the body gesture or the clothing gesture. Needless to say, the clothes merely react to the stresses placed upon them by the action of the body. Elementary, but sometimes overlooked.

And not to complicate things — keep it simple! Each action usually has just one motive behind it. If anything detracts from that one motive (story point), leave it out — save it for some gesture that it will fit into more appropriately. Don't try to put everything you know into one gesture. Put in just those things that enhance the action (the story).

Speaking of enhancement — every drawing should be considered a caricature. The degree of exaggeration depends on the character and the story, but no drawing, no not one, should be without some caricature. There is no place for photographic copies in cartooning. As Walt said in his memo, "I have often wondered why in your life drawing class, you don't have your men look at the model and draw a caricature, rather than an actual sketch."

Well, in one gesture class we did just that and it was very rewarding (and revealing). Each of us took turns posing, each striking the same pose so we could get a feel for the differences in character and structure. I am reproducing one artist's rendition of four different people to show what happens when not thinking caricature how they all look alike. If the hair were removed from the female figure in the lower right corner, it would look like the male figure in the upper right corner. Thinking caricature would have brought out the personality and individuality of each person.

I then showed that artist a sketch of that same pose by Gilda Palinginis, which more nearly approached caricature.

On the next pose, the artist, having "seen the light," broke away from her "standardized" figure and came up with this commendable sketch.

Gilda, inspired by Disney's suggestion, was "cooking" on that pose, too. Here is her version — a nice, loose, caricatured figure. Also, whether consciously or unconsciously, she got a lot of nice straights against curves, the abdomen against the back, the face against the back of the head, the shin against the calf, and the front of the arm against the back. There is weight on the left arm; the head is nicely tucked into the upper chest area. If you'll excuse the expression, it's a "damned nice sketch."

It's refreshing when we get a good model who inspires us to reach for our creative extremes. Such a model came to us in the person of Vickey Jo Varner who, while she was a temporary training coordinator, modeled for us. And did she model! Here is a sketch of her by Jane Krupka, who somehow captures gestures with a minimum of line and fuss.

Here are a few delightful sketches by Mike Swofford.

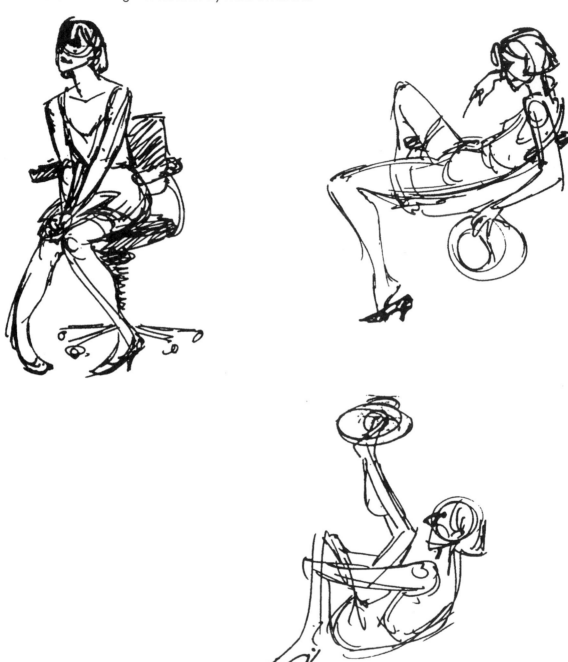

Wish all of you could have been there.

46 Going Into That World!

In a few plainspoken words (plus some typically expressive gestures), Glen Keane told an interviewer on television recently that, "When my pencil touches the paper, whooosh! I go into that world, and if I'm in that world, you (the audience) will be in it too."

In that brief statement, Glen voiced what our Gesture Class is all about, i.e., trying to enter the model's intention for the pose (or to make one up of our own) and to relate that to the (potential) audience. Glen said it all there, but sometimes truths have to be elaborated upon to be fully accepted or made personal. That is why we have endless classes on acting, drawing, writing, pantomime, and a library full of books on these and related subjects. The big problem is in translating all that "outer form" into the "inner working."

Let me try to suggest some of the things that might go through your mind while drawing from a model or while animating. Let's say you have to draw a person hitchhiking. You could of course stay "on the surface" and draw just the stock pose — the universally accepted cliché for hitchhiking: the expressionless waving of the thumb. But to get "inside" the gesture, you would have to add motivation and a whole series of related factors that suddenly involves you in acting and caricature. Okay, is the hitchhiker a tough, belligerent guy, shoved around (in his mind) by society? Does he stand with his feet far apart in a defiant gesture, thumb sticking up like he's saying, "Wanna know something — I don't care if you pick me up or not — I don't wanna owe nobody nothin!"

Or is it a young college student on his way to meet his girlfriend? He wills himself to look not only desperate for a ride, but also to appear trustworthy. He leans forward toward the oncoming car as if to force it to a stop. As the car passes, his body follows it in a defeated attitude. Each disappointment makes him look and feel shorter; his countenance begins to look like a withered tulip. But thoughts of his girlfriend spark him anew, and he continues to hurl psychic thoughts toward the oncoming motorists — "Stop for me...stop for me..." If you were animating, perhaps all that could go in, but what if you are making just one gesture drawing. Which part would you portray? Which part of the action would you feature as your choice of the best representation of the story? Would it be the anticipation or pleading when the approaching car is still at a distance, or the diminishing hope and realization that the car is not going to stop as it comes abreast of him without slowing down? Or will you pick the disappointment and perhaps anger when the car zooms past? To that last choice would you add insult to disappointment by having the wind, whipped up by the speeding car, blow his hat off and blow some dust from the road into his eyes or into his lungs, causing a spasm of coughing?

So you see, waving the thumb at a passing motorist for a ride is a kind of symbol for hitchhiking, but in drawing for animation, you must add motive — that's the kind of gesture we're talking about. There has to be a motive so you can draw what is on your character's mind. There has to be some reason for your character to be doing what he is doing, and for the way in which he does it; depending on his physical characteristics, the gesture will take on a mood of its own. For instance, Mickey would hitchhike in a different manner than would Goofy or Roger Rabbit.

Any character an artist draws should be analyzed with deep interest and concern. Let me reprint for you animator Art Babbitt's character analysis of the Goof (as Goofy was called in those days). Art is one of the greats in animation and the thoroughness displayed in this analysis is one reason for his greatness.

"Character Analysis of the Goof"

In my opinion the Goof, hitherto has been a weak cartoon character because both his physical and mental make-up were indefinite and intangible. His figure was a distortion — not a caricature, and if he was supposed to have a mind or personality, he certainly was never given sufficient opportunity to display it. Just as any actor must thoroughly analyze the character he is interpreting, to know the special way that character would walk, wiggle his fingers, frown, or break into a laugh. Just so must the animator know the character he is putting through the paces. In the case of the Goof, the only characteristic which formerly identified itself with him was his voice. No effort was made to endow him with appropriate business to do, a set of mannerisms or a mental attitude.

It is difficult to classify the characteristics of the Goof into columns of the physical and mental, because they interweave, reflect, and enhance one another. Therefore, it will probably be best to mention everything all at once.

Think of the Goof as a composite of an everlasting optimist, a gullible Good Samaritan, a half-wit, a shiftless, good-natured boy, and a hick. He is loose-jointed and gangly, but not rubbery. He can move fast if he has to, but would rather avoid any overexertion, so he takes what seems the easiest way. He is a philosopher of the barber shop variety. No matter what happens, he accepts it finally as being for the best or at least amusing. He is willing to help anyone and offers his assistance where he is not needed and just creates confusion. He very seldom, if ever, reaches his objective or completes what he has started. His brain being rather vapory, it is difficult for him to concentrate on any one subject. Any little distraction can throw him off his train of thought and it is extremely difficult for the Goof to keep to his purpose.

Yet the Goof is not the type of half-wit that is to be pitied. He doesn't dribble, drool, or shriek. He is a good natured, dumb bell who thinks he is pretty smart. He laughs at his own jokes because he can't understand any others. If he is a victim of a catastrophe he makes the best of it immediately and his chagrin or anger melts very quickly into a broad grin. If he does something particularly stupid he is ready to laugh at himself after it all finally dawns on him. He is very courteous and apologetic and his faux pas embarrass him, but he tries to laugh off his errors. He has music in his heart even though it be the same tune forever and I see him humming to himself while working or thinking. He talks to himself because it is easier for him to know what he is thinking if he hears it first.

(This is me, Walt, breaking in. Stay with me, I'm trying to put over a point. The point is that such devotion to character analysis should not be the exception. Think over some of the wonderful Goofy cartoons you've seen and you will appreciate this kind of thoroughness. In the Gesture Class I try to get the students to determine the type of characters that're drawn and how best to execute the gesture they are performing. "No fuzzy thinking is allowable, if you are to create a full emotional effect of the character on the reader." That is a quote from *Characters Make Your Story*, by Maren Elwood. Okay, back to the Goof. Bear in mind this thing was written sometime in the 1930s when the character had not yet been fully developed.)

His posture is nil. His back arches the wrong way and his little stomach protrudes. His head, stomach, and knees lead his body. His neck is quite long and scrawny. His knees sag and his feet are large and flat. He walks on his heels and his toes turn up. His shoulders are narrow and slope rapidly; giving the upper part of his body a thinness and making his arms seem long and heavy, though actually not drawn that way. His hands are very sensitive and expressive and though his gestures are broad, they should still reflect the gentleman. His shoes are not the traditional cartoon dough feet. His arches collapsed long ago and his shoes should have a very definite character.

Never think of the Goof as a sausage with rubber hose attachments. Though he is very flexible and floppy, his body still has a solidity and weight. The looseness in his arms and legs should be achieved through a succession of breaks in the joints rather than through what seems like the waving of so much rope. He is not muscular and yet he has the strength and stamina of a very wiry person. His clothes are misfits, his trousers are baggy at the knees and the pant legs strive vainly to touch his shoe taps, but never do. His pants droop at the seat, and his vest is much too small. His hat is of a soft material and animates a little bit.

(As I type this my mind wanders back to our gesture workshop and the great variety of models we are privileged to draw. I have them come in street clothes, costumes, and work clothes and also have them bring hats and sweaters, all of which have distinguishing characteristics. Should we not treat these models with the same consideration as Art Babbit was asking the animators to give to the Goof?)

It is true that there is a vague similarity in the construction of the Goof's head and Pluto's. The use of the eyes, mouth, and ears are entirely different. One is dog, the other human. The Goof's head can be thought of in terms of caricature of a person with a pointed dome — large, dream eyes, buck tooth, and weak chin, a large mouth, a thick lower lip, a fat tongue, and a bulbous nose that grows larger on its way out and turns up. His eyes should remain partly closed to help give him a stupid, sleepy appearance, as though he were constantly straining to remain awake, but of course they can open wide for expressions or accents. He blinks a bit. His ears for the most part are just trailing appendages and are not used in the same way as Pluto's ears except for rare expressions. His brow is heavy and breaks the circle that outlines his skull.

He is in close contact with sprites, goblins, fairies, and other such fantasia. Each object or piece of mechanism which to us is lifeless, has a soul and personality in the mind of the Goof. The improbable becomes real where the Goof is concerned.

He has marvelous muscular control of his fanny. He can do numerous little flourishes with it and his fanny should be used whenever there is an opportunity to emphasize a funny position.

This little analysis has covered the Goof from top to toes, and having come to his end, I end.

—Art Babbitt

I hope I haven't bored you or scared you by making it all seem so complicated — it really isn't. All you have to do is forget the bones and muscles for a little while, form an impression of the model and the pose, then keep that impression clearly in mind as you draw. As an example, here is a drawing where the student seemed preoccupied with lines and muscles, forgetting to enter into the spirit of the gesture. Here, the left brain took over saying, "This is a hand, this is a pectoral muscle, etc." In my accompanying sketch I allowed the right brain full command in using those things to create an entertaining gesture. You can't feel what a thing looks like but you can feel what it does.

Here is one that has a lot of what seems like good drawing in it. But as I pointed out, this is a self-deprecating girl, in a kind of apologetic stance. She is thin, emphasizing her vulnerability. We should take advantage of these suggestions in the model's personality.

47 Understanding What You See

I often reflect on my audacity in coming to the studio and posing as an instructor. Many of you artists draw better now than I ever have or ever will. Yet I come, bringing my "handouts" for everyone to read and conduct some drawing classes where I make bold to criticize your drawings. How utterly offensive!

On my quote-adorned writing desk is a dilly by Destouches, a French physician and novelist, "Criticism is easy, art is difficult." It humbles one to read such incisive acumen. But what is one to do? One cannot just retire and carry what little one knows to one's grave. That would be more unforgivable than criticism. So, another handout unfolds with one old timer's attempt to pass on some hints that he wishes he had been exposed to when he was young and trying to get it all together. Listen to this — when I started at Lantz studio in 1937 we used nickels, quarters, and half-dollars to lay in the heads of those stiff old cartoons we drew. Since then, thanks to Walt Disney, the art of animation has come a long way. He introduced acting, drawing, caricature, and entertainment which are the name of the game.

At some point along the way, I have come to realize that forming a clear picture of the idea or story you want to put over gives you something to shoot for. This picture or first impression is accompanied by a kinesthetic awareness of the gesture (or action). In other words you are not just observing the pose optically but also kinesthetically, which is like mimicking the pose or action without actually moving. Glen Keane put it so aptly when he said: "...I get into that world..." It would be difficult to get into that world if you were just trying to copy what your eyes see.

One way to free yourself to "...get into that world..." is to avoid trying to make a finished drawing too soon. Trying too hard to make a "good" or "pretty" drawing will cause self-consciousness. Self-consciousness draws your attention to self, rather than to your character. To go into "that" world requires that you become a sort of surrogate actor; that is, you become a catalyst that uses certain elements (the physical body and costume) turning it into an idea or story for someone else to see and enjoy.

In his book *The Natural Way to Draw*, Kimon Nicolaides said:

As the pencil roams, it will sometimes strike the edge of the form, but more often it will travel through the center of forms and often it will run outside of the figure, even out of the paper altogether. Do not hinder it. Let it move at will. Above all, do not try to follow edges." (He was saying do not copy.)

It is only the action, the gesture, that you are trying to respond to here, not the details of the structure. You must discover — and feel — that the gesture is dynamic, moving, not static. Gesture has no precise edges, no exact shape, no jelled form. The forms are in the act of changing. Gesture is movement in space.

He goes on and pretty closely explains kinesthesia.

To be able to see the gesture, you must be able to feel it in your own body. You should feel that you are doing whatever the model is doing. If the model stoops or reaches, pushes or relaxes, you should feel that your own muscles likewise stoop or reach, push or relax. *If you do not respond in like manner to what the model is doing, you cannot understand what you see.* If you do not feel as the model feels, your drawing is only a map or a plan.

(I get all tingly when I read this stuff...)

The focus should be on the entire figure and you should keep the whole thing going at once. Try to feel the entire thing as a unit — a unit of energy, a unit of movement. Simply respond with your muscles to what the model is doing as you watch, and let your pencil record that response automatically, without deliberation. (The right brain working.) Loosen up. Relax. Most of the time, your instinct will guide you — sometimes guide you the better, if you can learn to let it act swiftly and directly without questioning it. In short, listen to yourself think; do not always insist on forcing yourself to think. There are many things in life that you cannot get by a brutal approach. You must invite them.

Here are a couple of illustrations from the Nicolaides book that serve to illustrate his thinking. One is by a student of his, and the other is by Paolo Veronese, Italian painter (1528–1588).

It is essential for an artist to be keenly aware of the functioning of kinesthesia, the sensation of movement and positioning. We live with those sensations as long that they become unconscious. It's like when we do an action over and over — it becomes dull and the newness of the sensation leaves us. We can, however, re-awaken those "first time" feelings if we make ourselves conscious of kinesthesia. You've seen how thrilled young children are when they take their first steps. The kinesthetic feeling is new and exciting. After many years of walking — we take it all for granted, but the proprioceptors are still in there measuring every move we make, balancing, refining, and seeing that the move is performed just the way we desire it.

We go to drawing classes. The models pose. They may do some way out posing, but we have seen it all — it is just another pose. But you see, it isn't just another pose. To the artist who can arouse those kinesthetic sensations, each pose is a magnificent reminder of the thousands of nuances the human body is capable of. Each modulation of movement becomes a thing to see and enjoy and marvel at, and to capture on paper. If we don't personally experience the pose, we will more than likely miss the essence of the gesture and straighten everything up, all our figures looking like soldiers at attention. I'm kidding, of course, none of us do that.

Actually, it is the desire to do that that starts all this stuff to working. You desire to raise your arm and all the propriocepters in your body begin to measure the task. These impulses activate the muscles in hundreds of parts of your body, and like radar, they send their messages to the brain and your brain sends messages back, ordering all the intricate adjustments necessary to carry out your desires. And this same desire will allow you to experience another's action — vicariously.

Perhaps you'd like to hear it in more scientific terms. Here's a page or two from *The Thinking Body* by Mabel E. Todd:

Awareness of our own motion, weight, and position is obtained from within the body itself rather than from the outside world. It is accomplished by means of sensations arising in certain nerve end organs, which are as definitely specialized to record them as are the sense organs in communication with the outer world for seeing, hearing, smelling, feeling, and so forth. Otherwise we should be unable to stand or move about with any certainty without guidance from some outside source through the sense of touch, sight, or smell. But the body possesses the power of reacting to gravity, inertia, and momentum, the primary forces of the physical world, by means of the part of the nervous system known as proprioceptive, or "perceiving of self," as distinguished from the exteroceptive mechanisms by which the outer world is perceived.

The proprioceptive sensations, also called "organic," are grouped, according to their origins in various parts of the organism, into three general types: the "feeling of movement," in all skeletal and muscular structures, called kinesthesia; the feeling of position in space, derived from organs in the inner ear and known as labyrinthine; and miscellaneous impressions from various internal organs, as of digestion and excretion, called visceral.

Altogether, the proprioceptive system, acting in conjunction with all the outer senses, serves to guide our total reaction to the outside world in terms of motion toward or away from particular objects, and to give us our ideas of space and time. More than any other factor the proprioceptive system is responsible for the appearance of the individual as an organized unit when he is moving about.

Kinesthetic sensations from extremely numerous and scattered end organs in muscles, tendons, joints, ligaments, bones, cartilage, and other tissues of the supporting framework, make us aware of movement, whether passive or active, resistance to movement, weight pressure, and the relative positions of the parts of the body.

Awareness of our orientation in space is derived from sensations arising in special end organs of the inner ear, which are closely associated with, but not part of, the acoustic sense. These organs are located in a bony chamber called the labyrinth, or vestibule, and the sensations from them are therefore termed labyrinthine, or vestibular.

The labyrinthine sensations record two kinds of impressions: the position of the head and thus of the body, in relation to the earth, and the direction of movement in space. Two distinct organs are involved, the otoliths and the semicircular canals.

The precise way in which labyrinthine sensations are transmitted is not known, but it is agreed that knowledge of the position of the head in relation to the horizontal plane is derived from movements of the otoliths, little particles of lime imbedded in tiny hairs in the vestibule of the ear; whereas the direction of movement of the head, particularly its rotations in any given dimension of space, is perceived by means of fluid moving in the semicircular canals. The semicircular canals, of which there are three in each ear, together represent the three dimensions of space.

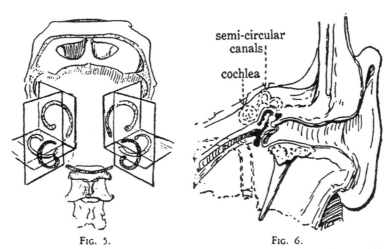

FIG. 5.   FIG. 6.

FIG. 5. Diagram of semi-circular canals in skull of pigeon. (Redrawn after Ewald.)
FIG. 6. Osseous labyrinth of left human ear, containing fluid and membranes
which serve the sense of balance. (Redrawn after Morris.)

However the result is accomplished, the fact is well established that the otoliths and semicircular canals are the seat of impressions of position and direction of motion in space; and that they are combined in the brain with the kinesthetic sensations of movement, weight pressure, and relative position, coming from other parts of the body, to give us our minute-to-minute information as to the movements of our limbs, neck, and trunk, where we are at any given moment, and how we can get somewhere else.

And from another chapter, this interesting bit:

As a working mechanism, the skeleton cannot be understood if considered only as a bony framework. Since ligaments bind the bones together at the joints, and muscles move them, and the activities of the whole are governed by the nervous system, no one of these elements acts independently.

In my class critiques I try to show how, when using the gestural approach, you can keep your mind on the gesture (the acting, or the story), which is a right brain activity. The left brain is right there trying to elbow its way into the process by trying to get you to make a photographic copy, which is mighty tempting but pointless. Here below is one of those critiques. The student's drawing is a fairly good one — as far as left brain involvement is concerned. The anatomical parts are very identifiable. Now consider my critique sketch — it is all right brain stuff — no bones or muscles or style in the dress. I concentrated on having the model lean on the table. To accomplish this I bent her more in the direction she was leaning. This accomplished several story-supporting objectives. It put weight on her right hand, it leaned her whole body in the direction she was looking, intensifying the look, and put her face more in the clear so the look is featured. Every part of the body helps to establish that story-point — the look. Notice the simple straight of her right side against the curve of her left side; a curve which helps to thrust the attention in the direction of her look. I tried to do as Nicolaides suggested, "...think more of the meaning than the way the thing looks."

Here is a pose where the model was *"resting."* This gesture requires that the body slump forward. The hands are hanging below the lap, dragging the shoulders with them, which in turn pulls the muscles of the back taut, around, and forward. The artist should feel this action happening, kinesthetically, as he is drawing. It doesn't matter how well the muscles (or details) are drawn, the important thing is to transmit that whole kinesthetic feeling to your audience.

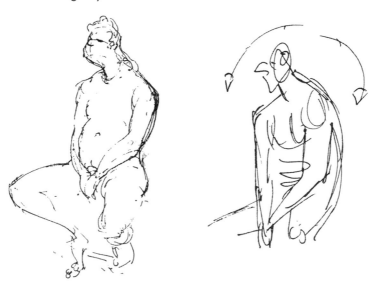

An automobile can get around by going straight or by turning from side to side — the only visible thing that happens is the front wheels turn. When a person moves, hundreds of bones, tendons and muscles are activated. Skin is stretched, flesh and fat are squashed, angles are altered, and balance is constantly adjusted. If all these things aren't attended to, what you get is a passport photo; that is, "Stand on the X. Stand up straight. Eyes on the camera. And don't move!"

I don't mean to sound like the "parent," but this just happens to be the technique I know best to arouse your determination to think gesture, or as the title of this handout suggests, to *Understand What You See*.

The cartoonist Al Kaufman evidently understands the importance of feeling the pose in one's own body, kinesthetically, as one draws or paints.

I have done it again! I have given credit for some drawings to the wrong artist. My apologies to Gilda Palinginis, who was and is the creator of these excellent sketches.

48 An Inspirational Journey

In this handout, I have compiled a potpourri of quotations, some of which you may find suitable for clipping out and pinning up. Some of them were taken from art books and some from a book called *Writers on Writing*. Writers are artists, so what they say can be construed to apply to us (drawers), too. Some of the quotes are from *The Power In You*, an inspirational book by Wally "Famous" Amos (the face that launched a thousand chips), to whom I often turn for a mental uplift. I refer to some of them as 1,000-volt jump-starts.

Some have a definite "religious" overtone for which I do not apologize. The word "spirit" has a vital place in everyone's life.

And so you may know exactly who it is that has assembled these aphorisms, maxims, and guides to a happier and brighter future — here I am depicted by the penetrating pen of Mike Gabriel.

Alaska. Walt Stanchfield

We must renew ourselves constantly. Like water in an isolated pond that soon becomes stagnant, we too become sluggish and unimaginative when we become satisfied with where we are. And like a moving stream that becomes purified as it moves over its rocky river path — so we must gather inspiration on our path to keep the channels open — the creative juices ever flowing.

There are numerous sources of spiritual and mental reinforcement. And no two people have the same psychological needs, but for sure, we all need some inner sustenance. Here are just a few that I present for your perusal.

And oh, yes, some of them are mine.

In the beginning was the word, and the word was made visible through the miracle of drawing. Those who draw use the basic materials of creation to express themselves. Their product is highly visible but is formed in the unseen and brought to fruition through the phenomenal process of creative thought.

The position of the artist is humble. He is essentially a channel.

—Piet Mondrian

Without art, crudeness of reality would make the world unbearable.

—George Bernard Shaw

For God sake, keep your eyes open. Notice what's going on around you.

—William Burroughs.

I don't know what there is about this one, but it has a soothing effect on me:

Going home, boy — going back where I belong.

I have so many quotes pinned up on my writing table that I am sometimes pleasantly surprised when I spot one I had forgotten, like this one.

I carefully guard my thought.
I refuse to permit anything antagonistic or
unlovely to enter my consciousness.
I am learning to live in joy, in peace and in
calm confidence.
I am putting my whole trust, faith, and confidence
in the good.
I think with clarity, move with ease, and
accomplish without strain.

That's an old one, brown and brittle from exposure. It probably came from one of those little devotional booklets.

Here's one close to the previous quote that I am extravagantly paraphrasing.

Put vitality in your drawings and they will be like catnip to your audience.

Love the inner you and keep moving ahead because you can't stand still and improve at the same time.

—Wally "Famous" Amos

As you strip away layers and layers of negative attitudes and replace them with positive attitudes, your horizon broadens and your capabilities increase. You go to success, success does not come to you.

—Wally "Famous" Amos

A positive attitude says success is a journey, not a destination. With a positive attitude you know that throughout each day you experience success.

—Wally "Famous" Amos

When working from a model it is best to do many quick sketches rather than going for a "masterpiece." You will get more practice, learn more, and be less inhibited than when spending a lot of precious energy on a drawing that may not "come off" anyway.

If you think you're out there all alone, maintaining a positive attitude about life can be a lost battle. Acknowledging that a higher power exists for you to work with can remove the fear. Personally, I know that my life constantly flows and is shaped in positive ways through the guidance of that higher power. Whether you call it God, Allah, Buddha, or "Larry" does not matter. The importance lies in the faith and acceptance placed in that force. Armed with that kind of faith, you will find it impossible not to keep a positive attitude about all of life's adventures.

—Wally "Famous" Amos

Acting: How much thought has each of us given to our acting career? Sometimes we even forget we have one! But, we have — each and every one of us — and our "roles" are of great variety and everyone makes a positive demand: *get into character*. Getting into character is no small assignment. It's like changing dress for different moods of the day, but not quite so easy. It can't be done with a brew such as Dr. Jekyll used to create Mr. Hyde. It isn't a physical transformation — it's an image born of observation and imagination.

—Eric Larson

I glory in my growing appreciation of God, acting in and through me.

—Dr. Carleton Whitehead

"Creative Meditation"

Drawing is, in a sense, a graphic form of acting. Actors, whether comic or dramatic use their bodies and voices to tell a story — artists rely on drawing to do the same. Years are spent studying life drawing, still life; how to draw animals, birds; how to use pencil, charcoal, and pen, plus many other facets of art. In the end, if the "audience" grasps the idea — the story — then the drawing is successful, if not, it's just another illustration gone awry.

For a drawing to be good, gesture is indispensable. By gesture I mean body language that portrays emotions such as love, hate, anger, jealousy, sorrow, sadness, fear, despair, happiness, satisfaction, and pride. Without that, a drawing is merely a collection of facts looking for a reason for being.

—Guru Stanchfield

It's a very excruciating life facing that blank piece of paper every day and having to reach up somewhere into the clouds and bring something down out of them.

—Truman Capote

I like to do and can do many things better than I can write, but when I don't write I feel like shit. I've got the talent and I feel that I'm wasting it.

—Ernest Hemingway

"Four Basic Steps for Effective Creative Visualization"

1. Set your goal.
2. Create a clear idea or picture.
3. Focus on it often.
4. Give it positive energy.

And then say, "This or something better, now manifests for me in totally satisfying and harmonious ways for the highest good of all concerned."

—Julia Cameron, *The Artist's Way*

A work of art is not a matter of thinking beautiful thoughts or experiencing tender emotions (though those are its raw materials), but of intelligence, skill, taste, proportion, knowledge, discipline, and industry; especially discipline.

—Evelyn Waugh

You can lie to your wife or your boss, but you cannot lie to your typewriter (*pencil*). Sooner or later you must reveal your true self in your pages.

—Leon Uris

I am profoundly uncertain about how to write. I know what I love or what I like, because it's a direct, passionate response. But when I write I'm very uncertain whether it's good enough. That is, of course, the writer's agony.

—Susan Sontag

Hey, there's artist's agony, too…and typist's, accountant's, manager's, secretary's, and etc. We sympathize, Susan, we've all been there.

49 Comic Relief

Kevin Klein met his hero, Sir John Gielgud. Kline was in awe. "Mr. Gielgud," he said, "Do you have any advice for a young actor about to make his first film in London?" Gielgud stopped and pondered the question for some time. At last he spoke, "The really good restaurants are in Chelsea and the outlying regions — you want to avoid the restaurants in the big hotels."

Draw ide

One of my handouts greatly enlarged.

Here are some of my "fractured classics."

More "fractured classics."

I could go on like this for hours.

I'm taking a once a week class at Hancock College in Santa Maria under the wild tutelage of Robert Burridge. He shared this advice from the artist known as SARK.

HOW TO BE AN ARTIST

STAY loose. learn to WATCH snails. plant impossible GARDENS. invite someone Dangerous to teA. MAKE little signs that SAY Yes! and POST them All over Your HOUSE. MAKE friends with FREEDOM & uncertainty. look FORWARD TO DREAMS. Cry DURING MOVIES. Swing AS HiGH AS YOU can On A swingset, BY MOONLiGHT. CULTiVATE MOODS. refuse TO "Be responsible." DO iT FOR love. TAKE loTS OF naps. Give money AWAY. DO iT NOW. THe Money will Follow. Believe in MAGiC. lAUGH A loT. CELeBRATE every GORGEOUS MOMENT. TAKE MOONBATHS. HAVe WiLD iMAGinings, TransFORMATiVe DReAMS, AND perfect CALM. DRAW On the WALLS. reAD everyDAY. iMAGine YOURSELF MAGiC. Giggle with CHiLDren. listen TO OLD people. Open up. Dive in. Be Free. Bless YOURSELF. Drive AWAY FEAR. PLAY with everything. entertain Your inner CHiLD. YoU Are innocent. BUiLD A FORT with BlanKeTS. GeT WeT. HUG Trees. write love letters.

♥©SARK⁹⁰

SA 172 Copyright ©1990 SARK published by Celestial ARTS PO BOX 7327 Berkeley CA 94707 printed in USA World rights reserved

Terri Martin keeps coming up with these splendid gesture drawings that in a graphic way, serve as a surrogate to the written positive thinking statements. They are in themselves a testimony of the life force we are attempting to capture in all our drawings.

Tomorrow (and each tomorrow of the year) is a blank canvas. On it you will paint, by word and action, a picture that will correspond to what you consciously and unconsciously envision. You are creating tomorrow today, but you have the privilege of changing any color or detail before the word is spoken or the action taken.

What is your picture of tomorrow? What do you consciously and unconsciously expect to happen? Does it correspond to the desires of your heart? Before the brush touches the canvas, paint out what does not; paint in what does, using lavishly the colors of harmony and beauty and joy.
—Dr. Carlton Whitehead, *Creative Meditation*

Mind is forever creating anew. The formless is eternally taking Form. Unconditioned Life is continually becoming conditioned. Mind, moving as my thoughts, creates my experience. The Formless takes the Form of my ideas. Life flowing through my whole being is conditioned by qualities in my consciousness. This creative forming, conditioning action is neither past nor future, it is always now."

—Dr. Carlton Whitehead

First is the desire for a new or different experience, expression, or manifestation. Second is an idea, at least a general one, of the form the fulfilled desire will take. (Note that the result usually far exceeds your expectations). Third is a conviction or faith that results will appear. Desire, idea, conviction — when your demand encompasses these three, the response is inevitable.

—Dr. Carlton Whitehead

Ask, and it shall be given you; seek, and ye shall find; knock and it shall be opened to you.

—Matthew 7:7

Terri Martin keeps coming up with these splendid gesture drawings that in a graphic way, serve as a surrogate to the written positive thinking statements. They are in themselves a testimony of the life force we are attempting to capture in all our drawings.

50 If It Needs to Lean, Then Lean It

Many problems in drawing are very stubborn and so, they plague artists over and over and over. One of the pesky problems is a tendency to straighten things up, which will take the guts out of any pose. Recently I went through previous handouts and picked some of the critiques that addressed that very nemesis. I am reprinting several in the hope of shocking you into realizing how unmindful we can be at times.

I would hope to convince you that drawing is as much a mental thing as it is physical. If you get involved in just the physical side of drawing you may miss the very thing you are attempting to capture — a drawing that tells a story. But if you proceed, concentrating on your mental concept of the gesture, you will surely hit it on the nose. And it is not enough to hear these things and merely agree intellectually — you must apply them as you are drawing. Not just when you happen to think of it but at all times and, yes, even when you are not drawing.

Ollie and Frank say it succinctly in their book, *The Illusion of Life.*

Conveying a certain feeling is the essence of communication in any art form. The response of the viewer is an emotional one, because art speaks to the heart. This gives animation an almost magical ability to reach inside any audience and communicate with all peoples everywhere, regardless of language barriers. It is one of animation's greatest strengths and certainly one of the most important aspects of this art for the young animator to study and master. As artists, we now have new responsibility in addition to those of draftsman and designer, we have added the disciplines of the actor and the theatre.

Farther on they speak of the added problem the animation artist has to overcome — that of chemistry and charisma.

The live actor has another advantage in that he can interrelate with others in the cast. In fact, the producer relies heavily on this. When he begins a live action picture, he starts with two actors of proven ability who will generate something special just by being together. There will be a chemistry at work that will create charisma, a special excitement that will elicit an immediate response from the audience. The actors will each project a unique energy simply because they are real people.

By contrast, in animation we start with a blank piece of paper! Out of nowhere we have to come up with characters that are real, that live, that interrelate. We have to work up the chemistry between them (if any is to exist), find ways to create the counterpart of charisma, have the characters move in a believable manner, and do it all with mere pencil drawings. That is enough challenge for anybody.

The problem I have chosen to feature this week is that of leaning — leaning for pressure, leaning on an arm for rest, leaning for emphasis, etc. You might reason that shortcomings are bound to creep in occasionally, but this problem is like a bad case of athlete's foot — it itches (as I said above) over and over and over. And, of course I'm talking about the tendency to straighten things up. It's *most* obvious when the character is resting on a knee, or a chair, or table. If there is not enough weight distributed over the area being rested upon there can be no rest. As a matter of fact it would be very un-restful to straighten up a bit, leaving nothing to lean on, as in the first example. The student's drawings will appear on the left, my critique on the right. Bear in mind, mine is not *the* way to draw it but just *a* way to overcome the problem. Remember, in all drawings you are trying to say something to an audience; you are acting in *every* sense of the word.

This will sometimes happen — the student will realize something is amiss and will try a couple of more times, often repeating the error. Oftentimes, I will suggest they actually assume the pose so they can experience the kinesthetic feeling in their own body.

Admittedly a tough view but notice how the upper body of the student's figure is straightened up.

Talk about straightening the pose up — look at this one. In my sketch I went a little beyond and I caricatured the gesture.

This student's drawing is quite well done, but I felt the "resting" action could be plussed by gathering the upper body into a more cuddly posture. In this kind of pose you make a resting place with the hands to rest your head upon. It carries the leaning action a tad further.

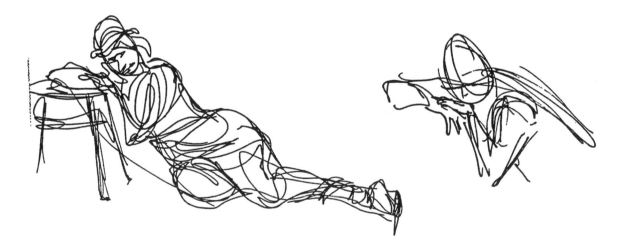

How about if your character is leaning on a chair back? Straightening him up is not going to cut the mustard. It can, and probably should be a subtle lean, but a vertical is not going to shift the weight enough to form a lean.

In the handout where this originally appeared, I explained the action a little more in depth, and by action, I mean what each part of the body does to execute the gesture.

Analyzing a gesture doesn't take a long time, nor does it use up a lot of energy (actually it's quite invigorating). All you have to do is decide what you want your character to do (that should take but a split second) and then without getting sidetracked by fascinating and eye-catching details, get it down on paper. For instance, here's a student's sketch of a character supposedly leaning on the back of a chair, in a somewhat reflective attitude. His head says "reflective mood," but cover up the head with your finger tip and then name the pose. In my sketch (and this only took about ten or fifteen seconds), he is leaning back on the chair, his left hip is jutted out because all the weight is on his left leg, and the arm is relaxed along the left side with the hand dangling free. Between the support he gets from leaning on the chair and the placement of the weight on the left leg, he can relax and reflect to his heart's desire.

There are many types of "leans." For instance, here's a lean on one elbow to take advantage of the light from a window to read by.

Here's a lean on a pole to propel a gondola.

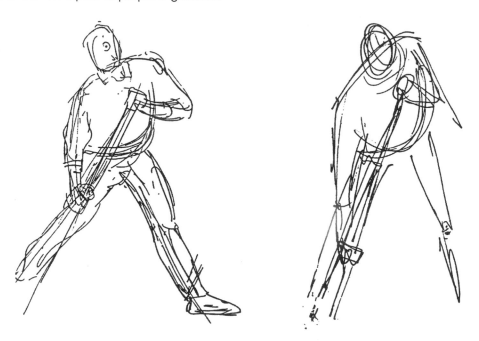

Here is a classic realization pose, one we all use, probably daily, meaning we should be kinesthetically acquainted with it. But here in the student's drawing you will see, what, a fear of being off balance, the fetish for straightening everything up, maybe deep down it is a quest for safety, equilibrium, conservatism, symmetry or balance…Who knows? I do not know, I am not a psychologist. I am just a ham actor.

Leaning into the action is a good way to emphasize the point. Here is a chap about to smash some small threatening creature. You would not back away as if it were going to bite you on the nose — you would lean into the action getting a better look at the wee beastie and thus shorten the hitting stroke.

Also, and this is important — if anyone is watching you, which happens to all actors, you do everything you can to caricature the action to entertain your audience.

A typical opportunity to lean into the action is when your character is offering something. Here's a clown offering someone a feather duster.

When a clown leans on a cane he *leans*! They exaggerate every action, to the point of defying gravity.

Here's a case where "double lean" was called for. The model was on the model's stand and was reaching clear to the floor.

This next one was from a session where we were drawing heads and shoulders. What little of the body that shows should explain that he is leaning forward. Just because it is a head drawing doesn't mean it's not performing a gesture — every drawing is a gesture drawing!

There is always a bonus when you dramatically lean your character into the action. Part of it is psychological and part is physical. (It takes both to make the story.) Take this character, who could be pointing to something on a blackboard. (Obviously, I've forgotten what she was doing.) A good lean makes a more interesting connection to the audience (psychological) and it affords an opportunity to do something with the clothes. In this case I let them sort of hang down (physical). Notice how I have *everything* leaning into the action.

How about one more and then you may go in peace. You don't always lean *into* the action. Sometimes, like the character taking a swig from a bottle, leaning *away* from the action is called for.

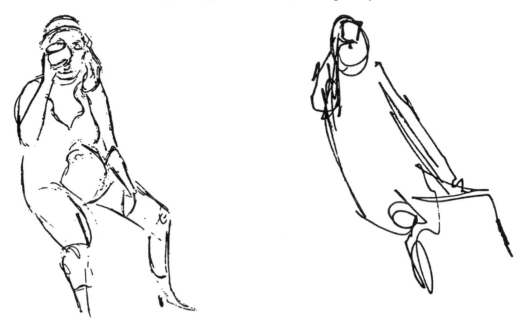

But whatever, don't ever, ever, ever take all the guts out of a gesture by straightening it up, PLEASE!

51 Don't Tell, But Show!

There's a rule in the arts — "Don't tell, but show." Which means don't just tell your audience about some event; rather show them what is happening so they can participate vicariously. Applied to drawing from a model, sketching, or animating, it means it is not enough to record the facts of a subject's construction and details, but it is important to show what the characters are doing.

Here is an overly simplified example. This is a hat.

This is a head.

I'm *telling* you what we are dealing with. Put the two together, and I'm still just telling you about them.:

But if I want to *show* you something that is *happening* with these two things, I might draw something like this.

or there are numerous other possibilities.

You might think of it in this way: the hat and the head are nouns, things that can be named. But when those objects do something like tilt, or the hat blows away, they become *verbs*. I always advocate, "If you can't turn a noun into a verb, then don't draw it." Drawing nouns is *telling* your audience something; drawing verbs is *showing* them.

Harvey Dunn, that great illustrator of the recent past (1884–1952) put it this way.

Merely having all the objects in your picture that belong there and having them well drawn is not sufficient. A man who is dead is entirely complete in the physical sense, and yet he is not there at all. The same can be true with a picture.

Concentrating on the anatomy of each part of the body will not make a good drawing, but relating each part to each other part, in accordance with a gesture, will make a good drawing.

Often students in the gesture class attempting to render a photographic copy of the model become mired down in confusion. Usually there is no thought of gesture in minds. I pounce on them, shrieking, "Quit trying to make a photographic copy, and just make a drawing!"

On the following page are some rough gesture drawings by Norman Rockwell. In them, he is searching for ideas for *The Saturday Evening Post* magazine covers. As an artist who could carry a detail to its "nth" degree, he was still able to put aside all of that expertise, and just go for the gesture — that all important ingredient (foundation) for professionally finished work. But even Rockwell, professional as he was, could not have arrived at those delightful *Post* covers without having gone through that rough stage. That is the very stage I am trying to instill in the Gesture Class. There, most of the drawings that founder are those where the artist went for the final polished rendition too soon, having neglected the necessary, all-important rough foundation.

Rockwell's search for picture ideas followed an evolutionary course.

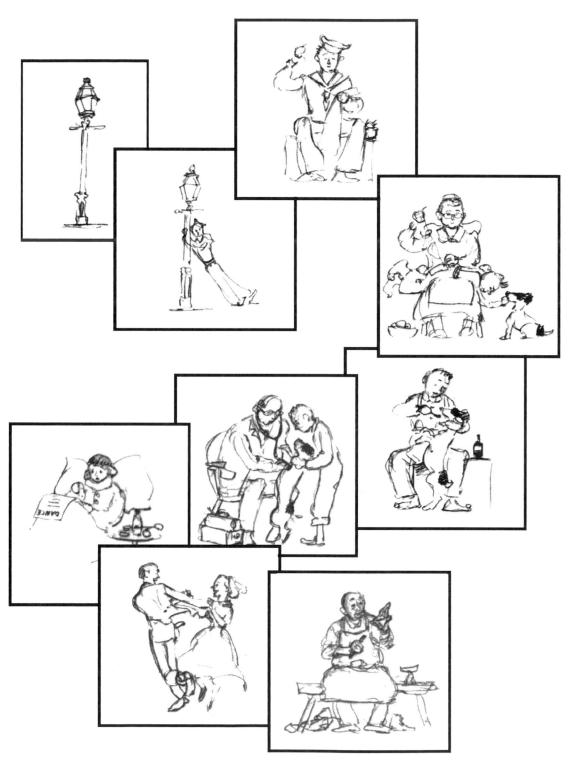

Illustrations by Norman Rockwell from *Rockwell on Rockwell*, © Famous Artists School, division of Cortina Learning International, Inc.

Drawing is as much attitude as it is skill. As I pondered this weighty concept one day, I sat down and wrote some aphorisms which might help to sort out some priorities in your approach to drawing.

- Drawing gives me an insight into how I see people.
- The fastest way to learn to draw is to learn about yourself then you will know others and can draw them.
- As I draw, the pen or pencil allows me to check my thinking.
- Whatever goes into a drawing, only gesture will give it meaning.
- Draw, draw, and draw, and then combine all those into another drawing.
- A drawing may not be a composite of all drawing that came before it, but it is a prelude to the next drawing.
- When drawing seems difficult, go back to the simplest possible form. It is like plowing a field for the next planting of seed.
- If you enjoy drawing, your audience will sense it.
- Be positive while drawing and the gesture will bloom.
- Every drawing becomes a push/pull between inactivity and gesture.
- We make marks with a pen or pencil, but we make drawings with our emotions.
- When fear engulfs me, I go for realism, but when I feel freedom, I go for the gesture.
- A tight photographic drawing lies there like a stop sign, while a gesture drawing takes off and carries the viewer with it.
- A photographic copy is like an embalming, while a gesture drawing celebrates life.
- Though the pencil moves on a two dimensional plane, the illusion must be one of third dimensional space.
- Tension makes a drawing exciting and interesting, because all gestures are created by tensions.

Let's get into some critiques. Hopefully, it will be like vicariously attending the class — without being harassed by the instructor.

Earlier I mentioned the tendency to try to make finished drawings before setting the foundation. That's like trying to nail the windows in before the walls are up. Here is a pose where the model had a small radio held against her ear, in a kind of dance-like attitude. The artist, with pen tightly grasped down near the nib, was laboring away at the area around the head. I quickly "threw in" the overall gesture, conveying the idea that it would be easier to relate the other parts of the body while everything was still in the rough stage.

Kinesthesia is really quite a phenomenal help in drawing. The word means the sensation of movement or strain in muscles, tendons, and joints. I can't imagine trying to make a drawing without it. In this next drawing the student was looking for structure but saw a lot of meaningless curves. In contrast, I imagined myself striking that pose and drew the kinesthetic feeling I experienced. It revealed the tensions inherent in the pose and I was able to get a nice stretch on the front part of the body, while the backside became a squash.

This next artist was starting to do the same thing as the first example, so I pounced on him, encouraging him to get the whole gesture first before honing in on one area.

Here's the kinesthetic matter again. Feeling the pose in one's own body is the #1 priority. That constitutes the first impression that one forms when starting a drawing. Notice on this, as in a previous sketch, it allowed me to get a nice long stretch on one side, while the other side becomes a squash.

Squash and stretch have long been recognized as a vital element in animation, and have their place in single drawings, too.

This next drawing appears to be a very solid drawing, but actually it is a very much-straightened up version of the pose. In my sketch I introduce some twists, tension, and weight shifting to bring it closer to the model's gesture. The artist was a layout person, who, I suspect, having spent most of his time drawing structures of an inorganic nature, saw the figure from that perspective. It's a beautiful drawing, but it needs a little life force. Study your acquaintances and actors on TV, notice how they mince about from gesture to gesture. The life force in them keeps them gesticulating constantly. Time enough to settle down to one stiff pose when that life force leaves you. Once again, by raising the left shoulder and lowering the left knee, I accomplished a stretch, while the right side becomes a squash.

Here are a few stimulating quotes to read and re-read when your zeal sags. This one is from Howard Pyle (1853–1911), famous for his pen-and-ink drawings and carefully detailed, colorful romantic paintings.

The artist should climb over the frame of the picture and become one with the characters he is painting.

Here are a couple of perceptive quotes from Joseph Hirsch, successful realistic painter during the 1960s and 1970s nonobjective furor.

The alert eye everyday can catch hundreds of glimpses, any one of which might serve as the seed of a possible picture. For centuries the whole tradition of sketchbooks, in which artists store these seeds while the memory is fresh, has been based on the validity of brief revelations of glimpses.

And Hirsch also observed,

The Danish philosopher Kierkegaard put great value on having one thought only. (I assume he meant "one thought" at a time.) In painting (also drawing), it is disastrous to give equal importance to a number of things at the expense of the one overall theme.

Here is one by Austin Briggs, illustrator for *Cosmopolitan* magazine, etc., sometime around the 1940s when the stories were all illustrated by similarly great artists.

It is the business of the artist to see the common everyday experiences of people in a new and fresh way, and to show them as if they were being presented for the first time. Since each of us is a unique individual, if we are truly aware of our experiences and the world in which these experiences take place, we cannot help presenting the old themes in a fresh way. Unfortunately, most of us tend to see things through other's eyes. We relate our own special experiences to the standard experience pattern of our fellows, and for this reason we tend to fall into the cliché.

…most successful pictures deal with basic human feelings and experiences. Beginning artists often feel such themes are trite. They are — in the sense that they are the common experience of humanity. The more trite the basic theme of your picture, the better. The cliché to worry about is the visual cliché. Search for subtle variations, which present the old theme in a new light. Comedians know the truth of the saying, "An old joke is the best joke. It is all in how you tell it."

And lest you students of the gesture class decide to come in and merely copy the structure and details of the model, remember this quote by Harvey Dunn, another of the old *Post* illustrators.

Pictures must be held together with spirit.

I close with a juice-stirring quote from one of my metaphysical books.

Back of every event, the slightest effort you make, the smallest concept you entertain, there is an inexhaustible reservoir of life, of imagination, energy, and will, flowing through you into action.

Wow! Let's do it!

52 Mainly Mental

I am well aware that my handouts sometimes become wordy. I justify that tendency by contending that drawing is mainly mental and that ideas and concepts can be both communicated and assimilated through the written word. It just takes a little effort on the part of the communicator and the recipient. Not all books on art have illustrations to illustrate the text, and there are two books in particular that I have treasured that have no illustrations. One is that wonderful book by Bob Thomas and Don Graham, *The Art of Animation* which contains a wealth of vital wisdom, analysis, and enlightenment for animators. Don had planned for illustrations but the work was never published.

Read this from his chapter, "The Analysis of Action.". He speaks of gesture, a subject dear to my heart, and the raison d'être for the drawing classes I conduct.

All real actions have some meaning to us but most do not arouse in us emotional responses. We observe innumerable actions daily; we accept them; forget them. When, however, a real action has special meaning and arouses us emotionally we refer to it as a gesture.

A gesture always implies an idea — she carries her head "regally," the horse prances "proudly."

In nature most actions are not gestures, for most actions are not performed to arouse other people's interest and emotions. In animation, however, the interest and response of the audience must never be lost. Consequently, few actions are utilized that in some way do not resolve themselves into gestures.

The unfortunate and limited use of the term "gesture" to imply only hand action is widespread. Except in rare incidents the hand action is to an animator merely part of the gesture. The mood or spirit of the whole action dictates the hand actions; and the total impact of the action — body, head, hands — is the gesture.

In nature the eye is accustomed to catching the slightest gesture, the most subtle expression among thousands of unrelated actions. In animation every gesture, every action must be planned to read to the audience. Extraneous actions are ruled out. Nothing will kill a scene faster than an unrelated action; a hand, for instance, that moves for no apparent reason. Down to the smallest detail, the motion of a piece of drapery or of the blink of an eye, every action must be accounted for. Gestures don't happen in animation; they are drawn purposefully.

"Old hat" stuff you may be thinking, but if you're like me it stirs the juices and renews a sensibility to gesture — whether it's a human, animal, or rock.

The second book, which is actually a collection of lessons, is a tome of sensitive analysis of animation-related writings by Eric Larson, who spent the later years of his life teaching and helping young animators. Most of his writings were, appropriately, concerned with entertainment. Here is a sampling from his chapter, "Entertainment IV."

Our drawing and what it "says" is our communication with the audience. It is the visual factor in our efforts to entertain. It interprets life, caricatured and alive. Our drawing is a statement of personality and attitude — be it saucy, bold, impudent arrogant, accusing, happy, sad, quizzical, embarrassed — whatever mood the story demands, our drawings must express it simply and clearly.

As we have often discussed, in our drawing we must search for interesting, expressive poses that make strong, easily understood statements, all in keeping with our character's personality and physical structure. Will not a child and a grown-up, experiencing similar emotional reactions, show their feelings in different body attitudes? We know that in adults, children, animals, or birds, no two are alike, similar maybe, but not exactly alike. So let's let nothing become "stock." We can't afford to be lazy and follow the thinking, "It was good enough in that picture — so why not in this?" Given the same situation and mood, no two characters will move, stand, sit, or laugh in the same way. We must always consider this fact so our drawings will reflect good analysis and will be more interesting and entertaining.

Sometimes we might say, "I know all that, I know my drawings must appeal to an audience and convey a thought — how else can I communicate?" Knowing all this as we do, we still so often minimize their importance and our efforts. We "slough off." Don Graham used to say in a quiet but positive way, that we were lazy when we failed to constantly search for the very best way to present an action and an emotion on the screen. Today, we, too, might pay attention and give heed to his words.

We must always be fully aware of the life a good animation drawing can project — of the emotional experience and sincere response it can induce. It takes nothing from reality — it flavors it — it makes it more exciting, more imaginative, and more enjoyable. As animators, do we not secretly wish to put something extremely humorous or dramatic on the screen — to create a bit of lasting entertainment?

I confess that now as I review these writings, I translate them from animation drawing to the single drawings — such as from a model, and event to painting, which I am now mainly involved with. But, you see, they don't require illustrations — they are mind expanders, mind motivators, mind energizers. They encourage you to visualize how you would implement the postulations.

But me, I stick in an illustration now and again. For instance, here is a nice one by Terri Martin.

I'm not letting you off easy, though. Here's one you'll have to study to understand. I talk a lot about kinetics, kinesthesia, etc., and also how angles in your drawing can cause tensions and movement — how lines can slow an action or speed it up. Here is a reviewer's analysis of a 24" × 40" bronze sculpture called The Ridge Runners by Dave Hodges. I made a pen copy of it so you could look from horse to horse, head to head, leg to leg; and see how the angles of each create a sensation of movement. There's even a bit of squash and stretch at work.

Here's "Kinetics, Many Ways to Movement," by Jack Hines:

The orientation of all living creatures to their surroundings is fundamental to survival. Environment touches every aspect of existence, whether it be bird, fish, or human being.

Taking environment to its most basic element, we encounter the force of gravity and its corollary, movement. These two aspects are at the foundation of existence, and they likewise play an important role in art. For me the word "Kinetics" expresses the relationship in art. Many of you might know the term with regard to kinetic sculptures, or the application of moving parts that respond to motorized movement, the wind, or balance weights — the cuckoo clock, for instance. I prefer a broader conceptual definition. Kinetics need not be only three-dimensional and mechanical. *Drawings*, paintings, and sculpture *should also suggest kinetic forces at work*, whether they be wild action or more subtle movement (emphasis mine).

In Dave Hodges' bronze "The Ridge Runners," we encounter what can only be described as violent action, awesome in its speed and power. Hodges is a Montana rancher who has ridden and herded horses for years, thus accumulating a storehouse of knowledge about their strength and modes of behavior — the factual elements that impact horse anatomy.

What is more important in this sculpture, however, is how Hodges has manipulated kinetic associations within the forms, lines, and shapes of the six running animals. Notice how the movement of one animal has a catalytic effect upon the others in the group and how each reaction is passed on to the herd. This overall reactive motion counters the static base, providing an ingredient without which art does not exist: contrast. The immovable anchor of the ground and rocks compounds the sense of rushing in the horses; whose heads comprise an agitated line, punctuated by angular negative spaces.

"The Ridge Runners" goes beyond simple depiction of movement to a powerful statement of kinetically dynamic forces. Working from knowledge and gut reaction, Hodges delivers doses of contrast in variable strengths that breathe life into this work.

You can easily spot those kinetic forces Hines spoke about. Now for some closer-to-home examples that I have concocted, using drawings from various past handouts. Once you become aware of these kinetic forces, they will appear by the dozens to you. Every drawing, I repeat, every drawing you'll ever make will need them, whether in wild or subtle amounts. Become aware of them, caricature them, and you'll have yourself a memorable, entertaining gesture drawing. Here are the first drawings.

In this example the model is reaching. I include the student's drawing so you can get the feel of caricature and how important your mental concept of the gesture is. My correction drawing (on the right) features the upper body bending forward and the arm swinging down for the reach. Notice the arm is slightly bent. Bending a line (or shape) seems to suggest a move in the direction of the bend. It's a psychological thing, maybe, because we associate it with the bow and arrow.

a drop of liquid,

or pancake batter which moves in all directions as it settles in the pan.

Sometimes in animation, a fast moving object's leading edge will be rounded (bent) with effects training aft.

Anyway, do you feel the right arm still moving down? That's one of those kinetic illusions.

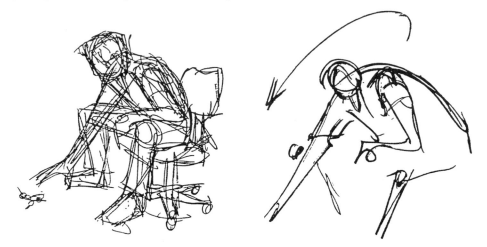

In this second example (same pose, different angle), I caricatured the reach by stretching the arm out straight and lowered the shoulder, which would happen anyway, but also helps to emphasize the force of the thrust. The knees were spread apart to make room for his upper body to fit in as he bends forward. See how the angles of the lower legs set up a kinetic force — can you feel a tension around the hips and groin?

There is a strange illusion the "V" suggests to us. When the V's angle is less than 45 degrees.

the sides tend to draw together, while when greater than 45 degrees.

they appear to be moving apart. Here's a fairly clear example of that. In my drawing I closed the angle of the face to the right arm, while opening the angle of the left arm. The straightened-up verticals of the student's drawing become static. In my drawing the right arm seems to be moving in toward the face (doing its task) while the left arm pushes the mirror out where it will show more of the face in it. Get the feel for it by acting it out yourself.

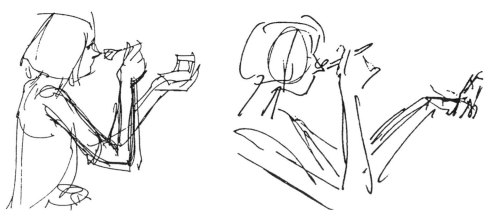

You don't want good gesture drawings to be accidents that just happen once in a while. With a bit of kinetics (pertaining to motion in the drawing) and some kinesthesia (the sensation of movement in your own body) you can steer your drawings into the realm of "impressive."

A friend always advised anyone who had a strain or sprain that, "Motion is lotion." That goes for drawing, too — keep a feeling of motion in your drawings. It takes a lot of involvement, accompanied by a lot of thinking. Like the little child who said, "I think and then I put a line around my think."

Now I'm trying to apply my gesture knowledge to painting. In a recent book, *Strengthen Your Paintings with Dynamic Composition*, by Frank Webb, he says, "Feel the gesture of a shape. You are not only a spectator but also a participant. Even a rock should have gesture. Try to feel the forces a rock 'feels.'"

In *The Natural Way to Draw*, Kimon Nicolaides says,

The study of gesture is not simply a matter of looking at the movement that the model makes. You must also seek to understand the impulse that exists inside the model and causes the pose that you see.

The drawing starts with the impulse, not the position... what the eye sees — that is, the various parts of the body in various actions and directions — is but the result of this inner impulse, and to understand, one must use something more than the eyes. It is necessary to participate in what the model is doing, to identify yourself with it. Without a sympathetic emotional reaction in the artist there can be no real, no penetrating understanding.

Limerick!

Put down a line of your liking.
Add action to make it enticing.
A curve and a straight,
Some angles for bait,
And you'll catch something really exciting.

Stanchfield (of course)

And now, to paraphrase Dave Pruiksma, "Back to the drawing boards with ya now."

53   The Shape of a Gesture

Often in the Gesture Class, I suggest the artists first sketch in the "abstract" of the pose. Basically, that would be the essence of the gesture — without the details. Another way to approach the gesture is to look for its shape. Not the outline, but the shape of what's taking place inside. Every pose or drawing of a pose does have an outline, but what is really happening is the tension and muscular activity within, and that determines the shape. When more than one figure is on stage, they collectively form a gestural shape. One exciting and ever changing gestural shape is a flock of birds. It might be stretching things to call them gestural, but if the poses of humans and animals can be called gestures, surely birds qualify.

Even landscapes form a unified gestural shape. Here are a couple of my woodcuts (on page 237). The composition forms a simple "gesture."

A guy sitting in a chair forms a shape according to his gesture. Here are a couple of rough examples. Look back and forth and you can see the shape change.

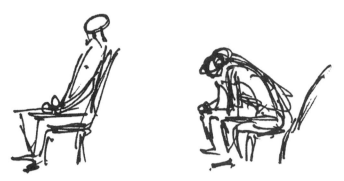

If you want to go beyond the stretch position, that is, caricature it, you would have to consider where the "normal" position was and then carry the stretch farther — in line with the action.

Anytime two figures are relating to each other, they are separate figures, but one gesture. Here's an extremely active relationship involving three characters — the painting, *Stag at Sharkey's* by George Bellows. There is a very vivid, descriptive, exciting shape to this gesture. (My pen sketch doesn't do it justice.)

In the last handout (Chapter 51), I quoted Don Graham as saying, "In nature most actions are not gestures, for most actions are not performed to arouse other people's interest or emotion." With all due respect for Don's perspicacity, I must differ with that statement. Many times we are aroused emotionally by someone whose "gesture" moves us, though they were not aware of us at all.

Look at the shape of this gesture, *American Gothic* by Grant Wood. Unlike the action-packed painting by Bellows, this one is very subtle — yet so strong. You'd recognize it in the fog at 500 feet, just by its shape. (I once profaned this bit of Americana by rendering it in a cartoon style with a caption that read, "If that traveling salesman comes around here again, I'm going stick this pitchfork in him.")

As you look at these paintings you are moved by the inner motivations that prompted the gestures, and though they are very different in physical flurry, one is no more powerful in its message than the other.

I go on and on, but let's not forget my original premise — gestures have a shape and the shape is determined by the forces within the body that are called upon to express them. When a figure assumes one of those shapes we recognize it immediately.

Every so often I reprint these drawings by James Fujii. Each time it is to illustrate a different point. A good drawing is good when viewed from any angle. Anyway, here are the drawings, each with a distinct shape, all constructed to fit the character and the motivation that prompted the gesture.

Here is a batch of sketches I did for a handout to suggest a simple approach to laying in a drawing. As you look from figure to figure, the gestural shapes become very apparent. Try to concentrate on the shape, and how that shape communicates the gesture.

No matter what character you are drawing, the basis of a good drawing is not the model, the costume, or the detail; it is the shape of the gesture that counts. To illustrate this I took a variety of class drawings and turned them into, albeit roughly, the cook in *The Little Mermaid*. The shape of the character changed, but the shape of the gesture remained.

Whenever you make a drawing of a human or animal, think of it as being a character in a story, your story if you're drawing in the Gesture Class. Treat it as a living character, one whose idiosyncrasies you are working out; as a character who is solving a problem or carrying out some, perhaps, mundane, task; as a character who has certain qualities and traits that you want an audience to see and feel; as a character who has logical reasons for doing what he does in keeping with his or her dominant character traits. If he is a villain, show it in the attitude of the drawing; if a hero, make his gesture strong and purposeful, in a way that the audience will root for him.

In stories that have audience appeal, there is a hero and a villain, maybe two, or three. Each must be true to their destiny — otherwise the audience will become confused. Think "hero." Think "villain." But also think ordinary, mundane, or humdrum — whatever class your character fits into. No character deserves the contempt of indifference. A farmer can be a sort of hero — tilling the soil, planting seed, nurturing the crops, fighting pests, droughts, and finally reaping the harvest. That is symbolic of all positive, constructive, time-honored heroes.

Joseph Campbell, in *The Power of Myth*, says of the trials and tests and ordeals of the hero, "The trials are designed to see to it that the intending hero should be really a hero. Is he really a match for this task? Can he overcome the dangers? Does he have the courage, the knowledge, the capacity, to enable him to serve?"

The characters we draw in the Gesture Class have no earth-shaking destinies to fulfill, but they deserve the same kind of character consideration that the "big guys" get. Otherwise... why draw?

In animation the shape changes with each change of gesture. You might say the story itself takes on shapes, the layouts, the actions, even the dialog — but let's not get too esoteric here.

In the Gesture Class, I was trying to get the artists to loosen up, draw more freely, and try to feel the shapes of the poses. Here are two very relaxed (in more ways than one) sketches that I intercepted in the early stages, while they were just a shape, sans any details. The first is by Terry Naughton, the second by Tamara Lusher-Stocker.

54 Dreams Impossible to Resist

To set the mood for this handout I have chosen a poem from *Mud Woman, Poems from the Clay* by Nora Naranjo-Morse, an Indian artist from New Mexico. She is a sculptor whose works are both social commentaries and humorous. But, to the point, I see a parallel between her attitude toward sculpture and what ours might be toward drawing. Think of your having written the poem, using the word "drawing" in place of the word "clay" as you read. I especially love the last two lines.

> There is nothing
> like an idea
> that comes to life
> through clay.
>
> Each step
> a personal investment of
> thought
> labor
> and time.
>
> Hands
> moving quickly,
> rounding curves
> setting up in clay
> skillful responses
> educated
> by Gia's
> simple instruction
> and immense knowledge
> of her own work.
>
> Letting dreams come true
> from songs
> born from within,
> sounds
> inviting irresistible challenges.
> There is nothing like an idea
> that comes to life
> through clay.
> There is nothing better than a life
> whose dreams
> and ideas are
> just too
> impossible
> to resist.

The crux of that poem, I think, lies in the first line that states, "There is nothing like an idea that comes to life..." For we artists, and for that matter, everyone in the studio, bringing an idea to life is what it's all about. If we can't do that, we have nothing. Nita Leland in her fabulous book, *The Creative Artist*, says, "Drawing is about communication, insight, feeling, emotions, not just a recital of facts." In other words, bringing an idea to life.

It is a problem! We spend years studying proportions, muscles, and bones of the body, then suddenly have to use all that to convey some idea — some emotion. We are confronted with the need to act, to caricature; to translate a story into drawing form. That's why we also study acting, pantomime, character development, and gesture drawing. From my viewpoint, gesture drawing encompasses all the other aspects of drawing. In the gesture class, we don't just practice drawing the parts of the body from different angles — we learn that those different angles relate some kind of body language that is applicable to a story. We never make a drawing without it telling a story, even a simple one: a person resting, a king showing his superiority, a gal talking to her boyfriend on the phone, etc. The success of these drawings hinges, not on the factual depiction of the figure, but rather on an entertaining portrayal of the gesture.

Any physical likeness to the model is a bonus. Oh sure, we take advantage of the character of the model, for usually the build and personality of the model dictates the manner in which she interprets the pose. But that is part and parcel of any faithful rendition of a gesture. We are constantly honing our sensitivity to such things. Yes, it's a problem, but a pleasurable one and you should be having fun doing it!

That's why I so often say that drawing is mental. It's a switching over from the left brain categorization of life seen as rational, verbal, scientific, and linear to the right brain which sees life as intuitive, visual, artistic — full of hunches and feelings and how things relate to other things — and playful!

Of course you can't function with just half a brain — though I've known some that have come close to it. One fellow was a "perpetual" college student who was short on original thoughts, but was a walking encyclopedia of facts. Another was an artist who had scant contact with what we know as reality. He could draw and paint, but he was a flake away from the drawing board. There has to be a balance between the two spheres. In Virginia Cobb's book *Discovering the Inner Eye,* she writes, "The time spent in practice is time spent integrating your artistic nature with your more analytical mechanical skills, the side of you that creates with the side that designs."

Too often the left side takes on the "parent" role and tries to dominate the right side — the "child" role.

Parent: "Draw it like it is. Measure it, plumb it, and copy it faithfully."
Child: "I don't want to copy it. I want to draw it doing something interesting."

Oh, if we could just bring the "child" to class, with its sense of wonder and play rather than the stifling, intellectualizing "parent."

When we were kids we "play-acted" with great abandon and child-like involvement. When I was young, I emulated Bill Hart, Tom Mix, and Tim McCoy of the silent movie days. There was an organ in our neighborhood theater and a neighbor of mine played it for mood. I think since there was no dialog, we were not told what was happening — we had to feel it. So later, when we got a gang of kids together to play cowboys and Indians, it was easy to mimic their actions and emotions. Maybe that's why I have always had a problem memorizing verbal things. Emotions through sight are more important to me than through words. Words are vital, of course, I love words, but remember, one picture is worth a thousand words.

Here is a model, dressed in some costume, acting like some fictitious character, doing their best to fabricate a tiny portion of life for us to work up into a gesture drawing. We should consider that just the beginning of an exciting adventure and take it from there — let the right brain or the "child" take it where he or she will.

I have said many times that drawing is mostly mental, but I also feel deeply that drawing is spiritual. That is, a super-refinement of thought and feeling as opposed to a religion or church. If some are interested — I'll take the plunge and get into it. For now, here are a few teasers.

Creativity is the natural order of life. Life is energy, pure energy.

—Julia Cameron.

The position of the artist is humble. He is essentially a channel.

—Piet Mondrian.

We undertake certain spiritual exercises to achieve alignment with the creative energy of the universe.

—Julia Cameron

What moves men of genius, or rather what inspires their work, is not new ideas, but their obsession with the idea that what has already been said is still not enough.

—Eugene Delacroix

Critique time. Here's a drawing by a student that's quite well-proportioned, and the parts are well-depicted, but it lacks a kinesthetic involvement. Compare it to my version on the right, where I felt the slouch of relaxation, the slackened drop of shoulders, the more "curled-up" attitude of a reader who is absorbed in his magazine. I let his head sort of hang relaxed onto his chest, as if his whole body was melting into the article. That's the story! He is interested in what he is reading. In the last handout (Chapter 52) I had a child say something like, "First I think the gesture, then I draw a line around my think."

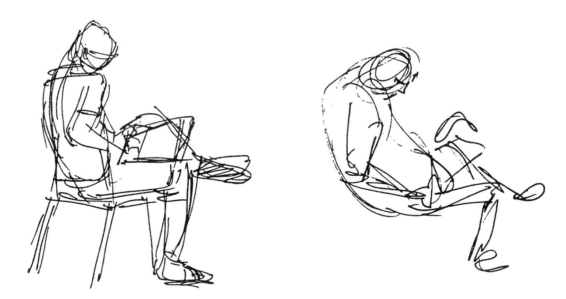

In this drawing session David Roon came as a regal, pompous, imposing, proud, smug self-important, boastful, egotistical, contemptuous king — sword and all. It was a difficult character to draw. But to try to capture all the above, or even some of it, by trying to find some shapes in the drapery, leads to a dead end. Without thinking of any of the above characterizations, the student's rendition ended up rather soft and apologetic. In my brief sketch, I went inside the confusing robe and came up with a pose I figured he was flaunting, one that portrayed his character. In a sense, I was trying to mimic his arrogance.

There is a logical sequence to drawing. First comes the gesture, then the details. If you let the details dominate your thinking, you may end up with a lot of details floating around looking for a gesture to attach themselves to.

In this next drawing the student tried to draw some details (the King's cape) with no gesture beneath and as a result, third dimensional space and perspective were lost altogether. Again, in my sketch, I simply went for the gesture, which included the "stage" on which he is acting. Crude as it may be, I have captured the pose, and I can add whatever details are necessary to complete the story, later.

Wherever you happen to be at this moment, as you read this, become aware of your pose. Look at that part of it that is visible. Observe how it occupies space. Notice the space between your feet, knees, elbows, and all the various parts of your body. Have a sensation of the space between them. *The positioning of those parts in space is what constitutes your gesture.*

I'd like to share with you some drawing by a former Disney Studios artist. His name is Dan Boulos, and his drawings illustrate my attempt to get my students to draw the gesture with a minimum of detail. Dan never goes farther than just getting the gesture down, and when that is done, he goes on to another sketch — another version of the same pose.

Dan never copies the props used by the model, but alters them to display them more clearly or in accordance with the story or gag.

Copying something photographically does not denote a good drawing. Good drawing is simply putting over an idea clearly and in an entertaining way. It can have a lot of detail, or none, depending on the needs and the style — but in the gesture class there is no need for details.

Study these drawings for their simplicity, inventiveness, and for how they go straight to the gestures.

I started this handout with a poem — let me close with one. This one is by Dan Boulos, who is as sensitive with his emotions as he is with his gesture drawings.

Caught myself,
Sipping images of you,
Swirls in my coffee;
I caught myself,
Tracing words,
Of our once conversation,
Our once upon a time romance,
Beneath the stars and eyes,
Of a watchful night.

55 Short Book on Drawing

INTRODUCTION: ONE PICTURE IS WORTH A THOUSAND WORDS

To encourage my students to inject as much "story telling" into their drawings as possible, I have used a version of a Chinese saying that goes, "One picture is worth a thousand words." When you think of some of the brilliant authors whose writings we so admire, it is hard to believe one drawing could equal even a dozen or so of their words. Read these lines (with *less* than a dozen words) for instance:

His wry smile was hidden under an umbrella of a moustache.
A pair of icy blue eyes radiated hatred and torment.
I couldn't get over the obsessive sense of everything going wrong.

Those are difficult things to portray in a drawing, are they not? Even descriptive things are not easy:

His dark hawkish face seemed never to have known a smile.
He looked like a hawk with mumps.
A square wall of a forehead with heavy brows for a base.

Each of those descriptions evoked a definite physical attribute — to illustrate them in drawing form would require some rather inspired sketching.

Actually, according to Alan Watts, the proverb goes, "One showing is worth a hundred sayings." In his book *The Way of Zen,* he explains it thus:

> The Chinese written language has a slight advantage over our own, and is perhaps symptomatic of a different way of thinking. It is still linear, still a series of abstractions taken in one at a time. But its written signs are little closer to life than spelled words because they are essentially pictures, and as a Chinese proverb puts it, "One showing is worth a hundred sayings." Compare, for example, the ease of showing someone how to tie a complex knot with the difficulty of telling him how to do it in words alone.

This is not to suggest that we learn to use a series of diagrams to illustrate our meanings, our stories — but that we strive to pantomime our drawings to the point where words are not necessary to grasp their full meaning. Almost as if the sound went dead during one of our pictures and the drawings by themselves would carry the story along.

SHOW US HOW TO DRAW!

We yearn for the ultimate book of drawing, or the teacher who can, once and for all, show us how to draw, so we can get on with our lives. We study anatomy, vanishing points, and overlap; we study distribution of weight, balance, shape, design, etc., and drawing is still a frustrating experience. We call out in pain and disappointment — our efforts should have reaped a better harvest.

We mediate, searching for mental blocks from the past that keep us from victory. If we could just identify the devils that thwart our progress so we can administer the emancipating blow. Or better yet, if we could somehow form a partnership with the source of all creative energy.

Enjoy these drawings – they are fun and pure entertainment.

CRITIQUES

In the suggestion/correction sketch (mine on the right), I tried to think in the same terms that Shepard must have, as he worked out the gestures in his "Decorations." It's, maybe, like assuming the role of director who has to explain to his actors the meaning behind the story, and how best to put it across to an audience.

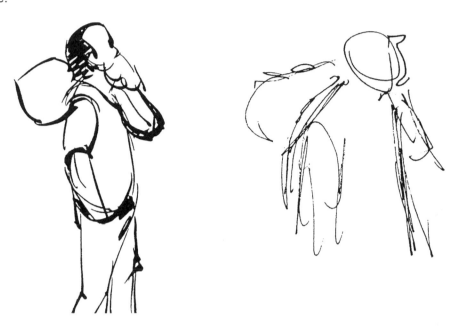

Here the hands are spread apart, together forming a triangle which directs the look to the object being held there — the center of interest.

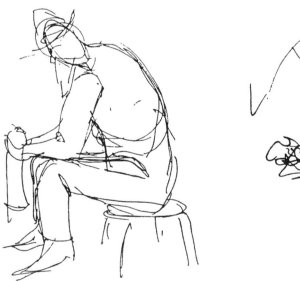

In Nita Leland's book *The Creative Artist,* in the chapter called, "Drawing: Don't Leave Home Without It," she says, "In drawing you define something you cannot quite describe in words." Later she says,

Drawing helps you to see and seeing helps you to draw. You think that when your eyes are open you are seeing, but your brain plays tricks on you, reporting stereotypes instead of what your eyes actually see. It gives you a quick and easy symbol — the tree looks like a lollipop, the eye looks like an almond — so it won't have to work so hard searching for individual differences.

Drawing on the Right Side of the Brain, by Dr. Betty Edwards, suggests that most people see and draw more accurately when they shut down the time-oriented, verbal left side of the brain and allow the space-oriented intuitive right side to function more freely.

You do this by confusing the left brain. One way is to change the labels. Don't call what you're drawing by name; think of it as "a curved line about so long" or "a space this high and that wide."

And this from Walt Stanchfield's unwritten book, "Buy a bunch of sketchbooks and draw, draw, draw, and...draw!"

56 Encompassing Reality with All Your Senses

For the past five years I have been doing these "handouts," which have covered many approaches to drawing. My suggestions have been directed mainly to those who were and are still struggling with the art and those already professionals who desire to improve or "bone up." Some of the things I have tried to cover are found in a handout from the dim past called *28 Principles of Animation.* A few of them pertain only to animation but the rest are essential to drawing from a model. Here is the list as it appeared.

POSE AND MOOD	PLANES	STRAIGHTS AND CURVES
SHAPE AND FORM	SOLIDITY	PRIMARY AND SECONDARY ACTION
ANATOMY	ARCS	STAGING AND COMPOSITION
MODEL OR CHARACTER	SQUASH AND STRETCH	ANTICIPATION
WEIGHT	BEAT AND RYTHEM	CARICATURE
LINE AND SILHOUETTE	DEPTH AND VOLUME	DETAILS
ACTION AND REACTION	OVERLAP AND FOLLOW THRU	TEXTURE
PERSPECTIVE	TIMING	SIMPLIFICATION
DIRECTION	WORKING FROM EXTREME TO EXTREME	POSITIVE AND NEGATIVE SHAPES
TENSION		

It's scary to think that every time you make a drawing you have to think about all these things simultaneously, but it's really not all that bad. As long as in your training stages you don't get stuck on just a couple of the principles and concentrate on those to the neglect of the others. As long as you are aware of the prerequisites of a good animation drawing, you can stay loose while studying and eventually bring all these things together into expressive, meaningful, and entertaining drawings.

The directions I have taken in these handouts have depended on the work the students do in the gesture classes. You have seen my reactions to their work in the handouts in the form of critique sketches, where I make suggestions as to what might have been done in their drawings to make them more dynamic or expressive of the gesture. I have tried not just to sketch my version of the gesture, but also to explain the thinking behind the choice in the hope of encouraging the artist to reason in a similar fashion — not exactly like me, but in their own personal way, mainly to break them of the habit of just copying the model.

Things don't just happen — they are thought into happening. For instance, when you physically perform some action, hundreds of bones, muscles, tendons, and parts of clothing are involved, plus the thing that started it all — motivation. Your body responds obediently and automatically to your desires. But when drawing that action, you have to have some information about all that is required to pull off that gesture (the 28 principles), plus an actor's ability to perform it convincingly on paper. There's no book of rules, so there's no one "proper" way, for instance, for a character to thrust his hand out to test for rain.

Speaking of testing for rain — here is a pose where the model was doing just that. Naturally, I think, you would lean back, look up toward the source of the rain, and extend a palm to test for drops. In leaning back and looking up, the belly would protrude, causing the back of the coat hem to hug the calves while the front would be projected forward. That is what I meant by, "…the details must follow the articulation set forth by the gesture." This requires not just "looking at," but "feeling," the gesture kinesthetically.

Recently, while breakfasting in Los Olivos, I looked out the window and here was this guy in a rain-coat, with an unopened umbrella in one hand, paying no attention to the sky — just to the drops that were falling on his outstretched palm. Hardly a cartoonist's approach, but I thought, "Hey, that makes sense. You don't have to know what the sky looks like, you can see how hard it is raining by the number of drops that dampen your palms." You could figure, it's not what is happening up there that counts, but what's happening down here. And after all, as Don Graham said, "It could have been done a hundred different ways and any one of them could be right — depending on the situation."

This leads to a couple of important questions you can ask yourself on any drawing:

1. Where should the attention be directed?
2. In what part of the body is the primary action taking place?

Ultimately, of course, the object is to make a drawing that fits the action called for and to make it as entertaining as possible.

This reminds me of a scene I animated in a Winnie the Pooh picture where Christopher Robin is holding an umbrella in one hand and, if I remember correctly, the other hand is outstretched testing for rain. Christopher Robin is saying, "Tut, tut, it looks like rain...tut, tut, it looks like rain."

Here is a pose where the model is observing some scene or object. His hands are thrust forward into his pockets, forcing his shoulders back, while the coattails are pushed forward in line with the action, and also down from the force of the thrust — also pulling the back of the collar tight against the back of his neck. The head and neck naturally project forward to maintain equilibrium. The stomach juts out characteristically as he bends back to look forward in this relaxed but active manner. The angles of all the parts add a feeling of life to the pose. In other words, it becomes a gesture.

The student's drawing to that point took probably around five or six minutes. (You can see that most lines have been gone over many times.) My critique sketch took maybe thirty seconds, meaning of course, that if you can feel the gesture in your own body, kinesthetically, it won't require a lot of searching around for the proper line here, the proper line there — which will never materialize if you don't see/feel it to start with.

It's sometimes amazing what you end up with if you become involved in recording various parts of the figure for the sake of the gesture itself. Here is a student's drawing that recording-wise has some very nicely drawn facts. As you can see, the whole figure was brought around to a more straight-on view.

(The chair is correct.) Notice how the model's left elbow is not leaning on the knee, while the right elbow is off somewhere in space. My critique sketch was made to encourage the student to get the basis of the gesture down before attempting to draw any of the details.

When drawing from a model, one must learn to cheat. That is, if you are struck with a straight-on view, it is sometimes better to shift your drawing slightly to one side or the other. Here is an instance where it allowed me to show the all-important bend of the back, and resulted I think, in a more pleasant over-all shape.

You've probably seen that sign that counsels "Plan Ahead" where not enough room was left to finish the word "Ahead." Well, artists have to take heed to that advice as well as anyone else. Next are two cases of this kind of planning — both by different artists and both of the same pose. The logical thing to do when faced with a horizontal shape would be to turn the paper to a horizontal format. Theses two artists did not and as a result they let the right edge of the paper dictate the angle of the body and the length of the legs. I think my critique sketches show a more exciting angle and overall length (the model was Vicky Jo Varner, a tall, thin woman), and also reveals the pleasure I had in making the sketches. If you want your audience to be entertained, some entertainment has to be injected into your drawing.

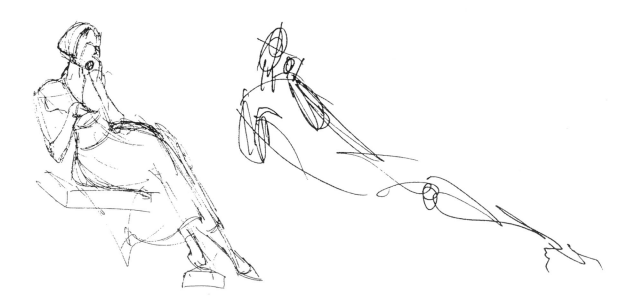

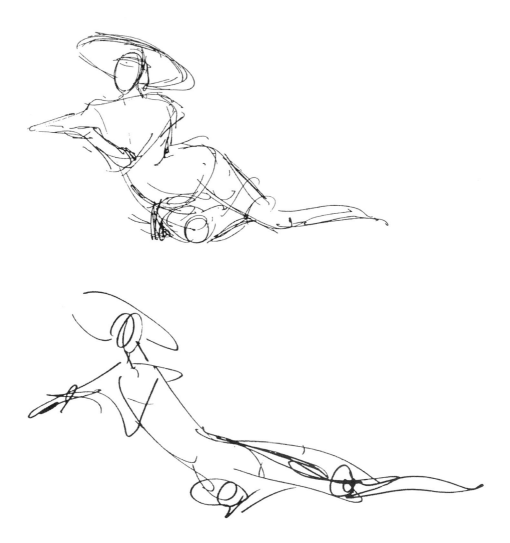

Doing these critiques always reminds me of Don Graham telling us, after one of his ego-shattering critiques, "So what. It could have been done a hundred ways, and they could all have been right."
I've talked enough, so let's listen to Kimon Nicolaides. He seems to speak so clearly.

You are attempting something that might be called simplification, but I choose to call it emphasis. Try to select those lines, those forms, those rhythms that speak specifically of the meaning of the whole gesture. A figure has one gesture. The parts are all there, but each plays a particular role — some the leading role, others a very secondary one. Others are silenced completely or become temporarily merged with other forms.

Let's repeat what I said the very first time you sat down to draw. That is — drawing depends on seeing. Seeing depends on knowing. Knowing comes from a constant effort to encompass reality with all of your senses, all that is you. You are never to be concerned with appearances to an extent which prevents reality of content. It is necessary to rid yourself of the tyranny of the object as it appears. The quality of absoluteness, the note of authority that the artist seeks depends upon a more complete understanding than the eyes alone can give. To what the eye can see the artist adds feeling and thought. He can, if he wishes, relate for us the adventures of his soul in the midst of life.

Wow!

57 Gestures, Moons, and Tangents

One of the practical benefits of a gesture class lies in the fact that it condenses nearly all the steps of animation into the making of one sketch. So instead of just copying the model (or studying anatomy and drapery) the artist is asked to create a one-drawing scene — complete with story, motivation, and inner forces that constitute a gesture.

A gesture would be impossible without some real or imagined motivation and a kinesthetic feeling for the physical moves needed to express that motivation. Motivation involves acting, while the physical moves involve action analysis.

As an example, in a recent session we had David Roon come as a farmer. One of his jobs was to hoe some weeds. (The hoe was real but the weeds were imaginary.) The students were doing a pretty nice job of copying what was before them, but weren't really involved in the story — what came before and after the "pose," that is, what they would have had to consider if they were animating a scene. Even in a single drawing they should have included action–reaction, weight distribution, tension, squash and stretch, overlap and follow through, primary and secondary action — which are all principles of animation — but also stress, thrust, twist, balance, and leverage, which are principles that are present in almost any drawing.

So I gave a short lecture on weed hoeing. The story behind the action was to eradicate a weed. The physical manipulation necessary to do this is to bring the hoe forcefully down on the weed and then pull it slightly back to make sure the weed is properly decapitated. This requires that the hands be quite far apart on the handle for good leverage for the downswing, then the whole body helps in the pull back; the back and knees bend into the thrust, then straighten up as the body pulls back. The feet are quite far apart for stabilization and leverage.

My premise is that no drawing should be made without considering all the things that constitute a good animation drawing. In other words any drawing should express either anticipation, action, or resolution. To ignore those vital ingredients and just blindly copy the model's lines gains nothing but a superficial facility with the pen or pencil.

It is only when these principles of drawing are used that a drawing really grabs you. Copying the model is like reading a list of words:

moon
proud
night
across
speckled, etc.

Rather than a poetic juxtaposition of those words.

The moon, prima donna of the heavens,
In its proud fullness took
Its place on the state of night,
And performed its slow, graceful way
Across the dark blue, speckled sky
In a costume of borrowed light.
From a poem by Yours Truly

Having hopefully put over that point, let me bring to light the many possible moves the human body is capable of (like the many words available in verbal communication), with which we can express an infinite number of gestures. I'm going to skim over this part because it gets so complicated I'd lose you before the 20,000th combination. Basically, the head has seven positions: straight ahead, turn right, turn left, tilt right, tilt left, look down, and look up plus combinations of all these, plus an infinite number of nuances of each combination.

Now add to that the chest, which has the same basic seven positions with the same amount of combinations and nuances. Then the possible combinations begin to compound themselves when each head combination is added to each chest combination. But now add each hand, foot, upper arm, lower arm, upper leg, lower leg, hip, fingers, and toes, with all their changes, with all the others with each of their changes. What you end up with (besides a headache) is an inexhaustible variety of bodily movements to aid you in drawing the gestures you desire to express.

Actors have the advantage of using the body first hand, that is, they only have to think an emotion and the body automatically assumes a gesture to express it. The artist has to think the emotion, then has to translate it to his kinesthetic sense, and then transcribe that to paper via pen or pencil. Being aware of the bodily moves that represent certain emotions is a necessary part of drawing. And though there are tens of thousands of possible variations the body is capable of — even when you strike a pose — the raising of one finger, or a smile, or a frown can change the whole meaning of the gestures.

In February the Gesture Class was fortunate to have the Berger and Diskin Mime Class as a model to draw. This was another challenge for the artists — to capture moving targets onto paper, and to single out some of those thousands of bodily movements taking place while the student mimes writhed through their skits.

The subjects were made especially difficult because of the fantastic roles the students were asked to perform. There were about a dozen of them, so some of the artists sketched quickly to cover as much of the "bedlam" as possible; others worked out the drawings more fully with the aid of memory. Here are a few of the artists' work. The first is by Geoffrey Everts, who sketched quickly and moved on. Bear in mind the mimes were working in groups of three.

This next group is by Raul Garcia who ignored detail and went for the gesture.

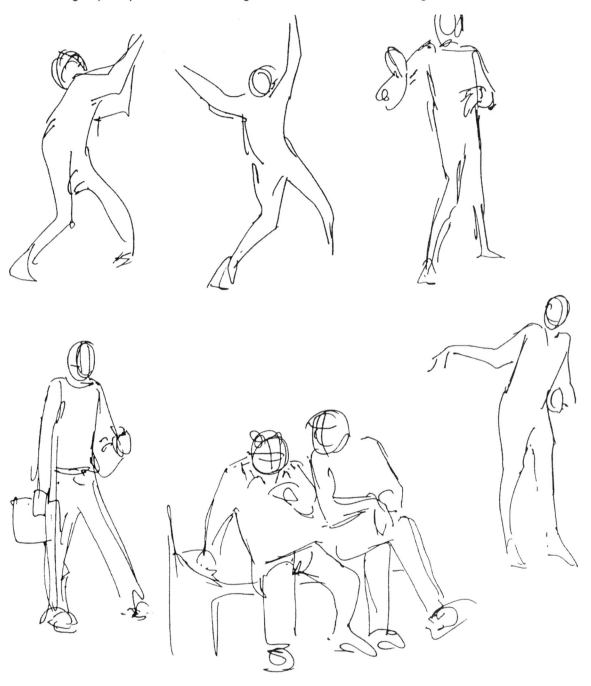

Terri Martin, a long time member of the Gesture Class, was not only able to capture the gestures but also add a little finesse.

For the critique section, I'd like to talk a little about a big problem — tangents. In the first illustration, there is a drawing where some objects were placed in positions where no tangents occur. A path can be clearly seen traveling unobstructed, and third dimensional space is felt. In the second illustration, the tangents make it difficult to even get started on the path, and third dimensional space is almost nil.

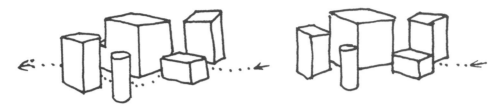

Basically, it's just a matter of using the perspective rule — "Overlap," that is.

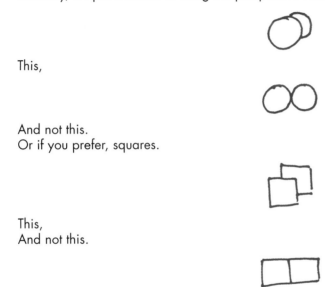

This,

And not this.
Or if you prefer, squares.

This,
And not this.

Here are some drawings from the Gesture Class, which contain tangents, with my accompanying critique sketches to show a possible solution. In this first drawing, the hat brim tangents with the shoulder line.

Notice here how both arms line up (tangent) with the sides of the body, also the umbrella handle sort of lines up with everything.

This is a nice drawing but would have read better if the face was not quite so lined up with the body.

As you become more aware of tangents and see the devastation they can cause, you will be more inclined to avoid them.

Better watch that tangent!

58 Include Your Audience

In the last handout (Chapter 56) I spoke a little about tangents. Later, as I was thinking about the subject, it occurred to me that a stationary vantage point such as you get when drawing from the model, may tranquilize you into drawing tangents if they appear before you. The remedy for that kind of entrapment is to assume (mentally) a moving point of view. Don't think of the model as an immobile bronze statue and that you are chained to your seat. Think of yourself as ubiquitous in that you have the option of altering your view of the pose, or that the model is pliable, and you may move an arm, or whatever, to clarify the pose.

The thing you want to portray is not just the parts of the body, but how the parts of the body function together. A gesture is just that — various parts of the body in some intricate combination of attitudes. Each of the parts, due to their individual characteristics, plays a role peculiar to themselves alone; that is, an arm can be made to do such things as plead, point, and clap with joy. An orchestra conductor can impart all kinds of emotional and rhythmical signals to the musicians through his gesticulations. In the meantime the legs go along with the moves, but mostly for stability or mobility, foundations on which the rest of the body depends.

When you think of legs, you think of running, jumping, and kneeling whereas the arms have a much more varied repertoire of gestural moves. Even an animal's front legs are more versatile than its rear legs. So whichever parts are to be featured as the gesture's "main event," or primary action, they must be pliable and adjustable so they can be placed in the best possible attitude. It will help in conveying to your audience that the character is not a statue, but is indeed a live being with feeling and spirit.

Always try to bring your audience into the process of drawing. Say, "Hey, look, I'm turning the body so you can see both shoulders, clarifying the pose; and here I'm using the rule of overlap so you will get a feeling of depth, etc." There should be harmony between you and your audience, not *the* audience — but *your* audience.

It has been said that a picture is worth a thousand words, but if you're not careful, twenty or thirty words might paint a better picture than your drawing. Modern fiction writers have a knack for paring down a description for their reading audience so they can move right along. For instance, here are a couple from Ross Macdonald's book *The Blue Hammer*.

She had deep black eyes, prominent cheekbones, prominent breasts. Her long hair was unflecked black. She was a very handsome, and quite young.

And another example:

A heavy old man opened the door and peered out at me through the screen. He had dirty gray hair and a short growth of moth-eaten gray beard. His voice was querulous.

Extremely brief descriptions, but enough to allow you to form a mental image of the characters. Not a thousand words — just twenty-two in one, and thirty-three in the other. Could you make a drawing that would be worth that many words, much less a thousand?

Look at these drawings by Terri Martin. I didn't ask her, but I truly believe that at least subconsciously she was saying to herself, "Hey, audience (my audience), this is what was happening — I'm not making this up. This is a real person doing real things. If it were a different person doing the same thing it would have been drawn differently so you would get the flavor of the "other" person. Notice how the tourist appears to be actually rubbing his sore foot, not just posing and the lady seems to be tipping the teacup slightly?"

He're some more of Terri's drawings. There's no confusion as to what the stories behind the poses are. For instance, consider the lady putting on mascara — notice how still she seems to hold herself so she doesn't mess up the job. Any good drawing will kindle that kind of response in your audience.

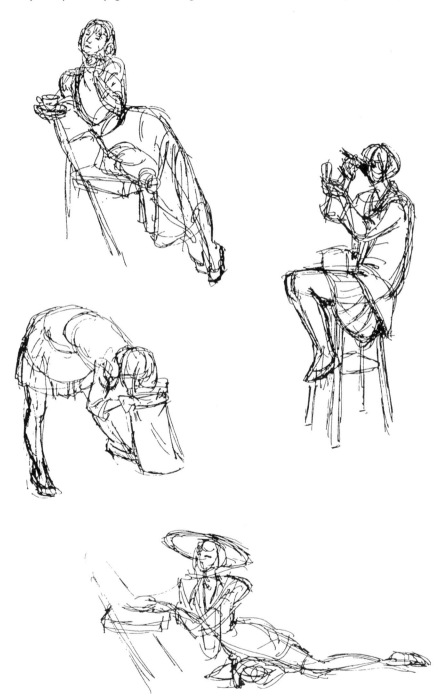

Here are a couple of very nice sketches by Jean Morel. Enjoy them, but also study them for how she used overlap,

size,

and surface lines.

Check out the thrust of the hips, the crisp angles of the legs, arms, and upper body. Observe how the details become a part of the action. And hey, no tangents! Jean managed to stay loose so the drawings have a spontaneity that keeps them alive. In *The Golden Book on Writing*, Lambuth says, "Snail-pace writing never catches up with spontaneity." And this goes for drawing, too. If your mind is on anatomy and details, spontaneity is apt to die a slow death with each stroke of the pen or pencil. Behold these spontaneous sketches.

You don't have to know Bobby Ruth Mann, the model, to appreciate this drawing by Robert Biggs. It's not your everyday type pose, and it presented some drawing problems, but this drawing says it all — this drawing is Bobby Ruth.

An artist's material for a drawing comes from without, but the ability to make it "work" comes from within.

Most of the shortcomings in drawing come not from laziness — everyone works hard for the full two hours in class. The most common problem is having nothing to say. One must have something to say and proceed to say it in no uncertain terms. For instance, here is a drawing problem that should have been felt in the artist's own body before attempting to draw it. The model is sitting on a stationary spot and is leaning over to rest on her right elbow. The hips are the anchor point, while the upper body leans to whatever extreme is desired (or necessary). Elementary, my dear Watson. Eh, what? Well, only if you are thinking in those terms. Also one should take liberties to twist the body slightly to one side or the other to avoid those straight-on "crotch" shots.

Below is a drawing where the model is sitting in a chair, playing a tiny stringed instrument. If the student were intent on showing the audience what was happening, he would have spread the knees, making a lap for the instrument. (See the previous drawing.) I call that area where the action (the story) is taking place the "stage." As you draw, think of yourself as a storyteller — that is all — a storyteller. Not a copier of models, or a recorder of mere facts, not an elucidator of anatomical wonders, but just a teller of stories. It may help to have an audience in mind as you draw — even if the audience is yourself. After all, we do work in the entertainment industry.

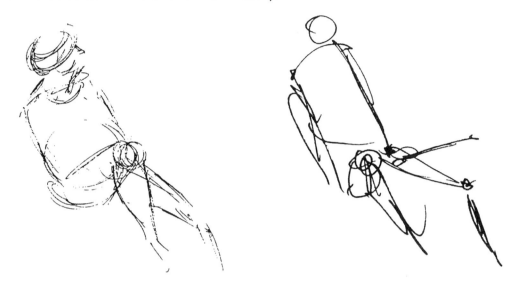

Here's a drawing that I interrupted in its early stages. The first few lines of a sketch should be the foundation for the gesture. If the artist has only time for, say, 15 lines in his sketch — there should be enough there to enable him to finish the drawing at a later date.

I suppose there were always some know-it-all's who thought they could teach drawing.

If you had studied the twenty-eight principles of animation, this wouldn't have happened.

59 The Wonders of the Right and Left Hemispheres

Some time ago I did a handout on drawing verbs not nouns. Just now, two or three years later (I'm slow and steady), the thought occurred to me that nouns might be dealt with mainly in the left hemisphere of the brain, while the right hemisphere prefers the verbs. A short, easy experiment will verify this premise. Think of a noun — dog, man, deltoid muscle. Your mind immediately presents you with some familiar breeds of dogs, a man in some form, and the deltoid muscle probably conjures up an anatomy book illustration (typical left brain conceptions). Now, think of some verbs — running, cooking, or acting. Suddenly there is activity, life, and gesture on your mental screen (right brain reflection).

So it stands to reason anytime you face a drawing project, whether it is training oriented or work related, approach it mainly through the right brain channel and it will be more like an actor on stage, and less like a display in a wax museum.

Even our language evokes gesturing. Words, plus the way we say them, work together to produce a double-edged expressiveness. Charles Darwin was evidently interested in such things. In his book, *The Expression of the Emotions in Man and Animals*, there is a photo of a man saying, "Ugh!" and a lady saying, "Sn...," probably the first two letters of the word "sneer." Here are some crude pen sketches of them.

Have you ever considered the physical feelings that words evoke? It's not only the meaning of the word, but also its sound that prompts certain kinesthetic feelings. You feel like doing something with your body when you say, "gloomy," "bright," "teeny-weeny," or "huge." Certain sounds, vowels, and consonants seem appropriate to the meaning. You feel a definite need to form a gesture when you hear, "stern," "stiff," "stubborn," or "strut." The very sounds of words suggest activity or movement, like, "activity," "declare," and "gesticulate;" though some require less exertion: "comfort," "rest," "docile," or "ease." These are some of the kinds of words that are inextricably linked to the gesture that our models assume in drawing classes, and the story lines of our animated films. If you can formulate a relationship or word and pose in your "first impression" of the gesture — it will help in drawing it.

Here are a couple of nice drawings by Terri Martin. It is obvious how having a word, an emotion, or a story line in mind would help in drawing such expressive gestures.

In a stimulating book, *Teaching for the Two-Sided Mind* by Linda Verlee Williams, there's a mandala that shows quite clearly how the two hemispheres of the brain process information. Notice how the left half of the mandala, an analysis of the flower, results in a sort of scientific breakdown — a "laboratory" view; whereas, in the right half, the flower is perceived as a whole — as a flower.

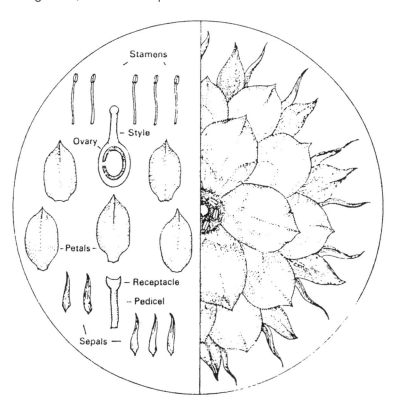

When you don't have a model to draw from, you have to visualize the pose or action. Visualization is in cahoots with kinesthetics, for when you visualize you are not using your eyes, but you are using every cell in your body. It's as if you create a whole 'nother world in your imagination — one that can be translated to an audience through your drawings. But even with a model in front of you, the same process has to take place; otherwise it is just copying.

In the book *Psycho-Cybernetics* by Maxwell Maltz, he says, "...your nervous system cannot tell the difference between an actual experience and one that is vividly imagined. If we picture ourselves in a certain manner, it is nearly the same as the actual performance. Mental practice helps to perfect."

He tells how "C. G. Kop, of Holland, a recognized authority on teaching piano, recommends that all pianists 'practice in their heads.' A new composition, he says, should be first gone over in the mind. It should be memorized and played in the mind, before ever touching fingers to the keyboard."

Alex Morrison said "You must first clearly see a thing in your mind before you can do it. When you see a thing clearly in your mind, your creative success mechanism within you takes over and does the job better than you could do it by conscious effort or will power."

Maltz tells about how many athletes, who practiced by imaging while sitting in an easy chair, greatly improved their game. He (Maltz) may not have been aware of it, but it was fine tuning the kinesthetic sensibilities that helped improve those athletes.

You who type will agree that you can tell when you've misspelled a word even before your machine flashes "error." You can fell it kinesthetically — the sequence of movements in your fingers was wrong. Typing any word "feels" a certain way. Consequently, if you "feel" a new word, you will be able to type it correctly the first time you try.

So, my friends, are you not convinced that if you "feel" a gesture, you will be able to draw it? It's not only the information presented by the model, but it is also the way you "feel" it. That "first impression" you form when you observe the model is your kinesthetic "feel" for the pose.

Feeling, fantasizing, or imaging is a right brain activity. If you ask a person *about* a noun, they will respond with information from the left hemisphere. If you ask them to *become* a noun and tell you how it "feels," suddenly fantasy and kinesthesia come alive, and they will call up the insights of the right hemisphere.

This is from *Teaching for the Two-Sided Mind*:

Kinesthetic awareness is an inner sense, an awareness of how the body (or another's body) feels as it moves.

The importance of kinesthetic awareness was demonstrated in an experiment in 1952 by the late Lloyd Percival, director of Toronto's Sports College. Coleman R. Griffith, a psychologist, had observed that basketball players depended too much on sight when shooting and didn't make enough use of feedback from their muscles. Percival selected two groups of basketball players of matching ability, with an average score of twenty to twenty-one baskets in fifty attempts. The first group practiced predetermined shots for twenty minutes in the regular way. The second group practiced the same shots for the same amount of time, but they shot five minutes with their eyes open, ten minutes blindfolded while an observer told them exactly where each shot went and urged them to attend to muscle sensations, and then five minutes without blindfolds. After four weeks, the first group averaged twenty-three out of fifty baskets, while the second scored thirty-nine out of fifty.

Though we can be consciously aware of the separate functions of the two hemispheres of the brain, we should not obscure the fact that it is their complimentary functioning that gives the mind its power and flexibility. We do not think with one hemisphere or the other; both are involved.

The power of the two-sided mind is demonstrated most dramatically in accounts of creative discoveries. Any significant creative breakthrough is usually preceded by a good deal of primary logical, linear thinking as an individual defines and redefines a problem. Then there comes a moment of insight where an answer presents itself.

I suppose that's how we form those first impressions of a pose. We see the model dressed in a certain fashion, gesturing in a certain way, then after intellectualizing about it for a second or two — *voila!* "In a moment of insight," the first impression forms like a flash of lightning.

But it's not all that simple. Gestures are always performed for a reason. They are not just mere movements of body and limbs in some haphazard way, divorced from inner participation (motive); it is the visible manifestation of man's emotional or intellectual state. Also movement involves weight, time, space, and gestural significance, so actors, dancers, mimes, and animators have to be aware of all the things involved in an action, and be able to synthesize them into a meaningful and communicable gesture.

Gads! What a lot of test! But I'm only around for a little bit, so I have to pour it on when I get the chance. Perhaps it's time now for some aesthetic relief. For the last two noon-time classes we had Allen Chang, a martial arts pro, kick-boxer, and modern jazz dancer pose for us. They were exciting and inspiring sessions. I managed to confiscate a few of the excellent drawings to share with you. These first few are by Danny Galieote.

Here are a few perceptive sketches by Jane Krupka, who has an uncanny ability of capturing a gesture with a minimum of lines and details.

Terri Martin approaches gesture drawing with a solid background of classical art and a substantial understanding of the animation media. Here are a few of her sketches of Allen Chang.

60 Making the Rules of Perspective Come to Life

One of the most helpful things I've picked up over the years to improve my drawing is the "Rules of Perspective," as revealed by Bruce McIntyre. Bruce has written eleven books on drawing, made several television series, developed a self-study drawing program, and has produced two college courses in drawing. He considers drawing as not just for "artistic" purposes but, "a valuable community skill to show what things look like, how they work, and how they fit together." It's all very elemental stuff, but believe me, a lot of us have gotten quite far along in our careers without knowing all of the elemental stuff.

I've already done a few handouts on the rules of perspective but have never really done them justice. I'm going to try again. Here they are as they appear in their raw, dormant state.

Not too impressive, as they lie in that dispassionate form. They're like a blueprint of a sailboat — with no indication of the adventures the finished boat will bring once you set sail in it.

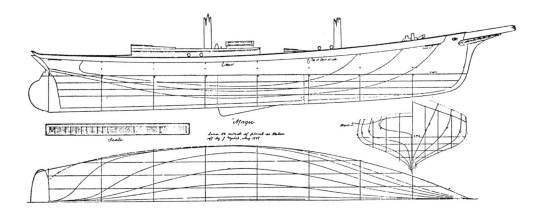

Anyone who has read Herman Melville, Joseph Conrad, and other authors of sea stories knows how a blueprint of a boat can be made to come alive and transport you into adventurous tales of the sea. To illustrate my point, here are a couple of boats bobbing, just waiting for their ocean-bound adventures.

Let's start with the rule of overlap. This is one I am extremely conscious of while drawing. It not only allows one to create the illusion of third dimensional space by drawing one thing in front of another, but it helps establish and control angles, plus is the basis for foreshortened figures. It is also helpful in drawing drapery. There are many ways to represent and use overlap. Let's analyze and expand on it a bit.

1. This is plain overlap. Notice how it creates a sense of space, whereas two circles (or objects) beside each other create a tangent and result in a two dimensional flatness.

2. Here is overlap plus diminished size creating a greater illusion of space.

Here's overlap with diminished size and surface.

And here is overlap with surface lines.

3. This is overlap with a bridge, or intermediate structure, separating the circles — which is my very own secret variation.

Now for some examples of overlap done in the Gesture Class. Here's a student's work that practices this.

The head tangents with the back, the forearm with the far arm, the shirtsleeve opening with the belly. In my correction sketch you can see how overlap has disentangled all those areas and creates a flesh and blood actor.

Whenever I draw shoulders or hips, I am conscious of overlap with the connecting structure. For instance, in the preceding drawing it provided me with an underpinning structure on which to attach the arms and legs.

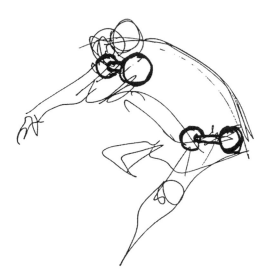

This imaginary device also helps in controlling angles. Here are three sketches with the shoulders on an angle. In the last one the shoulders are not drawn in but you can feel them, even as I felt them while drawing.

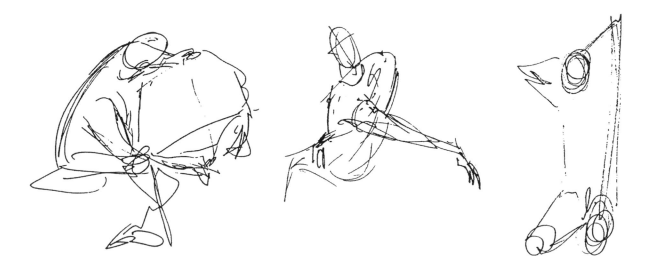

Let me show you two more student's drawings where I'm sure if they had been cognizant of overlap in general, and the "magic device," specifically, they would have come up with more solid drawings:.

One of the big problems in the gesture class, as I have often mentioned, is the tendency to straighten things up. If we were asked to imagine a figure, we probably, through the help of the brain's left hemisphere, would conjure up a man or woman, standing erect, with at head, a chest, two shoulders, etc., like a blueprint.

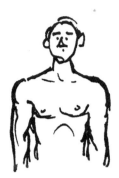

Unfortunately, while drawing, we unconsciously do the same thing, even though the figure might be at a 3/4 view. Here is a student's drawing in which this appears to have happened. In my correction sketch I avoided that tendency by concentrating on overlap. You can feel how the parts of the body seem to be packed on top of each other like clay. And you can feel how that invisible device stabilizes the upper body, both structure-wise and angle-wise.

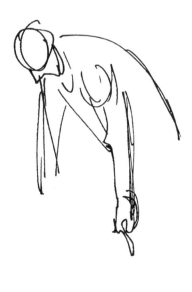

Okay kids, I really must turn it off — I can't write a book! And I haven't gotten to the other rules yet— maybe another time, eh? Anyway, until then, I have gathered a few drawings by Frederick E. Banbery that have most of those rules sprinkled throughout. Look for them — surface, diminishing size, overlap, surface lines, and foreshortening. Notice especially, as you spot them, how they actually *become the drawings*; how *they* make the drawings come to life; how *they* are the means by which the figures dwell in space.

61 In Further Praise of the Rules of Perspective

In the last handout (Chapter 59) I began a treatise on the rules of perspective as formulated by Bruce McIntyre who, incidentally, is a former Disney Studios artist. I had to stop after discussing only the rule, *Overlap*, and even that one was barely touched on.

I am making a big deal out of this overlap thing, am I not? Well, that is because I believe, though the other rules of perspective have their own individual applications, they can be thought of as just variations of *Overlap*. For instance, *Surface*, *Diminishing Size*, and *Surface Plus Size* are really *Overlap* with space between. For instance, if you lined up *Overlap* with *Diminishing Size*, like the traditional telephone poles, to illustrate how the vanishing point works, you would have a kindred diagram, but one with more of a feeling of volume — not only in the objects themselves, but also a feeling of third dimensional space between the objects.

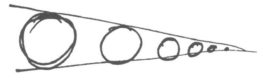

The *Surface Lines* rule can be applied to the *Overlap* motif to give both direction to the object and also create the illusion of depth.

After all, perspective is just a means of creating the illusion of third dimensional space in our drawings and paintings. Oh, I tell you, if there was ever an elixir for drawing third dimensionally — it is *Overlap*!

So

I would like to add a few very potent uses for *Overlap*. One is the obvious need for *Overlap* when drawing a foreshortened figure. If you can think of the figure as a few simple masses — head, chest, hips, plus arms and legs — you can lay those shapes down in whatever view you are interested in and that will give you a good foundation for your drawing.

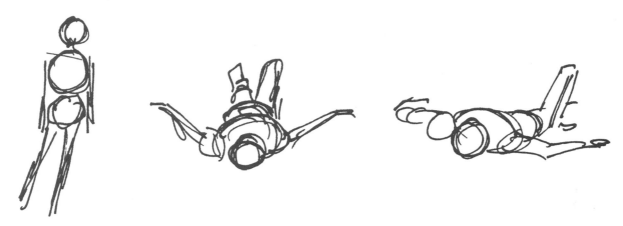

When drawing from a model, there is an irresistible tendency to copy the line that you see before you rather than build the figure with some integrity of structure. It reminds me of a time during World War II when I was between studio jobs (and the Navy). I tried to get a job drawing airplane parts assembly for people who couldnt read a blueprint. For my application, I drew in great photographic realism, different views of a pencil sharpener, and the engine of my car. I copied all the wires, spark plugs, and various parts — but I did not know diddly-poo about how the engine worked.

The purpose of drawing from a model is different in that we're trying to learn how the gesture (and clothing) works, so we can draw it at will and from any viewpoint.

Here is a student's attempt at a difficult foreshortened angle. The natural approach for the uninitiated is to look for lines on the model to transfer to the paper. But all too often the model's lines do not reveal very much of what is really happening, so the artist is lost, much like looking for some wispy cirrus clouds in a hurricane.

As you can see, the student jotted down some recognizable areas, but there is no underlying structure.

I pointed out that he should first choose the basic shapes he is dealing with such as head, chest, hips, and appendages, then using the rule of *Overlap* (encircled), line up those shapes as needed, or desired.

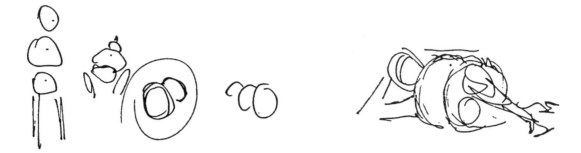

All individual parts of the body can be constructed in the same way. Here are some arms and legs (albeit crude) created with *Overlap* as a starting place.

Here are some more examples of hands from Bridgman's *Constructive Anatomy*.

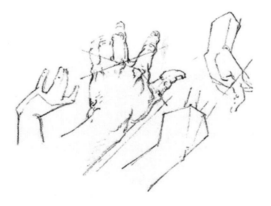

Disney artists need to be versed in animal anatomy as well. Here is a study from *Bambi* of a deer overcoming an obstacle and the impact of its movement.

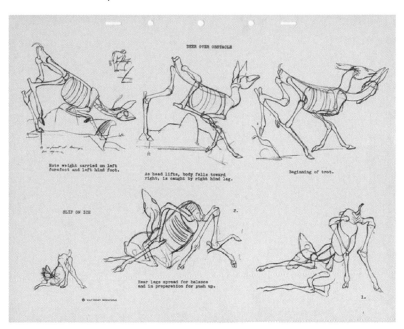

Drapery, we will all agree, is one of the most difficult things to draw. Thinking *Overlap* will not make it easy, but will help in forming wrinkles and will help move them around in animation. Think of wrinkles as shapes in space, overlapping and being overlapped by, other shapes. Here are some simple overlapping forms of drapery — cloth overlapping cloth.

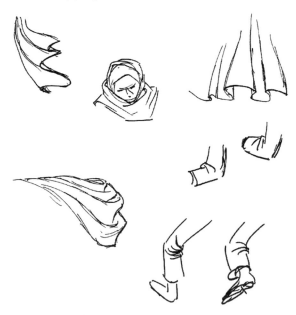

I contend that *Overlap* will help you in animation, too. Analyze these three drawings by Ollie Johnston — let your eyes wander from drawing to drawing and notice how those basic shapes (head, chest, hip, and legs) animate from position to position to reveal the action — but always maintaining an overlapping role. Follow the left leg as it overlaps the rear end to being overlapped by the rear end. Follow all the parts, observing how *Overlap* plays its role in clarifying the animation.

Overlap is important in drawing heads, too. The features are all stacked on at different depths — one in front of another. You should feel this "stacking" even in a front-on position or a profile. Here is a student's drawing of a head. All the parts seem to be on one plane. He also gave in to the proneness to straighten things up, making a profile out of a 3/4 back view. In my correction sketch I tried to show how the forehead overlapped the eyes and nose; the eyes overlapped the nose and upper lip. The ear was drawn with the thought in mind that it overlapped the side of the head, thus effecting the illusion that it is the nearest thing to us.

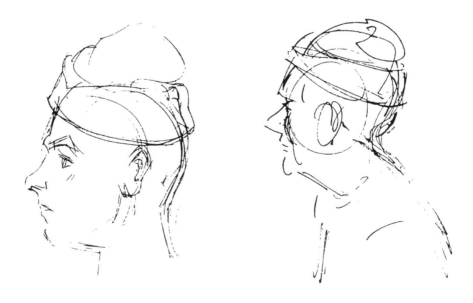

Remember, anytime an object is closer to you than another, it is going to overlap that farther object. It is going to be on "this" side of it — whether it is separated by negative space or not.

Everything exists in space, which means that everything, even different parts of one thing, is closer or farther from you than another. Thus the illusion is created that the closest thing is larger. Many modern artists go to great lengths to destroy that illusion. They proclaim that since they are working on a two-dimensional surface, any suggestion of three dimensions is an abomination. But needless to say, Disney Studios has pursued the goal of creating the illusion of realism, which requires a vehicle that replicates the audience's personal experience of space. That makes it easier to win over the audience to its storytelling.

Of course, along with all the physical principles that the artist has to wrestle with is the motivation and inner driving forces that impel the characters to perform each gesture. The only creative way to express these actions is for the artist to feel within him or herself the kinesthetic empathy for the motivation and the execution of the move. That is why I repeat so often that copying from the model, line for line, is an unreliable procedure.

Hey, my friends, I realize you know all this stuff. The reason I keep reiterating it is so that eventually these things will pop into (or out of) your minds effortlessly and will eventually become natural and unstudied — spontaneous. Try thinking *Overlap* on the next few drawings you make and I think you'll be pleasantly rewarded. I guarantee it'll see you through many a tough drawing problem. It's not a prop — it is basic three-dimensional structure. In geology, the rock that houses gems and minerals is called matrix. Well, space is the matrix that houses people and things. Remember we are not flat cutouts placed in this third dimensional matrix — it continues right through us as if we were... well, transparent.

Here are some interesting sketches by Terri Martin. They're interesting because they were drawn with the left hand. It's a good exercise because you can't be bothered with details — hard enough to get the main theme. Notice how as she sketched she seemed to concentrate on getting the main shapes to take their place in space. Notice, too how *Overlap* of the main shapes seems to be the dominant means to capture the essence of the poses.

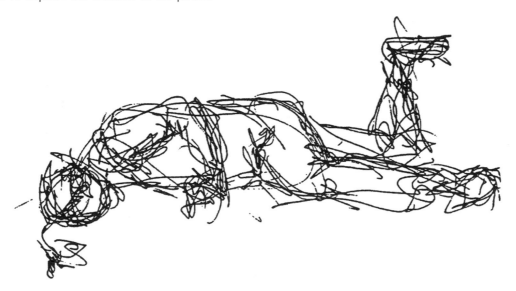

62 There Is No End to Thinking Overlap

In the last two handouts I have dealt with *Overlap,*

which I have stretched to mean anything that is closer to you than any other thing. I have stretched the word to mean that the closest thing doesn't necessarily have to touch or obscure the farthest. Think of it in the same sense that two lives can "overlap" each other. They lead separate lives, but at some junction they have something to do with each other. Well, everything in your drawing has something to do with everything else — so think of them as "overlapping." Therefore even 𝗢 𝗢 is *Overlap*! I talked about people and things in a matrix of space, so when you draw two separate things the space between them becomes a part of the composition or the drawing. You can't actually draw space, but it has to be there; otherwise those elements can't relate to each other.

When the characters, props, and space all work together to put over the story it forms what I like to call the "stage" of the drawing. It's just another way of saying staging. When the stage is set properly, the story is instantly readable.

Mike Swofford did these two nice sketches of two models posing together. The forms are intertwined and, in the case of the second drawing, quite complicated, but the third dimensional negative space that forms the stage is kept relatively clear so that the models' and your attention goes directly to the center of interest. Notice, too, how all the elements in the drawings either help to frame the center of interest or point to it.

Here is another excellent drawing. The female figure complicates the staging by covering up part of the male figure, but it is still quite clear because the overlapping figure forms a nice three-dimensional stage between the characters. The resulting focus on the subject matter is quite electrifying. As a matter of fact, knowing how hard it is to put over a story point so clearly, it ought to take your breath away. There is a lot of energy bouncing around in that negative space.

Here are a couple of Bill Berg's sketches where the relationship is between character and prop. Again, notice the stage that is established by arranging the elements so they direct our attention to the story point — the props.

James Fujii caught that coffee-pouring pose from another angle and seems to have been very conscious of "staging" it clearly; that is, stacking on the body parts and the space parts to create a three-dimensional stage.

Those drawings are successful because the elements are assembled in such a way that your attention is, in a sense, corralled. It's kind of like being drawn into the plot of a movie, play, or novel, not against your will — but in spite of it. There is no beating around the bush — the drawings come right to the point! As David Lambuth says in his book, *The Golden Book on Writing*, "If you have a nail to hit, hit it on the head."

Animals, more than humans, are subject to *Overlap*. The reason is the main forms — head, chest and hips — are horizontal and line up in diminishing size formation with a more obvious overlapping of the forms.

In *Drawing: A Search for Form* by Joseph Mugnaini, there is an interesting analysis of five animals, showing how those main body forms, the head, chest, and hips, are linked structurally. These are down-shots, or vertical views of things that ordinarily would be drawn horizontally. Knowing the spacing of these forms should make overlapping them easier.

A Bird   B Cat   C Horse   D Fish   E Frog

The bird is a shape of flight. The fused body cavity and the pelvis and thorax are close to one another. For flight, the forward appendages become wings. The entire head, neck, and beak, along with its other functions, is analogous to our arm. It is a tool and a weapon. It must have length. It must be flexible.

The cat is a springing animal, explosive; sudden in movement. Its neck can be short because its spinal column is the essence of flexibility; the pelvis and thorax are separated.

The horse is a stiff-legged animal designed for long distance travel. Its body cavity is rigid. The thorax and pelvis are spaced a bit closer than those of the cat, not quite so close as those of the bird.

Because the fish is supported by water, it needs no legs. The body rings, as indicated on the chart, are forward. It needs no pelvis to support the legs, no thorax to support the arms. The spinal column itself has become a lever for locomotion.

The frog is a flat-bellied, leaping animal. The character of its body is disc-like with built-in shock absorbers. The vertebrae are practically deleted; the body is therefore made rigid. It needs no long neck; its arms and legs are all-purpose appendages.

An illustration in the book, unrelated to the animal's structure chart, shows a breakdown of the overlapping shapes of a cat.

"Cat" by Joy Hankins. Colored wash drawing.

Notice the impression of volume based upon the principles referred to in the vertical view analysis presented earlier.

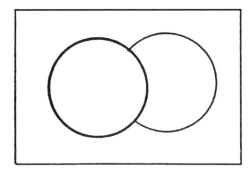

Here one circle is placed behind another and partially concealed by it. Solidity and space are suggested. The circles have become opaque and disk-like.

In the following examples, Mugnaini carries his line of thinking a bit further, but fails to refer to it as *Overlap*, that word that suggest a bag full of possibilities. Like, when I read or hear that word, I think of objects assembled in space — objects necessary to the story, that are consciously gathered and piled on, one on top of the other — like a three-dimensional display on a two-dimensional surface.

By reducing the size of one of the circles, the illusion of space is increased; the flatness of the rectangular picture plane has been penetrated.

The circles are turned into spheres by the simple device of adding stripes, which are spaced closer together as they approach the edges. Now the eye is carried completely around the objects, and one is aware not only of their solidity, but also of the space between the spheres and the other side of each sphere.

You might think of it like this — a sculptor sees his subject in a block of stone and chips away the negative space to reveal it. The artist sees his subject on a blank sheet of paper and with pen or pencil delineates *both* positive and negative space. Not a chipping away, but a piling on of both positive and negative, thus creating the illusion of space.

Let's leave *Overlap* for a change, and for old time's sake, do a few critiques. Drawing from a model is not easy, especially gesture drawing. It's not so much what you see as what you feel — and here comes that word kinesthesia again. It means "The sensation of position, movement, tension, etc. of parts of the body, perceived through nerves and organs in muscles, tendons, and joints." (Webster's Dictionary).

It's what divers feel when they hurl themselves into space from a high platform — every twist and angle must be felt to the nth degree. It's what a rodeo rider has to feel when he's being jerked, twisted, and bumped by an unhappy bronco. Hundreds of instant readings and adjustments have to be made, not only of his own body, but those of the horse also. And it's what artists have to feel when they draw a gesture. Kinesthetic readings are made within their own bodies to get a feeling for the action. It's a major maneuver, switching from *looking* to *feeling*.

Here is a student's sketch, and though basically well done, it lacks a certain kinesthetic involvement. Actually, the student's drawing comes close to the lines suggested by the model, but the feeling, the zing, is missing. In my correction suggestion, I simplified the pose and drew how it felt kinesthetically to me.

Here is another student's drawing that certainly did not go through the kinesthetic channels for its inspiration. And contrary to the mood of the pose, the figure was straightened up, when actually it should be leaning back in a relaxed manner. It appears that the artist was concentrating more on anatomy and shoulder straps than on feeling.

Here's another case where conjuring up a kinesthetic feeling might have solved the student's problem. Anytime a person lifts something out in front of themselves, out goes the belly! Whether it's a 50-lb weight, or a feather, out goes the belly. Stand up and try it. Then try it in the mind while seated. It may take a little mental effort, but, and I'm not making this up, the ability to do it mentally will make you a rich and famous animator. Well, at least it'll make drawing more fun.

Oh, and of course a cartoonist would push the belly out a bit farther.

The moral to that critique is "Don't let the model's rendition of the pose dominate your drawing. Put your kinesthesia to work. Feel the pose inside your own body and let that be your interpretation. And, if you can think of it, toss in a little caricature to spark up the drawing, and intensify its entertainment value."

Akin to that lifting action is a carrying action. To show the action of carrying — the sensation of carefully and thoughtfully balancing something (in this case a bed roll) on one's shoulder — one needs to lean forward slightly. You know that when carrying something, no matter how heavy your load, it would not feel as stable if you were standing erect.

Don't misunderstand me — I am no action analysis expert, but I figure if I can back up my drawings with some words that convincingly explain the action — I am in safe territory. Words are important tools; the story-people carefully choose words that express the action, emotion, or situation they are trying to describe. When those words are translated into drawings, they become the basis for reaching the audience. So if you can say in words the action or gesture you are attempting to draw, they will urge you on in the right direction. Usually the words are verbs such as reach, bend, run, lift, turn, sneer, laugh, etc. If you find yourself just copying lines from the model without attaching some verbs to your modus operandi, you could very likely drift off your course — if not completely astray.

Here are a few afterthoughts.

63 Space Is Created

My wife, Dee, who proofreads my writings, was bothered by my saying in the last handout (Chapter 62), "...this is overlap."

I concur that two separate marks on a page are not overlap, but I'm talking about something else. I'm talking about two objects, or parts of a figure in a drawing, that relate to each other and are embedded in this three dimensional matrix we call space. That space, though not actually drawn, is as real as the objects themselves. Thus an object

overlaps the space beyond it,

which in turn overlaps any object beyond it.

In landscape painting it's called aerial perspective and is painted as atmosphere. In line drawing it is dealt with by the rules of perspective, by making the far objects simpler and drawing them in a different scale; that is, drawing the farther object both smaller and of a finer line.

Besides, this

is not necessarily overlap — it could be two shapes like these.

brought together. (I'm kidding.)

Sometime ago in the Gesture Class I had the model hold a cardboard box out in front of his body. We drew it. Then I had the model drop the box and hold that box-shaped space. You could feel a density to that negative space. It became the center of interest, and when it was drawn well, it had real character; it had shape, volume, weight, and little mystery. The box, a "real" object that involved overlap was gone, but in its place was "real" third dimensional space — that still involved overlap — overlap of positive objects and negative space.

As for space being a real thing, check out this guy manipulating space.

Compacting it. Expanding it.

It rises.

He pushes it to the floor.

It's heavy.

It is light.

Of course you'll never be called upon to illustrate anything like that, but that very same negative space is going to be present in every drawing you'll ever make. It'll be there as space between one part of the body and another, and it'll be pulling or pushing, compacting or expanding, weaving in and out and around things, always expressing some kind of tension, creating a relationship between objects, and taking a tremendously important part in the staging. I am not talking about air. You don't have to create air — it is already there. But you do create space.

I remember when I was singing in operettas; the stage director would suggest positions for the actors to work in. A bird's-eye view would look something like this.

The participants would be placed at various distances from each other, creating a definite emotional and spatial relationship. Any tension created by the space between depends on the story and the characters. For instance, two enemies standing nose to nose would create quite a bit of hostile-like tension, while two lovers, nose to nose, would, well, create an unmistakably different kind of tension.

Here are several simple drawings that illustrate tension created by negative space. The first is a good example of a psychological use of space. In it you feel the parasol (humorously) buoying the figure up, while the bent rope presses down on space in weighty contrast. Notice the space between the model's right elbow and her left hand. They form a stage of space through which her look can travel unimpeded into the space that she is trying to keep from falling into.

There is moving space, too. Through a thoughtful handling of the positive shapes, the negative shapes will help create a feeling of something happening, something just happened, or the anticipation of something about to happen. The use of angles in your figures can create a sense of space being pulled apart or pushed together. It's a psychological thing. When we see this, we think of the hand of a clock moving, or two telephone poles — one of them leaning precariously. This one reminds us of the "domino" effect — one thing about to knock another over. But nothing has really happened yet, so you feel the space is changing, and a tension is created. Notice in this sketch, space was staged so you feel the ball and the arms moving toward each other, and vice versa in the adjusted sketch.

|/

/|

Here is space being squeezed. You can feel it happening between the left elbow and the right hand.

In this sketch of two friends meeting and greeting, you see the front of one and the back of the other, but you feel the space between the two.

Okay, one more. Here the space between the bodies has been virtually eliminated, but you feel it nevertheless. There is electricity, pressure, and psychological warmth there.

Have I gone too far with this? I would like to think not. I think artists have to hone their sensitivity to such things to create all the special emotions they are called upon to illustrate. Some of us are endowed with that kind of perception naturally — it flows forth unconsciously — while others of us have to learn it intellectually.

I posed for the gesture class in August and, boy, were there some nice drawings made. The class must have relaxed not having me hover over them with my nitpicking pen at the ready. Here is a partial gallery of them for your viewing pleasure.

Drawings by Christine Beck

Drawings by Terri Martin

Drawings by Steven Gordon

Drawings by Tina Price

Drawings by Mark Andrews

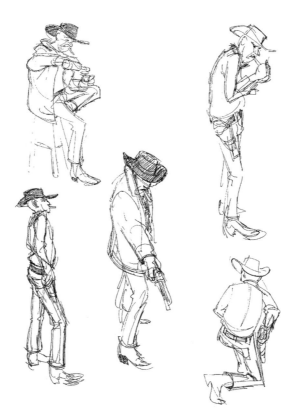

Drawings by Jean Morel

64   Words and Experience

These "handouts" have covered a multitude of rules and concepts that I trust have helped in some way. A recent one was about verbalizing the action or gesture you are attempting to draw, so as you repeat the words that electrifying "first impression" will be kept alive while you are drawing. That 1,000-volt first impression, which we so desperately want to record, is apt to start dwindling as soon as we get involved in drawing. Our minds get engrossed in the anatomy or the clothing. Some of us get intrigued by the facial features and spend several minutes on that even, heaven forbid, before we sketch in the overall gesture.

Even the model loses that first impression. When they strike a pose it is fresh and vivid in their minds and kinesthetic feelings, but after a few minutes, that initial flash of feeling beings to fade, and they begin to wonder if there're any guts at all in their pose.

So I suggested forming a word or phrase that describes the gesture as you see it, one you can hold on to — something that will constantly conduct you back to that intense first impression. Whatever you do, resorting to a "cookie cutter" copy of the model is a less than desirable compromise. After all, if the artist doesn't feel strongly about the gesture, then he can't expect the viewer to feel anything.

Michelangelo spoke of "…the hand that obeys the intellect," which implies the drawing comes not from the pen or the hand, but from the reasoning faculty. Reasoning and feeling join forces in the drawing process.

Anyway, to get back to verbalizing the gesture, we all know that no deep feeling can be adequately expressed in words, but if verbalizing, such as it is, helps even a little, it becomes a blessing. Artists don't use words to express the deepest of feelings, they use lines. Like words, lines can't adequately describe the deep feelings that we experience, but a series of well-selected lines can "verbalize" the idea in a very convincing way. The result is a drawing that communicates and entertains.

Lines and drawings are tools that we learn early in life — tools that are easily lost or forgotten if not used often. We use these "tools" to try to give expression to our experience and feelings as human beings. Yes the lines and drawings we use to express these feelings can be used to draw facts: A trash can in an alley, an airplane on a runway, a dog catching a Frisbee. These are all facts of life and can be captured like a photograph.

The real meat of drawing comes when we use line to capture not facts, but feelings. Just as a poet might struggle with a list of words to try to express deep feelings of love, joy, or sadness, so as artists we too must try to use our toolbox of line and shape to express deep human emotions that are more than just the facts of life.

A line is a way to express meaning, the meaning of our experience in a humble way on a piece of paper. The meaning of life the way we each see it, each one of us as individual observers of the universe. Line and shape seem pretty inadequate when we describe drawing this way. There is no amount of lines that can express how we feel about a sunset, or a romantic dinner. But as inadequate as line and shape are, they are as fundamental as the word in expressing our human experience. And line and shape is more ancient than the word as an effective tool to communicate.

It's our job as the interpreter of experience to not only take in the experience, but to become conscious of it, to know it and to trust our interpretation of it. When we draw a gesture, do we trust or distrust the character, is he or she real or artificial, vague or confident?

The novelist H. E. Bates has a habit of writing down quick biographies of people that he met who struck his imagination. The biographies were complete fantasy, or so he thought. The more he learned about the people in his biographies, the more he realized that his fictional accounts of these people were actually very close to fact in almost every case. There was an essence of the person that came through as a glance, a laugh, or a few words of dialogue that communicated a truth about that person.

Carl Jung, the great psychologist, describes a similar phenomenon. In a session with a person whom he had never met before, Jung was trying to make a point by creating a fictional character and situation to communicate his thoughts. His patient was shocked because Jung's story was uncomfortably close to the truth. This intuitive sense we have about people is a voice that we often dismiss. But these unspoken perceptions are quite often the essence of the character and our imagined biographies of people we hardly know, can be very close to the point.

What we search for in line and shape and gesture, is to unlock the key to the essence of our subject. The crush of information and fact about the subject is not always as interesting or necessary as is the subtle truth about a character. If we were writers, a few well-chosen lines about a character conveys more than an entire novel. It's these few chosen lines that we search for as artists.

There is an inaudible music that flows between humans. It is this fleeting music that we are trying to capture…not accuracy, not fact, not literal representation. We can get all of those things from photography. With our art we are looking for the inaudible music that emanates from our subject, and if we are lucky, we can capture the essence of that music with pen on paper. That's the lifelong pursuit of the artist.

The accompanying sketches are not meant to illustrate the text, but are just there to enhance the look of the page and to suggest that most people use words to express things — while artists use lines to express the very same things, and the end result is communication and entertainment.

Actually, there is poetry in these drawings — can you feel it? The viewer in her own imagination will experience the humanness, aliveness, and the distinctness of character in the drawings. In their minds, they fill in where the artist has only suggested. That is real gesture drawing. And, yes, it's a form of poetry.

Let's face it! When you chose to be an artist, you unleashed a gnawing and dreadful hunger to express yourself... *nothing less will satisfy*. The passion to bring real meaning to your audience, with all its extra levels of suggestion and emotion and humor, makes it necessary to keep growing as a "poet" in line. Thus the importance of studying gesture. (Plug!)

Here are a couple of student's drawings with my suggestions. Ted Hughes spoke of the "crowiness in the crow's flight," and that is what I try to bring out in the Gesture Class — the "humanness" of the human's gestures. For instance, in this first example the model becomes a gardener, in this pose he was raking leaves. To get that humanness in my sketch I mentally went through the process of raking. I leaned forward as I extended the rake out to reach as many leaves as possible, then pulled the rake toward me, having to straighten up (even lean back a little). The hands, because they are in a pulling action, are in advance of the rake (and leaves). His left foot is moved out of the way to avoid covering it with leaves. There is even a "stage" of compressed space created between the rake and the right foot. After all, this is the story, the center of interest, and it has to be in the clear. The pulling action swung his right arm around adding a twist to his body, also opened up the "stage" of third dimensional space in front of his body. It also alleviated the static lineup and even spacing of the feet and rake.

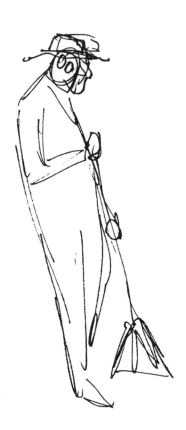

Of course, there are other ways to rake leaves. You needn't rake leaves my way. But in drawing, each move has to be designed to carry out a purpose, one that is done efficiently — unless of course it's meant to be humorous, then inefficiency would be the rule.

In this next example, the model held a hoe behind his neck as he rested from his weeding chores. Since the handle was behind his neck, it forced the head forward and the belly out. His weight was on his left leg which forced the left hip to be higher than the right hip. Also the left shoulder was lowered for balance. This is typical hip/shoulder body English for humans, so it brings out the humanness of the gesture.

We have the honor and the privilege to pass on what we see and feel to others who, by the way, need our expertise in interpreting the myriad bits of human drama and comedy. Thus the importance of studying gesture. Imagine that your viewers are cupping their ears to hear what you have to say, are squinting to see what you have to draw, and they are willing to go half way to make sense of the gesture you have presented to them. But, hey! Why not let them relax and only have to come 1/8 or 1/16 of the way?

So, study acting, gesture, human nature, kinesthetics, anatomy, mime, caricature, perspective, and words. The easy way is to... just do it!

65 Look, This Is What I Saw

Again, sorry if I get too wordy in presenting some of my ideas. A good drawing is summed up in the mind in a flash, but to explain how to arrive at that kind of visual statement takes, sometimes, many words.

Take for instance this sketch of Vicky Jo, as she powders her nose. The student's sketch is rather static as if the girl was doing it for the first time. In my sketch I first opened up the "stage" so you see both shoulders and consequently some third dimensional negative space. I angled her right forearm to appear to move toward the nose, intensifying the activity in that area — the thing she is concerned with. The image in the mirror, though, is the center of interest. Notice in the student's drawing the spacing is even and static between the face, hand, and mirror.

ı ı ı

Whereas, mine is spaced to suggest movement.

ıı ı

(In a former handout, I talked about how the spacing of objects can cause an acceleration or deceleration of movement.)

In this drawing the attention is whisked out to the mirror, where her attention, and ours, is directed. Just powdering the nose is a rather mundane pursuit, but with a little imagination it can be made to be quite a charming or even whimsical action. A little staging, some angles, some spacing or patterning, and some kinesthetic participation and you are sure to come up with an entertaining drawing. Oh, and also I raised the right hand and lowered the left to avoid the rigid straight line-up of the elements. It creates a kind of tunnel for the look to travel through.

This student's drawing needs to find its place in space. It is partly due to the tendency to (here we go again) straighten things up. The right arm and leg are presented to us in profile, flattening the drawing out, destroying any feeling of third dimension. In my sketch I simply lined everything up perspective-wise (3/4 view), which introduced the third dimensional stage I so often speak of.

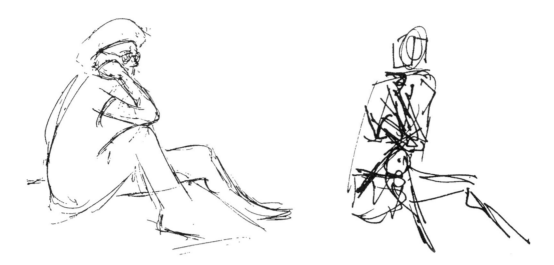

In this next pose, the model was stretched forward as if looking at something off stage, which becomes the center of interest. The student's version, though a fairly nice drawing, could have used some stronger storytelling action. In my sketch I leaned the figure forward more, and pointed the hat shape in that direction. It created a nice angle between the hat brim and the left shoulder. Can you feel it sort of leap out in the direction of the look? That negative space created by the hat and shoulder, the angle of the left arm, and the stretched back (remember squash and stretch?) with the belt being pulled forward on the right side, all work together to thrust the attention to the unseen center of interest.

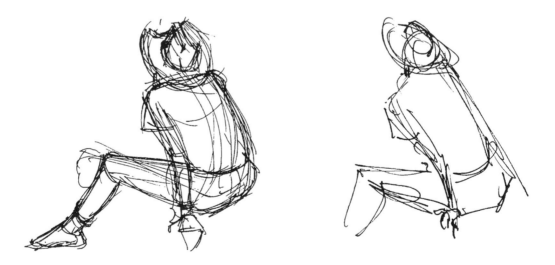

Has this guy got a headache or has his TV gone dead? Whatever, a sense of dramatics would help. Again, feeling the pose kinesthetically should have led to a simple squash and stretch configuration. Notice how in my sketch I used a straight line for the stretch and a squiggly line for the squash. If there is no distinction between the front and back of this pose, there can be no action. This should explain squash and stretch for all time and forevermore.

Even a still drawing can show action if verbs and not nouns are used. If you draw the parts of the body as nouns, you are drawing an arm, a torso, a leg, etc. But if you draw verbs, you are drawing an arm, stretching a torso twisting, or a leg bending. I suggested that if you can't express the part as a verb — don't draw it. It's a very exciting concept. When making a drawing for your audience, if it is full of nouns, it will be merely a presentation of the physical things present. But if turned into verbs there will be action, motive, story, human interest...life! It will, in the words of the great author, Maya Angelou, bring, "...truth beyond facts." Or in the words of that aged guru Walt Stanchfield, "It's like a basketball player who doesn't have to closely inspect the backboard construction or the weave of the net — all he has to do is aim for the hoop."

Here is that same pose from a different angle, but plagued by the same problem. If the student had formed even just one verb to describe the pose, it, beyond a doubt, would have been "stretch" (with its constant companion "squash"). And the mere thought of the word (the verb) suggests all the physical manipulations it takes to express it. This brings us back to my theory that if you can "verb-a-lize" the action, it will help you to draw it.

You've no doubt heard the old adage about not seeing the forest for the trees. Well, applied to drawing, that means not seeing the gesture for the parts. If your goal is drawing the forest, you have to start with it. If you get the shape of the forest — then you can work on the trees.

If you start with a tree — you may never end up with the truth of the forest.

If your goal is drawing a gesture you have to start with it. Get the shape of the gesture, then doll it up with details later.

One day in class I read a passage from the *The Joy of Watercolor*, by David Millard, wherein, speaking of a painting, said "I call it, 'A Stray Fisherman Soon Attracts His Customers At The Waterfront.' Try to give all your sketches titles from here on. It's easy to program into your thinking as you plan a painting (drawing)...*before you start it.* It will help you to paint it. It will also give you a feeling of caring about your subject in a way that is different from just sitting down to whack out another landscape (gesture drawing)."

It's important to consider your drawing worthy of a title or a mini-story to identify the action in your mind so you will have a goal — a good reason for drawing it — something to tell your audience. "Look," you are saying, "This is what I saw. This is how the model stretched her neck, how her hair hung down, how she twisted her body in a delightfully seductive attitude. I want to share this experience with you, my unseen audience. You may never have an opportunity to live through so wonderful an adventure as this — let me sketch it for you."

Here are three of the hundreds of excellent sketches made in the Gesture Class. I'm usually so intent on saving the critiques, I often pass over the faultless drawings. These seem to have been done in the spirit of "Look, this is what I saw and I want you, my audience, to experience it, too."

Drawing by Rusty Stoll

Drawing by Pres Romanillos   Drawing by Terri Martin

66 Breaking Away

We sometimes tend to get stale after doing the same thing, the same old way, time and time again. That's what vacations are for — to break away and do something different. In the Gesture Class recently, I suggested the students "break away" for a couple of hours and experience a refreshening in this drawing venture.

With all due respect to Steve Huston, the Anatomy Instructor, I encouraged the artists to forget anatomy for the time being, and to use the broad side of a broad pen, drawing as if they were having a seizure — going for a style of drawing that was foreign to them. Halfway through class we switched to a fine point pen, drawing as freely and delicately as we could. The idea was to get them to draw not a photographic copy of the *model*, but to draw their impression of the *gesture*.

I attempted to shock them out of their "status quo" habits by telling them how I, who have literally "broken away," carry on in my studio. I sometimes take a full sheet of watercolor paper and slop handfuls of water on it. Then I pour, splatter, or brush paint onto it, tilting the paper up and down, side to side and throw on salt and drop spray alcohol or turpentine on it. I push, scrape, gouge, and glue other papers on. If nothing comes of it — the next day I might draw into it with a twig, using black or colored ink. I use crayons to draw in a subject, then paint over it — that is a blast, for the wax in the crayon acts as a resist. If the thing bombs, I'll paint on a coat of gesso and start all over again. Or it may end up as bookmarks or in the collage box.

The wonderful thing is, I'm learning to venture where I was formerly too timid or hesitant to go.

I realize you can't go to that extreme in animation — you have to conform to the established style. Nothing wrong with that. I did it for 45 or 50 years, and enjoyed every minute of it. But some *nice* drawings may be just a slight experiment away from being *superb* drawings. "Breaking away," even a tiny bit, may work wonders for you.

I also gave the students a list of words and ideas to help them sidestep those taskmaster "censors" that hover over every drawing saying "Can't you make it a little more photographic?" "That's drawing?" Or, "You call yourself an artist?" And also to break away from some bad habits of which we are not even aware and those tentative, lacking-confidence periods of drawing that seem to be lurking at every drawing session. This is a technique I learned recently from my revered painting instructor, Bob Burridge, at the Hancock College painting class. Bob has a way of bringing out a little more than what you think you are capable of with his completely forward-looking method of both painting and teaching. His philosophy is if going at your problem head-on is getting you nowhere — make a left turn. Rather than type the Burridge list for you, I'm reproducing Nicole Strand's copy of them — it seems to visually epitomize the flavor of the "scheme."

NOW IS THE TIME!!!

Breakaway!   GO TOO FAR!

Simplify

make a Left S turn

Say "Yes"

cross the road

S== what happens?

Let the jesture EXPlode!

Break rules

get out of the way   Let your
drawing do what it wants.

Be crazy   Be different

a drawing has it's own Life don't force
your inhibitions on it.

Anyway, the students went along with the experiment and it turned out to be all fun and profit. I confiscated several of the drawings to share with you. I get gushy sometimes talking about how great the drawings done in the Gesture Class are, so you won't be surprised to hear me say "These are outstanding gesture drawings." I am in awe of the talent that I have been so privileged to work with. These drawings take my breath away.

Sean Jimenez

Jane Krupka

Tom Gately

Jared Beckstrand

Doug Post

This is the size Doug was drawing, so this is what he was seeing as he drew.

Tom Gately

Diana Coco

Jared Beckstrand

Clay Kaytis

Tom Gately

Of course, every drawing is not all "wine and roses." We sometimes forget that we are drawing gestures, that is, *acting on paper*. Often it appears that we are just trying to get enough lines on the paper so we can call it a drawing. This next drawing reminds me of when I sang in the Light Opera group. The director would say "Sing and act to the farthest person in the balcony." This meant not only project the voice but also the gesture. The student's drawing on the left, from 200 feet, would appear to be standing up straight. It needs a little pizzazz. I especially like how in my sketch the hand on the hip is not just cut out and stuck on, but is taking an active part in the pose, seeming to press the hip into that exaggerated gesture.

Here's another pose with a similar hip action, but for a different reason. In this one the hip is placed under the weight on the shoulder for stability. But even if this extreme a gesture were not really necessary, or vital, an actor would do it anyway just to make sure the people in the last row could "read" it, and to make his delivery entertaining. After all, actors (and artists) are entertainers. Even while talking to a friend, we don't just stand there at attention while relating our story — we gesticulate, sometimes wildly, especially when we want to be convincing....or entertaining.

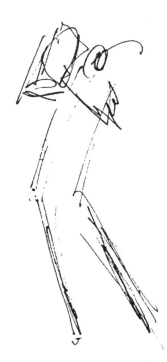

In this next drawing the student might have benefited by the knowledge and use of the golf term "Swinging from the socks." The principle is simple, if an arm is raised, the force is distributed throughout the whole body. The arm does not move independently. The farther away from the arm action a part is, the less influence the force has on it.

Did you like my "Fractured Classics" in last month's handout (chapter 48)? Here are two more.

67 The Shape of the Gesture II

Some months ago I did a handout on the Shape of the Gesture, but merely touched on the subject. Let's go a little deeper into this fascinating topic. When you look at these three shapes there is instant recognition: triangle, square, and circle. With a gesture drawing, the overall shape has to be especially well thought out to attain such clarity.

Take this gesture of Bobby Ruth Mann waving a tambourine, for instance. In this first drawing, the student seemed to be searching for the final shape with numerous pen lines, a technique not uncommon among Disney Studios artists. It's a good drawing, but it doesn't stamp a definite shape on your retina. It lacks a certain finality, one you might expect to see in an animation extreme. Both legs are similarly bent, both arms are paralleling each other.

Maybe if the upper arm was more extended it would lay up the tambourine, whereas now it gets tangled up with the hat. Nice drawing, but is the shape enhancing the story?

In this next drawing by Mike Disa, there is a clearer statement of the story. Notice how each leg has been given a different "part" to play, and the tambourine is in the clear. The fact that the drawing style is quite different from the prior one matters little — it's the end result that counts. However simple or detailed an animation drawing is, it must contain all the necessary information, or should I say *just* the necessary information, for an excess of detail will not plus a bad gesture drawing.

It seems that Marc Smith had this drawing well thought out before he applied pen to paper. There is an economy of line and each line contributes to the gesture. And the shape of the gesture tells you the story clearly:

In this last version of the same pose, Terri Martin has managed to give us the very essence of the gesture in a shape that is free from any divisive elements. The shape and the gesture are one. It hits you with a finality that you experienced with those symbols above, the triangle, square, and circle — except in this case, in the form of an entertaining female performer.

There were many magnificent drawings made that day. Here are a few of them. These drawings are by Marc Smith and Mike Disa.

Marc Smith

Mike Disa

This head is worthy of a close-up

David Pimentel

Joe Moshier   Diana Coco

David Pimentel

Danny Galieote

Marc Smith

On the following day, model David Roon became a cook for us. I brought a lot of cookery props and David's use of them was awesome. I had everyone name the gesture and write it down on their drawing paper to remind them that they are not just drawing things, but that they are illustrating a "story." Also we honed in on shapes — the shapes of the gestures. Since the critic in me must have its moment, here are some student's drawings with my critiques accompanying them. The first one, though a pleasant drawing, got muddled because the shape was not clear. In the student's drawing the cook's hands and the pepper mill are hiding his view of the salad. In my sketch I shaped it so the cook's view was clear enough for him to see that the pepper was making it to the salad. Basic to the student's problem was probably his choice of a title: "leaning over, holding pepper grinder." Perhaps it should have been "grinding pepper onto salad," which gives him something to perform; that is, a story to act out.

Next is one of the student's gestures named "What next?" His drawing seems to depict that idea quite well, but the shape gets a little mushy. There seems to be an overabundance of curved lines that send the attention off in various directions. Also the model had stretched himself to full height, as if to get a more overall view of the problem.

Below is another drawing of the same pose. It's called "standing, hands on hips, looking down, leaning back." That tells what he is doing, but doesn't suggest a story. I shaped my sketch to more cleanly direct his attention to the cooking paraphernalia. The title from the previous drawing seems to tell the story better: "What next?" In my perhaps overly simplified version, nothing gets in the way of his questioning look. The shapes are almost as simple and clear as the triangle, square, and circle.

Well, so much for nitpicking! Now for a gallery of delightfully light and humorous drawings for your viewing pleasure. I had coaxed, begged, harangued, and even insisted that the students lighten up — after all they work for a cartoon studio, don't they? So, they did attempt to inject a little humor into their drawing and the results were most gratifying. (In Xeroxing, I lost most of the titles. Sorry.)

David Pimentel

Joe Moshier

Tom Gately

LOOKING AT SPILLED MESS   TASTING

Tom Gately

68 A Tribute

This handout is in celebration of the young artists who have been attending the Gesture Class. It attests to their skills and to their determination to refine their artistry. Each artist has been striving to create entertaining drawings that relate an emotion or tell a story, rather than merely making faithful representations of the model. You sense that these drawings are not just reporting facts, but are, like great actors on the stage or in film, portraying a character engaged in some exciting adventure story.

I have relinquished my usual yakking and critiquing to make space for a representative look at the drawings done in one such session. As usual, I failed to collect something from everyone. And, the old demon *space* forced me to make some regrettable omissions.

Incidentally, I even gave up my usual hands-on critiquing to become the model for this session — so now add Walt Stanchfield to the model roster. (Just kidding.)

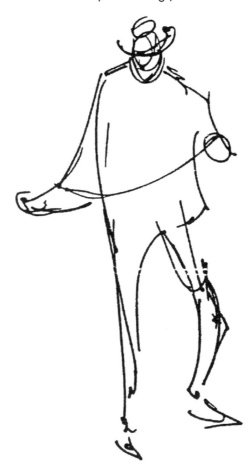

Diana Coco

Jane Krupka has a much more delicate approach, but nonetheless captures a good strong gesture. Models are Clark Allen and Wanda Nowicki:

Jane Krupka

Tom Gately is very versatile and can go from realistic through cutesy to comic. Here, in drawing Wanda Nowicki, he chose what I would call animation style cute. I say animation cute because the girls are cute; animation because they are three-dimensional and can be drawn from any angle. If you turn a flat drawing sideways,

you get this.

Tom Gately

Jane Krupka

Whitney Martin

Faris Al-Saffar

Jane Krupka

Jane Krupka

Cris Hurtt

GROUNDS
MURPHEY, CA.
5/28/97

Credit — Volume II